D1269825

# MEDIAEVAL CHANTRIES AND CHANTRY CHAPELS

I. EFFIGY OF LORD EDWARD LE DESPENSER ABOVE THE TRINITY CHAPEL, TEWKES-
BURY ABBEY

G. H. COOK

# MEDIAEVAL CHANTRIES AND CHANTRY CHAPELS

PHOENIX HOUSE LIMITED

LONDON 1947

TO
MY WIFE

# ACKNOWLEDGMENTS

THE author and the publisher acknowledge their indebtedness to the following photographers for the illustrations contained in these pages :

Mr. C. P. Cave, *57, 58*

Country Life, Ltd., *3, 49*

Dean of Windsor and Raphael Tuck and Sons, Ltd., *46*

Mr. Herbert Felton, *8, 9, 12*

Mr. W. J. Fullerton, *10*

Great Western Railway, *43*

Mr. F. E. Howard, *51*

Mr. R. P. Howgrave Graham, *1, 29, 30, 36*

Mr. E. C. le Grice, *17*

National Buildings Record, *7, 13, 14, 19, 26, 35, 37, 38, 41, 54, 55, 56*

Newtonian Illustrated Press Service, *28*

Photochrom Co. Ltd., *21, 22, 25, 31, 53*

Mr. Sydney Pitcher, *4, 5, 16, 45*

Walter Scott, Bradford, *2, 11, 24, 48, 52*

Mr. P. S. Spokes, *47*

Rev. F. R. P. Sumner, *18, 23, 33, 39, 40, 42, 44, 50, 59*

Valentine and Sons, Ltd., *6*

Mr. J. O. Webster, *15*

Mr. R. F. Wills, *27*

Illustrations 32 and 34 from the *Royal Commission on Historical Monuments, London, Vol. I,* Westminster Abbey, and 20 from the volume on Hereford Cathedral are reproduced by permission of the Controller of H.M. Stationery Office.

Special thanks are due to Mr Cecil Farthing, Conway Librarian, National Buildings Record, through whose kind help more than half of the illustrations were obtained.

All the plans were prepared by the author.

# CONTENTS

## 6

## PART TWO

## 7

## 8

## 9

## 10

## 11

# LIST OF ILLUSTRATIONS

# PLANS

# PREFACE

THIS BOOK IS an attempt to explain the purpose and character of chantries in the mediaeval English Church and of the chapels which often formed a part of their foundation.

The significance of the chantry in the religious life of the later Middle Ages can hardly be over-emphasized. The doctrine of Purgatory was no 'fond thing vainly invented,' as it is termed in the Book of Common Prayer, Article XXII., nor less readily accepted was the teaching that souls in that intermediate state could be benefited by intercessory prayers and the recitation of masses. In glass and in brass in our ancient churches is yet to be read the entreaty, 'Pray ye for the soul of ——"

The Doom painting, occupying a prominent position in so many churches, conveyed in a lively and no uncertain manner the terrors of Divine punishment, a subject which the Preaching Friars made much of in their vehement denunciation of evil-doing. The provision of soul-masses by pious and impious alike was a means of allaying fears of such retribution. For the two centuries following the Black Death, chantries and obits were the most remarkable manifestation of religious belief in this country. The considerable properties with which many chantries were endowed, the great care and deliberation with which their ordinances were framed, and the costly chapels that were built for the recitation of the masses afford evidence of the very real doctrinal belief underlying their foundation.

To-day a number of chantry chapels almost in their entirety are to be seen, mostly in the greater churches; elsewhere a window, a screen, a tomb or a piscina are all that remain. In the second part of this book, the majority of surviving chapels in our cathedral and monastic churches are described, together with a number in the parish churches.

For upwards of forty years the study of our architectural heritage has been the delight of the author, and it has been his privilege for the past twenty years to lecture in various parts of London on the cathedrals, monasteries and churches of the Middle Ages. More ample leisure and the comparatively easy means of travel have brought our historic monuments within the reach of the general public, with the result that a greater interest than ever is now manifested in the mediaeval architecture of this country, and that interest has been fostered by the many books on the subject that issue from the press from time to time. In a few such works scattered and incidental references to chantries are to be found, but rarely is more than a page or two devoted to their considera-

tion.* That being so, it is hoped that this book, the preparation of which
has spread over some years, may not be redundant. In no respect is it a
complete survey of mediaeval chantries ; much has had to be omitted
from lack of space. Where quotations of any length occur, the source is
acknowledged, but to give chapter and verse for every statement and
reference would overload the pages with footnotes, only to stub the
mental toe of the reader. Nevertheless, the author is conscious of his debt
to many who have laboured in the fields of ecclesiastical history and
architecture. He will not have failed if his book leads to an understanding
of the significance of the chantry and an appreciation of the lovely little
chapels, gems of Perpendicular Gothic, still to be seen in many of our
mediaeval churches.

* A concise account of chantries is given in Francis Bond's *English Church
Architecture*, and Professor Hamilton Thompson's *Historical Growth of the English
Parish Church* treats more fully of chantries in parish churches.

## PART ONE

# INTRODUCTION

EVERY RELIGIOUS HOUSE that was founded in this country from the eighth to the thirteenth century owed its origin to a royal benefactor or to some wealthy landowner.

After the Norman Conquest the military followers of Duke William, the feudal barons and their successors readily associated themselves with the founding of monasteries up and down the land, and these establishments became rich and powerful through the continued patronage of the great, who were fully cognizant of the dignity thus conferred upon their families. Nor were they less conscious of the spiritual advantages of the prayers which the brethren would offer up on their behalf. Such intercessions were one of the main obligations imposed upon the religious, for when a man founded or endowed any pious undertaking he would stipulate in the charter of foundation that intercessory prayers should be regularly offered up by the beneficiaries ; their lands and property were held on that condition. The religious houses were under legal obligation to fulfil their founders' wishes in this respect.

In the charter of Syon Nunnery, Isleworth, founded by Henry V in 1415, it was decreed that the sisters should ' celebrate Divine Service * for ever for our healthful estate while we live, and for our soul when we shall have departed this life, and for the souls of our most dear lord and father Henry, the late King of England, and Mary his late wife, our most dear mother; also for the souls of John [of Gaunt], late Duke of Lancaster, our grandfather, and Blanche his late wife, our grandmother, and of other our progenitors and all the faithful departed.'

In December 1537, when a large number of the monastic establishments had already fallen a prey to royal cupidity, the despoiler himself founded a Benedictine house ' to secure prayers for his good estate during his lifetime and for the soul of Jane, his late queen ; also for the souls of all his posterity and progenitors and for the souls of all faithful departed.' But what was ostensibly an act of piety, ' to secure prayers,' proved to be a piece of shrewd bargaining on Henry's part. In return for the surrender of Chertsey Abbey, Surrey, by the convent, he undertook to re-establish the brethren of that house as a Benedictine community at the Priory of Bisham, Berks., an Augustinian house which had been suppressed in the

* *i.e.* Mass.

1

previous year. However, the prayers of the newly constituted convent on behalf of the royal house were of little account, for the abbey was dissolved after a brief existence of six months.

In general, the brethren of religious houses duly observed the conditions laid down in their foundation charters and offered up prayers unceasingly for the good of their benefactors.

At the Augustinian Abbey of Bristol, Abbot John of Newland (1481–1515), compiled a record of events in the history of his house ; and the following extract from his roll is evidence of the convent's remembrance of the founder, Robert Fitzharding, some three centuries or more after his death.

For which good lord Sir Robert our founder, and dame Eva his wife, these be the special things due for them, besides the general prayers continually done in divine service by day and by night.

Firstly, a daily special prayer said for them and all other foundators and benefactors, at the hour of seven in the mornings, and also daily prayers by name in our chapter house openly. Also they have other rites solemnly sung with ringing on the eve of their anniversary, and on the morrow commendations—the abbot for the founder, and the prior for the foundress executing the divine service.

It was natural that such prayers should be desired equally by the less wealthy, who had not the means to found a religious house. Their desires were expressed in benefactions made to some convent or church, and these benefactions, to a lesser extent maybe, secured for the donors certain privileges, always including the prayers of the brethren.

The laity often sought ' to be joined with ' the family of the abbeys. These were the ' confraters,' or *familiares*, frequently alluded to in the monastic records : they paid in things temporal for spiritual benefits which they hoped to receive. Kings, queens, nobles, and men and women of all classes associated themselves in this way with the religious houses. It was so from Saxon days ; when Canute and his brother Harold were received into the ' family of Christ Church, Canterbury,' the King marked the occasion by presenting the convent with a copy of the Gospels, now in the British Museum.

When a building scheme was to be undertaken, the roll of confraters and benefactors was made to serve an immediate purpose. In the early thirteenth century, a project dear to the heart of Abbot Humez of Westminster was the erection of a Lady Chapel at the east end of the Abbey church. Before it was begun in 1220, Humez granted spiritual privileges to all who would contribute to the cost. Such benefactors were promised participation

in all good things and spiritual benefits to be made for ever in the church of Westminster, in masses, alms, vigils, psalms and all other good exercises ; also a participation in the good works done in all other churches bound to the church of Westminster by especially strong ties, namely Fécamp and its cells, the church of Hurley and the cell of S. Bartholomew at Sudbury. Certain of the benefits are definitely specified ; thirteen masses for the living, that is to say, three of the Holy Spirit, seven of the Blessed Virgin and three of the Saints whose relics are kept in the church ; while for dead brethren who had bestowed alms on the work, twenty masses a week were to be celebrated. . . . Furthermore, the abbot and convent of Westminster had obtained for the benefactors of the work from the abbot of Citeaux a participation in all goods hereafter to be made in the Cistercian Order for ever.' (Westlake.)

Assuredly, the building of the Lady Chapel at Westminster was regarded as an undertaking of great importance far beyond the precincts of the Abbey itself.

A roll of benefactors and confraters was kept in every religious establishment in mediaeval England, and the grateful brethren offered up prayers for their well-being whilst alive and for their souls after death. During the building or enlargement of a great church, the roll virtually became a list of subscribers to the Fabric Fund but the names also were included of donors of gifts in kind.

Amongst the muniments of S. Paul's Cathedral is a document which is an acknowledgment by the canons of S. Bartholomew's Priory, Smithfield, of gifts made in 1250 by Richard of Wendover, who held a prebend in the cathedral. Translated from Latin it reads :

To all the faithful in Christ, the prior and convent of S. Bartholomew send greeting in the Lord. Know ye that we have received by the gift of Master Richard of Wendover, imbued with pious charity, a psalter glossed in two volumes and the epistle of the blessed Paul, and an altar slab and an altar cloth, for the honour of God. . . . And we, imbued and full of pious charity, have received him to be a brother, with the consent and goodwill of the whole convent. And we grant and give him participation in all the benefits of our house, given and to be given hereafter, so that his name with the brethren of Christ may be inscribed in our roll.

Given in the year of grace 1250, on the day of S. John the Apostle and Evangelist. In witness whereof we have set our seal to this writing. (Webb's *Records of S. Bartholomew's.*)

The *Liber Niger*, or Customary, of the cathedral of Lincoln preserves the form of admission for members of the laity who desired to be numbered amongst the confraters of that great church. The following declaration done into modern English is an extract from this interesting document of the late 15th century :

And we here receive N. to be with us and all the brethren and sisters and the ministers and servants of God in this holy place, partner and partaker of all our and their prayers, suffrages, fastings, pilgrimages . . . and of all other good and meritorious deeds and works of mercy that we or they should pray or do by day or night in this holy place . . . that ye may be so guided and live that ye may come to everlasting bliss. Amen. (*Cathedral Statutes I.* Bradshaw and Wordsworth.)

The roll or register was known as the Annal or *Liber Vitae* and therein were inscribed the names and obit days of the benefactors for whom soul-prayers were to be offered.

At Durham Cathedral, the *Liber Vitae*, ' an excellent fine book ' containing the names of all the benefactors of S. Cuthbert's Church from the time of its first foundation, was kept on the High Altar. 'The daily and quotidien remembrance the monks had of them in the time of mass and divine service did argue not only their gratitude but also a most divine and charitable affection to the souls of their benefactors, as well dead as living.' The register, a richly bound volume shorn of its gold and silver binding, now reposes in the British Museum and there is preserved a similar record, the *Catalogus Benefactorum* from S. Alban's Abbey, which details at length the nature of the gifts against the donors' names. Included are the names of all persons who had been received into ' full fraternity ' of the convent up to the year 1463. When Bishop Hatfield of Durham was admitted to the family of S. Albans in 1350 he gave the brethren a *poculum charitatis*, or love-cup, that he might be remembered in their prayers *after meals*.

Serving a like purpose was the parochial bede-roll. It was the practice in parish churches for a register to be compiled of all benefactors for whose souls the prayers of the parishioners were desired ' according to the laudable custom used in the holy church.' This record, the bede-roll, was placed on the High Altar during the celebration of mass on Sundays and festivals and the names were read aloud by the celebrant to the assembled worshippers.

The frequent reference to the roll in mediaeval wills shows how eager was the desire of parish folk of all classes to be included in the list of those to be prayed for. The custom served as an inducement to make bequests for religious and charitable purposes. To quote an early instance. In 1246 a London cordwainer, Algrand by name, granted a piece of land to the church of S. Augustine by S. Paul's Cathedral for the enlargement of the church, to include an altar dedicated to Our Lady. In acknowledgment of the gift he, his wife Rose and his first wife Alice were to be made ' participants in all the benefits and prayers which should be made in that church for ever.' His name was to be added to the bede-roll and a special prayer said for his soul in all the masses sung at the altar which he had founded.

It is suggested by Aymer Vallance in his *English Church Screens* that the bede-roll was read from the rood-loft in the parish church, which

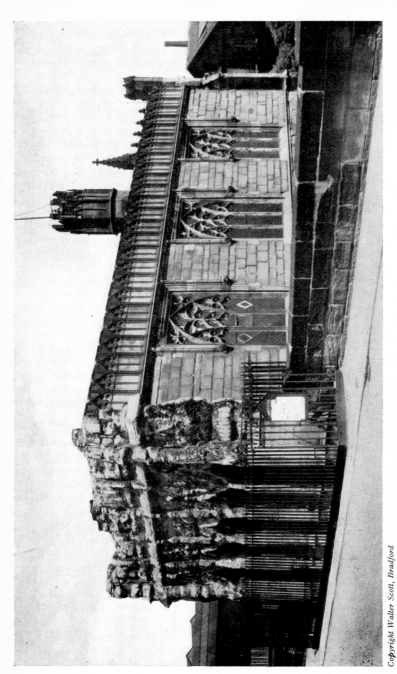

2. THE CHAPEL ON WAKEFIELD BRIDGE, YORKSHIRE

**3.** THE COURTYARD, S. WILLIAM'S COLLEGE, YORK

4. CHAPEL IN THE NORTH NAVE ARCADE, BURFORD CHURCH, OXON

5. PARCLOSE CHAPEL AGAINST THE ROOD SCREEN, SHELSLEY WALSH CHURCH, WORCESTERSHIRE

by reason of its elevated position was well suited to the purpose. A Thomas Jonys of Bristol, by his will 1464, ordained that the souls of his wife and himself be recommended to the prayers of the parishioners of S. Nicholas' Church ' in pulpito,' i.e. from the rood-loft.

A few original bede-rolls have been preserved. Too lengthy to be given here is that of S. Mary's Church, Sandwich, which will be found in Boy's *History of Sandwich*. Of particular interest is this roll, for it enumerates the various gifts made to the church by those named therein.

So esteemed were prayers for the dead that indulgences were some- times offered to those who would journey to the tomb of some great benefactor or person of saintly life. On occasion, prayers for the living earned indulgences. Bishop Beckington of Wells, for some reason or other, granted an indulgence of forty days to ' all true penitents who should go to the tomb of that worthy man, William Carent, in the prebendal church of Henstridge, Somerset, and should devoutly say a Paternoster and an Ave for the welfare of the same William Carent, his brothers and his son *during their lives* . . . and for the souls of the aforesaid after their deaths.' The canopied tomb on which lie the effigies of Sir William Carent (d. 1476) and his wife, and to which penitents made their way, is still to be seen in Henstridge church.

The monastic establishments themselves often assumed the enviable role of benefactor by founding daughter houses, whose prayers were duly expected by the brethren of the parent house.

Kilburn Priory, a house of Benedictine nuns, furnishes a case in point. It owed its foundation to a hermit, Godwyn, who c. 1134 granted his cell with the adjoining lands to the monks of Westminster ' as an alms for the redemption of the whole convent.'

Shortly afterwards, Abbot Herbert, with the prior and monks of West- minster, at Godwyn's request, assigned the hermitage and its possessions to three maidens, Emma, Gunilda and Christina, and to ' all the hand- maidens of God, hereafter living a holy life therein. . . . to hold it for the ransom of the souls of the whole convent of Westminster. The maidens are to pray for the souls of the whole convent and for the brethren quick and dead of Fécamp.'

There is a tradition that the nuns of Kilburn Priory enjoyed the privi- lege of having seats on certain feast days in the triforium of Westminster Abbey.

It was a common practice for the religious houses to make ' confeder- ations ' one with another, by virtue of which they were bound by mutual agreement to offer up prayers for each others' deceased brethren as for

2

their own. Abbot Humez of Westminster (1214–22), made a confederation
with the monks of Bury S. Edmunds and his successor made a similar
compact with Dorchester Abbey. When a brother died, the mortuary-
roll, on which his name had been entered, was conveyed to each of the
confederated houses by the roll-bearer, a monk who rode on horseback.
The mortuary-roll for an abbot or bishop would be an elaborate document, richly embellished and illuminated, as for example that of Abbot
Islip of Westminster.

II  The origin of chantries—Their endowment and provisions—Schools and
almshouses—Obits and perpetual chantries—Candles and altar lights—Ordinances for the conduct of chantries.

TOWARDS THE CLOSE of the thirteenth century, the piety which had
hitherto manifested itself in the founding of religious houses was directed
towards the more personal endowments known as chantries.

In mediaeval England when a man died, a mass was said for his soul
by the parish priest and not infrequently provision was made in money
or in kind for further masses to be recited periodically and on the anniversary. Thus it came about that bequests were made to a church or
to the priest solely for the purpose of securing prayers for the testator
after death. This cult of masses for the dead was the motive underlying
chantry endowments, the importance of which, in the religious life of
the later Middle Ages, was anticipated by Edward I in the endowments
he provided to commemorate his much-loved Queen, Eleanor of Castile.

When Eleanor died in 1290 at Hardeby in Notts., the King wrote to
Archbishop Romeyn of York desiring the prayers of the faithful for
her soul and the Archbishop immediately granted an indulgence of
forty days to those who responded. Provision was made for perpetual
services to her memory and for the repose of her soul, not only at the
places where her body rested en route to Westminster, marked later by
the Eleanor crosses, but in almost every part of the kingdom. At Hardeby
a perpetual chantry was founded for the Queen, for the endowment
of which 100 marks were granted the Dean of Lincoln in 1292.* The
prebendary of North Clifton was to receive 10 marks a year, out of
which he was to pay 100 shillings to the chantry priest, and to find him

*The mark was 13s. 4d. and its purchasing value in 1540 was equivalent to
about £30 to-day. In the thirteenth century its value was still greater.

a lodging and also to provide furniture for the altar. The *Valor Eccles-iasticus* records that the priest, Thomas Kyllyall, received a stipend of 103s. and a mansion and garden of an annual value of 4s. The King founded similar chantries at Edington and at the church of the Black Friars in London. But the greatest commemoration was that at West-minster Abbey, the final resting place of the lamented queen. To the monks there the King was profuse in his gifts, that the commemoration might be both splendid and perpetual.

To this end Edward enriched the convent with no less than twenty-two manors in the counties of Essex, Kent, Bucks., Warwickshire and Middlesex. The annual observance in the Abbey was one of the utmost solemnity, at which all the nobility and bishops were expected to be present. It began on the eve of S. Andrew, when 100 wax candles, each weighing twelve pounds, continued to burn until High Mass on the following day. All the bells of the Abbey were rung incessantly and divine offices were chanted unceasingly in the great church.

Daily, during the whole year, thirty massive tapers of wax remained on Eleanor's tomb. They were lighted on great festivals, but at other times only two were kept constantly burning day and night. On the conclusion of the commemoration, gifts of money were distributed freely to the poor and to the friars and hospitallers of many London establishments. Every abbot of Westminster was bound by oath to observe religiously and scrupulously the whole of the ceremonies, which con-tinued for two and a half centuries ' until the Reformation extinguished the candles and confiscated the money that kept them alight.'

The annual recurrence of so imposing a commemoration in the royal Abbey must have left a deep and lasting impression on the wealthy nobles and ecclesiastics who themselves might desire to be remembered after death.

A chantry was literally a mass that was recited at an altar for the well-being and good estate of the founder during his lifetime and for the re-pose of his soul after death. It kept the name of the founder and of his family fresh in the memory of succeeding generations, particularly when a special chapel was erected for the recitation of the masses.

During the fourteenth century the chantry movement established itself as one of the foremost manifestations of the religious life of the time. Royalty, the nobility, bishops, abbots, deans, lords of the manor and wealthy merchants in their turn sought such spiritual and posthumous benefits as the endowment of a chantry would confer upon them. In general, the endowment took the form of lands, tenements, rents and other possessions, or sometimes of money. It provided a stipend for the priest whose office was to sing masses periodically for the founder and for 'all the faithful departed' at a specified altar in a church or in a chantry chapel; and frequently part of the endowment was set aside to bestow a weekly dole upon the poor. Upon the chantry priest were often imposed other duties, such as assisting the parish priest in the normal offices in the church or teaching in a free school. He usually received a stipend of about £5 a year.

At the parish church of Walthamstow, Essex, Sir George Monoux, a London draper and mayor in 1514, founded a chantry in the north aisle which he had built. In the *Records of Chantries in Essex*, 1547, occurs the following entry : ' Lands and tenements put in feoffment by Sir George Monoux, gent., to the maintenance of a priest to sing mass in the church and also to teach a few scholars during the term of twenty years ; and one Sir John Hughson, clerk, of the age of forty years and of good conversation, literate and teaches a school there, is now incumbent hereof. . . . £7 yearly, value of the same doth amount to the sum of £6. 13s. 4d.' Set in the east wall of the chapel are brasses from the tomb of the founder and his wife, Lady Ann.

In chantry foundations of persons of rank and wealth, the endowment often provided for the establishment of an almshouse or hospital, as it was then termed. Here were housed and maintained a number of poor men or bedesmen, to whom the chantry priest, who was usually master of the hospital, served as chaplain and distributed their allowances, fuel and clothing. The bedesmen wore a distinguishing apparel, generally a long cloth gown of dark hue, and bearing the cognizance of the founder on one sleeve. They were all under obligation of attending church daily to pray for the soul of their benefactor. It was enjoined by the founder that they should kneel about his tomb and there make their supplications with the priest. The number of bedesmen in a hospital varied from five to thirteen.

To ensure an exact observance by the bedesmen of their duties, a precise ceremonial, almost a ritual, was often prepared by the founder. The bedesmen of Henry, Lord Marney (d. 1523) were to be :

such as shall say at least their paternoster, ave and creed in Latin . . . at their uprising they shall say for the souls of Sir Robert Marney, Knt., and his wife and of all my children, five paternosters, five aves and one creed, and every day go to the church of Layer Marney, and there hear Mass in the new chapel. Moreover, I will that at his first coming into the church, everyone of them shall kneel down before the Sacrament and say a paternoster and an ave, and then go to my tomb and there, kneeling down, say for my soul and for the other souls above named three paternosters, three aves and one creed in worship of the Trinity ; and then go down into the church and there in the time of Mass or else before their departure . . . say for the above-named souls, Our Lady's Psalter [*i.e.* the Rosary] and at night-time before their going to bed, every one of them to say kneeling on their knees five paternosters, five aves and the creed for the souls aforesaid. Also I will that such of them as can say De Profundis shall say it in lieu of the paternosters, etc. Also that every Wednesday and Friday, they go into the church at afternoon and there kneeling about my tomb say for my soul and the souls aforesaid, Our Lady's Psalter ; and if any of them can say Dirige, I will that they say it in lieu of Our Lady's Psalter.

The nature of a chantry necessarily depended upon the value of the endowment. Often the intention was that it should be of a limited duration, *viz.* for one, two, three or ten years. In 1533 Robert Astbroke bequeathed a sum of money for ' a priest to sing for my soul* in Wicomb church at Jesus altar for ten years.'

A moderate endowment would ensure the recitation of masses on the first, third, seventh and thirtieth day after the death of the testator, with an obit† once a year, a provision which seemed to be the most frequently favoured. Another person would desire a trental of masses, *i.e.* a daily mass for a month after his decease.

Obits became very popular, the endowment being less costly than that of a chantry. Payment for obits was usually made to the parish priest, who was responsible for the due observance of the rite and in most cases was required to distribute alms to the poor out of the payment received. Obits which made no provision for alms were the exception unless the endowment was very small. As a rule half of the bequest was set aside for charity.

The *Consuetudinary* of Norwich Cathedral gives an account of the use of candles at an obit. On the eve of the observance a pall was thrown over the tomb of the founder and a candle placed at the head and another at the foot, there to burn until the morrow, when four other candles were lighted and remained burning until High Mass had been sung for his soul. Then the four candles were extinguished and two others placed there until after compline, the last office of the day. Often, where there was no tomb, a hearse covered with a black pall was set up west of the altar.

In the ordinance for the obit of Henry VII at Bermondsey Abbey the use of a hearse is specifically prescribed.

The abbot and convent of S. Saviour at Bermondsey shall provide a hearse, to be set in the midst of the high chancel of the monastery before the High Altar, covered and apparelled with the best and most honourable stuff convenient for the same; and also four tapers of wax, each of them weighing eight pounds, to be set about the hearse—that is to say, on either side thereof one taper, and at either

---

*' To sing for a soul ' was a common phrase for the recitation of soul masses.
†An obit was a mass that was sung on the anniversary of the death, for a few years or in perpetuity.

end of the same hearse another taper, and all the same four tapers to be lighted and burning continually during all the time of every such Placebo, Dirige,* with nine lessons, lauds and mass of requiem, with the prayers and obeisances above rehearsed.

In an account of the obits at Waltham Abbey, given by Thomas Fuller, the church historian, in 1648, he exclaims : ' O ! the reasonable rates at Waltham. Two shillings and twopence for an obit, the price whereof in S. Paul's Cathedral was forty shillings.' Of the 2s. 2d. the bellman, who figures frequently in obit bequests, received 2d.

He was the parish bell-ringer or the town-crier and amongst his duties was ' going with the bell about the town ' to beg people to pray for the soul of some deceased parishioner on the occasion of the obit. By his will, 1403, John Baret of Bury S. Edmunds desired that two bellmen should be given 4d. each for ' going about the town at my year-day ' to enjoin the townsfolk ' to pray for my soul and for my father and mother,' and the same payment was to be made for ringing on ' the month's mind.'†

The bellman performed a like office for the religious gilds.

Obit bequests were made in kind as well as in money. At Bromley, Margaret White, by her will in 1538, ordained that her obit should be kept in the church ' out of the increase of two kine ' that she left. She also gave three hives of bees to maintain lights at the altars of All Hallows, S. Antony and S. Sepulchre in the church, and directed that bread, cheese and drink should be distributed to four poor parishioners.

Obits and anniversaries for persons long deceased would in course of time become wearisome affairs. This was apparently the case at Barking Abbey, Essex, where it was resolved by the abbess, Anne de Vere (1296-1318), and the sisters, that the obits of abbesses who had been dead for more than a century should be allowed to lapse ' for the greater alleviation of the convent.' Exceptions were made for abbesses who had provided obit pittances for the nuns, ' for these cannot and ought not to be removed.' Who would wish to deprive the ladies of an occasional delicacy to relieve the monotony of the frater ? Notwithstanding, after the lapse of a century, deceased abbesses can have been little more than shadowy figures and an economy was effected by the suppression of their obits.

---

*' Placebo Domine in regione vivorum,' I will please the Lord in the land of the living, Psalm cxvi.; ' Domine dirige nos,' Direct us, O Lord, in all our doings. Psalm v.

†The month's mind was the celebration of soul-masses for a period of thirty days, especially on the third, seventh and thirtieth days following death.

The founding and endowment of a perpetual chantry was a costly business, the privilege only of the wealthy. It made provision for masses to be recited for ever and often included the erection of a special chapel, which was reserved solely for the soul-masses of the founder and family. Within the chapel were set up an altar for the masses and the tomb of the founder. Stone for the fabric had to be purchased and payment made for its transport ; masons and carvers had to be employed, as well as craftsmen to colour and adorn the completed structure. The endowment would need to be ample enough to maintain the fabric and to provide a stipend for the priest. Vestments, ornaments, candles and missals were needed as well as money for distribution to the poor at the obit. Some idea of the ornaments and furnishings required is to be gained from the account given in Dugdale of the chantry of Canon Roger of Waltham in old S. Paul's Cathedral. The two priests who served the altar in Roger's chapel had for their use the following : two pairs of vestments, one for daily use consisting of a chasuble of gold cloth on canvas, the other a similar chasuble on silk ; albs, amices, stoles and manciples ; an altar frontal of gold cloth ; cloths to cover the altar and to wrap the vestments ; two altar towels, one with a frontal of gold bordering ; a chalice and patten of silver gilt weighing twenty ounces and valued at 30s. ; a missal worth 20s. ; two blessed corporals* in a case ; a box for altar beads ; two hand towels, two pewter cruets, a small bell, a brazier valued at 3s. and a ' good key ' to the chapel door. For these the chantry priests were ' for ever to answer according to the oath they took on their admission.' The brazier must have been most acceptable to the shivering priest when he sang early mass on a winter's morn. The good key was a necessity, for chantry chapels were often used as repositories for valuables and were locked when not in use.

In addition to the above furnishings, Canon Roger adorned his chapel with images of Our Lord, S. John Baptist and other saints and with pictures of the Heavenly Host and the Joys of the Virgin. His chapel was dedicated to Our Lady and S. Lawrence and stood on the south side of the choir of Old S. Paul's.

As lands and tenements most frequently formed the endowment of a perpetual chantry, a licence to alienate the property in mortmain had to be obtained from the Crown (page 55).

The vast majority of endowments, however, were for the recitation of masses at an altar already existing in a church, the particular altar being specified in the charter or in the terms of the bequest. The main end was ever to ensure prayers for the founder's soul, but part of the

---

*A corporal was a white linen cloth which covered the chalice and Host on the altar during mass. It was hallowed before use and was hence ' blessed.'

endowment was earmarked for other purposes. Sums of money were set aside for the tolling of bells, for the purchase of wax candles to be burned at the altar, for distribution as alms to the needy, for bread and wine and so on.

In 1509 William Plesyngton of Ipswich orders 'his body to be buried in S. Peter's churchyard ; a barrel of beer with bread to be given in the church at his cost to the poor of the parish ; Sir Jeffrey his ghostly father to say a trental of masses for his soul in S. Peter's church and to be paid five shillings.'

Candles, which were so important an item in Queen Eleanor's commemorations at Westminster, figure largely in bequests for chantries and obits. In 1414 Peter de Bolton, Rector of Scrayngham in the diocese of York, left ten pounds of wax in five candles, and two torches to be burned around his body on the day of his burial. To the priest celebrating mass for one year in the chancel for the repose of the rector's soul 100 shillings were bequeathed ' if my goods amount to such a sum when my debts are paid.'

The obit was the occasion for the burning of more candles at the founder's tomb. The prickets on which candles were fixed remain on some of the grates or grilles enclosing mediaeval tombs. In some churches so overpowering were the smoke and fumes from the great number of candles always burning that something had to be done to abate the nuisance. In 1466 twenty-two pence was paid a glazier for removing two panes from the windows (presumably the clerestory lights) of a church in Norfolk ' for to let out the reke of the torches at the Dirige and soldering new of the same.'

Less costly than candles were mortar-lights, i.e. wide bowls made of metal which were placed on standards and filled with oil or wax in which floated a burning wick. Both candles and mortars were used for altar-lights.

The chantry certificates of Edward VI contain many references to sums of money set aside for the maintenance of lights. In 1493 a chantry for one priest was founded in Cookham church, Berks., to sing masses for one year for the soul of William Norreys. The founder directed that he should be buried in the Lady chapel, to the north of the chancel, and he made bequests for the support of lights at the altars of Our Lady, S. Anne, S. Catherine, S. Nicholas, S. Clement, All Souls, the Holy Cross and for the torchlight in Cookham church.* The twinkling lights he had seen burning at the many altars doubtless caught this gentleman's fancy.

* The torch-light was a tall staff-torch which was held aloft at the elevation of the host during mass.

In one of the clauses of the Suppression of Chantries Act occurs the phrase 'to which chantries, obits, lights and lamps it is enacted . . . this Act shall extend.'

Another form of chantry was the anniversary, an office that was in the nature of a memorial service. The brethren of a religious house, in grateful recognition of some benefit conferred upon them by a pious patron, would pledge themselves to hold him in perpetual remembrance by celebrating a mass once a year for his soul.

Anniversaries were commonly maintained for deceased abbots, patrons and royal benefactors. In a charter of Romsey Abbey, dated 8 July 1351, the abbess and convent, much indebted as they were to Bishop Edingdon of Winchester, 'grant that, after the said Father's death, every year on his anniversary, they shall cause to be solemnly celebrated . . . a Requiem mass for his soul. . . .'; and the abbess undertook to distribute ten marks to the nuns who were present and to those absent from sufficient cause.

At Canterbury one of the obedientiaries was known as the anniversarius. He was responsible for the observance of all the anniversaries and obits by the brethren and frequently bequests were made to him for their maintenance.

The use of a hearse at anniversaries was customary, at any rate for those of royal and important personages. At S. Alban's the hearse and four tapers (i.e. candles), each weighing eight pounds, were used at the anniversary of Henry VII.

The ordinances respecting chantries as set out in the deeds of foundation vary not a little and in many cases are quite lengthy.

A good idea of the duties of a chantry priest on the eve of the Reformation is to be gained from the foundation charter of the Vavasour chantry at S. Mary's Church, Badsworth, Yorks. This was founded in 1510 for the soul of Isabella, wife of William Vavasour and daughter of Robert Urswicke. It was ordained that a priest of secular habit, not otherwise beneficed, should sing a requiem mass every week and a Placebo and Dirige—according to the use in the cathedral church of York—at the altar of S. Anne in the south arch of Badsworth church. At primum lavatorium* in each mass he was to turn to the people and, reciting De Profundis, then to exhort those standing round to pray for the soul of the founder; he should then say the collect inclina Domine for the same soul. Every year on the Tuesday after the octave of Easter there was to be an obit for Isabella, on which occasion the sum of 6s. 8d. was to be distributed to the poor of Badsworth under the supervision

---

*The lavatorium or lavatorie was that point in the mass at which the celebrant washed his fingers, reciting the while a part of Psalm xxvi. 6 et seq.

of the rector. The chantry priest was to be learned in plain-song and grammar and was to be present in the choir of the parish church every Sunday and festival at matins, mass, vespers and compline ; and was to wear his surplice and to read and sing as the rector appointed. He was not to absent himself from the said church for more than a month at a time and then only by leave of the rector. He should not play dice or other illicit or prohibited games except on the twelve days after Christmas, nor was he to frequent taverns and ale-houses at unseemly times. . . . He was not to alienate the goods, books, jewels or ornaments belonging to the chantry, but was to preserve and repair them and the buildings and other possessions. If guilty of crime or incontinence or prevented by loss of limb from performing the offices, he was to be removed by the rector of the parish. (Yorkshire Chantry Surveys).

Much in the above ordinance suggests that when their sacred duties were done some chantry priests were prone to indulge in relaxations unworthy of their office : and, as in this, many ordinances prescribed that the chantry priest should assist the parish priest in the daily or Sunday services in the church ; and as part of his duty, he was required to recite daily the office of the dead.

Of equal interest to the Vavasour ordinance and detailed at some length is that of the Daundy chantry. In 1514 Edmund Daundy, merchant of Ipswich, founded a perpetual chantry at the altar of S. Thomas the Martyr in the parish church of S. Lawrence in Ipswich, ' for the prosperous estate of King Henry VIII and Katherine, his queen, of himself, Edmund Daundy, Thomas Wulsy, clerk, Dean of the cathedral church of Lincoln,* and of William Daundy, his son, for the term of their lives and for their souls after their decease ; also for the souls of Anne, his late wife, Robert Wulsy and Joan his wife, father and mother of the same Thomas Wulsy.' The presentation was to be in the hands of the wardens of the parish and six other men nominated by the bailiffs. The chantry priest was to take the oath to keep the statutes of the foundation ; he was to perform the duties personally, not to be absent for more than twenty days except from infirmity, nor to accept any other benefice, office, stipend, trental or yearly service but the £11. 6s. 8d. granted by the founder. Further, the names of all those to be prayed for were to be inscribed on a tablet set up openly on the altar of S. Thomas. Daundy assigned for the priest's residence a messuage lately built in the parish ; he provided a mass-book, two complete vestments and a book called a coucher, and he directed that these and other ornaments of the altar

---

* In the same year, 1514, three bishoprics fell upon Wolsey, *viz.* Lincoln, Winchester and York ; and the next year the cardinalate. The name of the great churchman was variously spelt—Wolsy, Wulsy, Wulsey, Wolsey and Woulsey.

should be locked in a chest after the mass. He also willed that the priest should deposit 2s. 4d. in a box with two keys . . . for the maintenance of the house, furniture, etc. He made elaborate arrangements for his obit, on which occasion gifts of money were to be distributed to priests, clerks, singing children, the sexton and the poor of the parish. Two bailiffs of Ipswich were paid 13s. 4d. ' to control the said anniversary.' The founder spared no expense to ensure an adequate commemoration and he concluded, ' And because it is not in man but in God to foresee and provide all things, and oftentimes it fortuneth that what in the beginning was thought to be profitable, afterwards is found not to be so, he therefore reserves to himself the right to alter these statutes.'

The Wolsey family, whose names appear in the Daundy ordinance, was undoubtedly of some standing in Ipswich. In 1496, a few days before his death, Robert Wolsey made his will, by which he directed that ' if Thomas, my son, be a priest within a year next after my decease, then I will that he sing [masses] for me and my friends by the space of a year and he for to have for his salary 10 marks ; and if the said Thomas, my son be not a priest, then I will that another honest priest sing for me and my friends the term aforesaid and he to have the salary of 10 marks.'

Thomas was not ordained priest until 10 March 1498, at S. Peter's Church, Marlborough, so the office and the 10 marks went to ' another honest priest.'

The ordinance of a chantry at the priory of Newark in Surrey, a house of Augustinian canons, sets forth in considerable detail the obligations imposed on the prior, the canons and the priest. Nothing was left to chance or to the discretion of the prior. In 1382 John Newdigate and Laurencia, the widow of Peter atte Wode, made an endowment of £6. 14s. in rents to found a chantry for the good estate of King Richard II, Bishop Wykeham of Winchester and of Laurencia during their lifetime, and for the souls of the founders, the King and the Bishop after death. Obits for the founders were to be observed annually, when the prior would receive 14d. and each canon 7d. as pittances. The priest, who was to be a canon of the priory, was to celebrate a mass every Saturday at the altar of Our Lady, for which the prior was to pay him 7d. a week out of the endowment. If through pestilence—the Black Death was still in man's memory—a canon was not available for the mass, a secular priest was to act in his place. If no such could be found the prior was to distribute 3d. on each occasion to the poor at the priory gate, to pray for the souls of the founders. If a mass were ever omitted ' without lawful impediment ' a fine of 2s. was to be paid to the Bishop of Worcester to be distributed as alms. The convent was required to provide all the vestments, ornaments, lights, bread and wine and everything needed for the chantry. Every prior on assuming office had to swear on the Gospels to observe the ordinance of the chantry, which was to be read in chapter at Advent and Lent every year. Should the prior fail to take the oath as required within three days, he was to pay 2s. to the Bishop of Worcester for each day of default. (V. C. H. Surrey.)

Such precautions against ' breach of contract ' as occur in the foregoing were not unusual. Various methods were employed for ensuring that a founder's wishes were complied with. The most satisfactory was to entrust the chantry property to accredited administrators such as the Mayor and Corporation, a local gild or company. In 1504 the very large sum of £163. 6s. 8d. was left by a Hugh Pemberton for the founding and maintenance of a chantry at S. Catherine's College, Cambridge. One of the Fellows was to recite a mass every day ' while the world should endure.' Default was on each occasion to be followed by a fine of 6s. 8d., which was imposed on the Fellows by the Merchant Taylors' Gild, London, who were invested with ample powers to safeguard the testator's rights. (Coulton.)

Unusual obligations were laid upon the priest in the ordinance of the chantry of Avery Cornburgh at Romford, Essex. In addition to singing masses for the founder, the priest was required to preach at least twice a year in four churches in the county, viz. Hornchurch, South Ockendon, Ingrave and South Weald, as well as at Romford church. For all these duties he received a stipend of £12 a year.

Seldom was a benefactor of so uncharitable a nature as the Lady of Arringrosk, who founded a chantry in Cambuskenneth Abbey, Stirlingshire.

In a document dated 1507 she stipulated that :

Because we have thus by God's grace augmented divine worship in the said church of Cambuskenneth and have chosen our own sepulchre therein, therefore the said Alexander and his convent by unanimous consent have granted the whole choir as a free burying-place for us, our heirs and successors and the whole of our family, on condition that it shall not be lawful for any parishioner or any other person to be buried in the same choir, unless it be the abbot or one of his brethren, or some honourable servant or friend of the abbot, who might chance to die in the abbey or to choose his sepulchre there. (Reg. Cambuskenneth, 1872.)

The convent must have been much indebted to the dictatorial lady to have accepted such conditions.

2 Early chantry foundations—Increase after the Black Death—Distribution in England and Wales—Founders—Gild chantries—Grammar schools—Chantries in cathedral and monastic churches—In nuns' churches—In Carthusian houses—In the Mendicants' churches.

THE EARLIEST RECORDED chantries are those of Bishop Hugh of Wells at Lincoln Cathedral *c.* 1235 and of Bishop Stavenby of Lichfield *c.* 1238. Another early chantry was founded at Ely Cathedral by Bishop William de Kilkenny, 1254-7, who made a bequest of 200 marks for the support of two priests to sing masses for his soul. In the *Taxatio* of Pope Nicholas IV, 1291-2, only two chantries are recorded, one of Bishop Hugh at Lincoln and the other at Hatherton in the archdeaconry of Coventry. The endowment of the former was held by the sacrist of Lincoln, who, out of a sum of 32 marks, had to provide two chantry priests and alms for the poor at the Bishop's obit. No doubt other chantries were unrecorded at the time but very few date earlier than the fourteenth century.

The number of foundations rapidly increased after the Black Death, 1349. The frightful mortality of the pestilence and its attendant horrors remained long in the memory of man ; the uncertainty of life and the fears engendered by the plague and by recurring outbreaks turned men's thoughts to the next world : and so it was that during the second half of the century the provision of soul-masses multiplied greatly. The wills of the period are significant. Anselm de Fordele, a burgess of Great Yarmouth, by his will, dated 23 May 1349, ' willing to be prepared for a sudden change '—a timely phrase—desired to be buried in the chancel of S. Nicholas' Church and among many other bequests left ' five quarters of corn to be distributed for my soul and the souls of my benefactors on the day of my burial, by my executors ; also on the seventh day I bequeath five quarters of corn ; also on the thirtieth day I bequeath other five quarters of corn,' on which days masses were to be said for his soul. ' Also, I bequeath all my quit rents which I have in Great Yarmouth, for the support of a priest to celebrate for my soul and the soul of Margaret my wife and the souls of our benefactors ; also I bequeath all my mill-stones, spars, firewood, salt, etc., to be sold to be distributed for the souls before named.'

Of the two thousand or more chantries that existed at the time of the Suppression the great majority had been founded during the fifteenth century. By the beginning of the sixteenth century the chantry system in this country had become vast indeed. At the lesser altars in a cathedral or monastic church there was an unceasing recitation of soul-masses throughout every morning.

At Lincoln Cathedral, where there was but one chantry in 1290, the number had risen to thirty-six in the *Valor Ecclesiasticus*, Henry VIII's survey of the revenues of the Church. A grand total of 1,733 for England and Wales is given in the *Valor*, but the returns from the diocesan areas vary considerably in detail and no doubt in accuracy.

The following is a short list of the dioceses in which were the greater number of chantry foundations :

York (424) ; London (310) ; Lincoln (213) ; Coventry and Lichfield (106) ; Chester (127) ; Salisbury (72) ; Norwich (60).

How unequally chantries were distributed throughout England is apparent from the *Valor* figures. It would be difficult to account for such small numbers as twenty-three for the diocese of Canterbury and eighteen for that of Durham. In Wales there were very few indeed, the number given in the *Valor* for the Diocese of S. Asaph being nil.

Reference has been made to chantry chapels, the building and maintenance of which were often provided for by the founders of perpetual chantries. But it was not until after the Black Death that such substantial memorials of personal piety made their appearance in the churches of this country.

Only the wealthy—royalty, nobles, bishops, abbots, merchant princes and the like—were able to include a special oratory as part of a chantry foundation, as were also the many trade gilds and religious fraternities. Large numbers of chantry chapels which were once such prominent features in our cathedral, monastic and parish churches have long since disappeared ; but those that survive furnish us with examples of the several forms they assumed and are representative of the various estates of the founders.

Most of these are dealt with at some length in later pages of this book. Suffice it to mention at this point, the following: royal chantry chapels, of Henry IV at Canterbury, of Henry V and Henry VII at Westminster ; chapels of nobles, the Beauchamp chapel at Warwick and the Berkeley chapel at Bristol ; of bishops, the Audley chapel at Hereford and that of West at Ely ; of abbots, Ramryge's at S. Albans and Lichfield's at Evesham ; and of wealthy merchants, the Greenaway chapel at Tiverton, and the Lane chapel at Cullompton. Many a chancel aisle in the parish churches, *e.g.* at Chipping Sodbury, was originally built as the chantry chapel of a local gild or sodality.

A large number of the chapels in the cathedral churches were those of bishops, to whom the appeal of so lasting a memorial was more immediate than to the layman. The less fortunate parish priest seldom possessed the means to found a perpetual chantry. In a modest way he often could and did leave a small sum for soul-masses and obits, as is evident from mediaeval wills. Thus in 1412 Roger de Kirby, Vicar of Gaynford, desired to be buried in the chancel of his church and left £15 to a priest ' to sing for his soul and for the souls of all the faithful departed,'* for a period of three years after his death.

Sometimes a parish priest chose to have his chantry in the church of a neighbouring monastery, perhaps in the belief that the masses would be more faithfully recited there than if left to his successors in the parish church. In a deed of 1479 James de Newton, Rector of Bedrule, granted 10 marks a year from tenements in Jedburgh to Walter Henrison, chantry priest, and his successors serving the altar of S. Mungo in Jedburgh Abbey ; to sing a daily mass for the souls of James II of Scotland, James III and Queen Margaret and for the souls of the founder, his father and mother, etc. After the death of the rector the patronage of the chantry was to go to James Rutherford of that ilk and his heirs, and the presentation was to be made within twenty days, failing which, the provost, bailie and the convent of Jedburgh were to present within eight days.

A few instances are on record of chantries that were founded in expiation of some horrible crime, the perpetrator thereof providing the endowment for the soul-masses of his victim.

John Holland, Duke of Exeter and son of Joan the ' Fair Maid of Kent ' by her first husband, Earl Thomas, was guilty of a dastardly murder in 1385. Near York, one of his followers was slain in a brawl by an archer of Ralph, son of Earl Stafford. The next evening John, passing Ralph in the dark, drove his sword into his body and rode away to take sanctuary at Beverley. Richard II, John's half-brother, thereupon seized all his lands, and in February 1386 John was required to found a perpetual chantry for the soul of the murdered man. It was served by three priests, of whom two were to perform their office at the place where Ralph had been slain, and the other at King's Langley, where he was buried. Later, the king ordered that the three priests should serve the chantry at Langley.

> I Richard's body have interred new ;
> . . . and I have built
> Two chantries where the sad and solemn priests
> Sing still for Richard's soul.

---

* In nearly all ordinances occurred the phrase ' and for all the faithful departed.'

These lines from the king's speech in Shakespeare's *Henry V* refer to the atonement which he made for the guilt of his father, Henry IV. The chantries were founded at Shene and Syon. It may seem surprising that Henry founded none for Richard in Westminster Abbey, whither he had the body of the murdered king brought from King's Langley.

Personal chantry endowments being as a rule beyond the means of the vast majority of laymen, it came about that parish folk, not to be denied the benefit of soul-masses, banded themselves together into religious gilds, which made provision for what have been aptly called ' co-operative chantries.' The gilds were established for the purpose of mutual benefit, for works of piety and charity and for the celebration of masses for their brethren, living and dead.

In the thirteenth century at Bath was a religious gild known as ' the common chantry of Bath in the church of S. Mary de Stalles,' and its head or warden was the mayor of the city. It was endowed to maintain a priest to sing a daily mass for the good estate of the king and the royal family, for their souls and the souls of others, and once a year the gild members as a corporate body attended a mass for this purpose.

At S. Sepulchre's Church, Newgate, the gild of S. Stephen supported a priest and provided a light to be burned before the image of S. Stephen. Every member was to be present at the corporate mass on S. Stephen's day and make an offering of one farthing or more. On the death of a member a requiem mass was sung, for which the gild provided candles. Three trentals of masses followed and all the brethren were required to attend the Dirige.

The specific purpose for which religious fraternities were formed varied not a little. Some were established to repair the parish church, as for example at All Hallows' Church, London Wall, where a gild came into being, to undertake the rebuilding of the church spire and of a chapel attached to the church. Others repaired bridges, founded grammar schools, produced mystery plays or provided candles to be burned at an altar or before an image in the parish church.

Affluent and public-spirited was the ' Fraternity of the Holy Cross ' attached to the church of S. Helen, Abingdon. It was formed *c.* 1389 and was then served by two proctors and a priest. The gild erected a comely rood in the church and was instrumental in building the New Bridge of the town. In 1442 it was incorporated and was endowed with lands for the maintenance of the road from Abingdon to Dorchester in good repair. In 1446 the brethren founded a hospital (almshouse) for thirteen poor men and women ; and about the same time erected an octagonal cross in the market-place, adorned with three rows of statues, ' the whole ornamented with coats of arms painted and carved.' In 1457

6. CHAPEL OF THE BLACK PRINCE, CANTERBURY CATHEDRAL

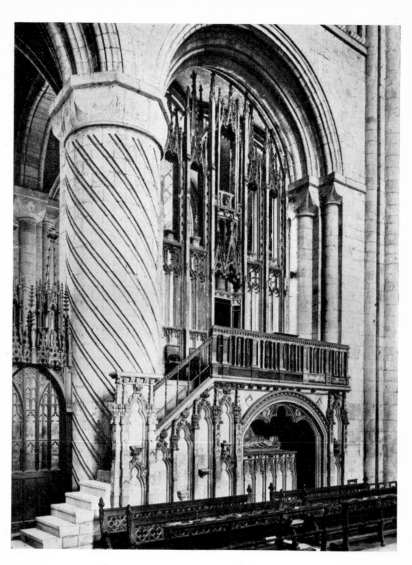

7. BISHOP HATFIELD'S CHAPEL AND THRONE, DURHAM CATHEDRAL

8. INTERIOR OF BISHOP ALCOCK'S CHAPEL, ELY CATHEDRAL

10. BISHOP WEST'S CHAPEL, PUTNEY CHURCH

9. HENRY IV'S CHAPEL, CANTERBURY CATHEDRAL

the fraternity supported two priests ; one, the road priest, who was to pray for the benefactors thereof, and the other the bridge priest, who sang masses for the brethren whose gifts maintained the New Bridge. Each of these received a stipend of £6. 13s. 4d. In 1539 the gild erected a chapel to the north of the chancel of S. Helen's Church, called ' Our Lady's Aisle.' The oak roof, richly ornamented and coloured, was the gift of Nicholas Gould, one of the brethren.

After the gild was dissolved, a new charter was granted in 1553 to maintain the hospital, which still remains—a low brick and timber building with a wooden cloister and a hall.

The Palmers' Gild at Ludlow, founded by royal licence in 1284 and dedicated to the Virgin Mary, not only maintained a college of chantry priests with singing men and choristers in the church of S. Lawrence, but also established a free grammar school in the town ; though the primary object of the fraternity was the celebration of masses for the well-being of its members and benefactors and for their souls, etc., after death.

The College of Corpus Christi at Cambridge, exceptional in this respect amongst university foundations, owes its existence to two religious gilds of the town, which in 1352 united for the purpose of founding a college for the training of a number of priests. The statutes, dated 1356, decreed that the chaplains and scholars should attend divine service in S. Benet's or S. Botolph's Church at certain times and all the masses were to be celebrated ' for the health of the King [Edward III] and Queen Phillipa and their children, the Duke of Lancaster and the brethren and sisters, founders and benefactors of the gild and college.' As Dean Stubbs wrote : ' This, perhaps, rather than the love of learning pure and simple, was the chief aim which influenced the early founders of Corpus Christi college.'

Sometimes a gild was formed to maintain a chantry which had declined through changing circumstances ; for it often happened that the property originally bequeathed for the endowment had depreciated so much that with the passage of time it proved inadequate for the purpose.

As a rule each gild was known by the name of its patron saint. The gilds of Corpus Christi, a very popular dedication, had as their special purpose the celebration of the Feast of Corpus Christi, which was made the occasion of a solemn procession of the Blessed Sacrament, in which all the gild members took part and was followed by a display of pageantry.★

★In Aldbourne church, Wilts., is a small brass in the chancel pavement to the memory of Henry Frekylton (d. 1509), the chantry priest who served ' Our Lady's Gild.' He is depicted in eucharistic vestments and the symbols of his office, a chalice and a missal, appear on smaller brasses on the same slab.

3

But, for whatever purpose a religious gild came into being, the provision of soul-masses was a *sine qua non*, and the maintenance of a chantry priest was a charge upon the gild treasury.

The number of brethren composing a gild necessarily varied with the size of the population of the place. At Colchester, the gild of S. Helen, the chief one in the town, numbered sixty-five brethren in 1418 and nearly ninety in 1491. The fraternity acquired for its use the chapel of the decayed hospital of the Crutched Friars in Colchester, and formed a co-operative chantry served by five priests in Holy Cross chapel, to pray for the souls of the king and all the brethren of the gild.

After the Black Death, the number of religious gilds rapidly increased. Few churches were without them and in many quite small villages there were three or four. The members of the gilds were expected to make bequests, however small, and not infrequently were required to do so. When the gilds became wealthy, they set to work erecting their own chantry chapels, which usually took the form of an aisle grafted on to the parish church.

From the middle of the fifteenth century onwards, the prosperous trade and craft gilds, notwithstanding their more secular aims, became equally active in establishing their own chapels, with chantry endowments. These chapels were generally attached to the parish churches, particularly in towns and populous centres where the gild membership would be considerable. The enlargement and maintenance of many town churches had been largely due to the munificence of the merchant class and the trade gilds.

The expansion and resultant irregularity of the plans of many town churches during the fifteenth century and the early part of the sixteenth are in no small measure due to the assimilation from time to time of the chantry chapels of the religious and trade gilds. The church of S. Michael, Coventry, of which only the outer walls remain, was an outstanding instance. The main body of the church was erected by the townsfolk in a period of about seventy years, from 1373 to 1450, and in the early sixteenth century outer aisles were grafted on to the nave to provide chapels for the various craft gilds associated with the cloth trade, on which the prosperity of the town largely depended. The new aisles were sub-divided to form gild-chapels and were enclosed from the inner aisles by timber screens, much in the same way as were the outer chapels in Manchester collegiate church.

Here the members of the fraternities met for corporate worship, here they celebrated requiem masses for deceased brethren and here their obits were kept. The most important of all the chapels in this large church was the Drapers', on the north side of the chancel, but the Girdlers, the

Cappers, the Smiths and the Dyers also had their chapels. The gilds set aside large sums of money for the support of the priests, who numbered six in 1522.*

Of equal interest, by reason of its accumulation of gild chapels, is the church of the Holy Trinity at Coventry. Here the Tanners, the Dyers, the Butchers, the Mercers and the fraternity of Corpus Christi were represented, their chapels being disposed in various parts of the church in a haphazard manner as dictated by circumstances.

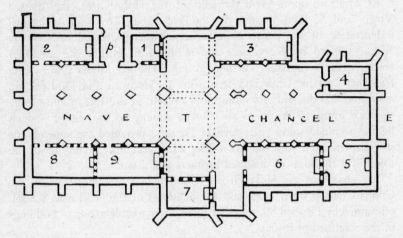

FIG. I PLAN OF HOLY TRINITY CHURCH, COVENTRY.

*1. S. Thomas Chapel. 2. Dyers' Chapel. (?). 3. Mercers' Chapel. 4. Lady Chapel. 5. Trinity Chapel. 6. Butchers' Chapel. 7. Corpus Christi Chapel. 8. Jesus Chapel. 9. Tanners' Chapel. The screens are conjectural*

The chapel of the Tanners' gild occupied the eastern part of the south aisle of the nave; that of the Butchers flanked the chancel on the south; the Mercers' chapel was off the north aisle of the chancel at the western end and was originally walled off from the aisle. The gild of Corpus Christi had the south transept and was also associated with the Lady chapel adjoining the chancel on the north, for the members undertook to find a priest 'to sing mass at the altar of Our Blessed Lady, for the good estate of King Richard and Anne, his queen, the whole realm of England and all those by whom the said altar is maintained . . . and for their souls after death.' This was virtually a

*S. Michael's, Coventry, was raised to the status of a cathedral in 1918 but was destroyed in the German air-raid of 14 November 1940. The western tower and the aisle walls alone survive.

chantry for the gild itself. There were in addition personal chantries in Holy Trinity Church, which were in no way connected with the crafts or gilds.

Scarcely less complex than the plans of the Coventry churches is that of the large church of S. John Baptist at Cirencester. The town gilds there maintained four chapels in the church, with which they were so closely associated that the rooms of the splendid three-storied porch at the south-west were used as the gild-halls.

At Stratford-upon-Avon the gild of the Holy Cross, the Blessed Virgin and S. John Baptist was opulent enough to build its chapel independent of the parish church, licence being granted in 1269 by Bishop Giffard of Worcester; and in the next century the members erected their own hall. Further, in 1482 Thomas Jolyffe granted the fraternity ' all his lands and tenements in Stratford and Dodwell on condition that the said gild should find a priest, fit and able in knowledge to teach grammar freely to all scholars coming to the school' which he had founded some years earlier. The gild provided the stipends for the chaplains and paid the town-crier 4d. a year for ' crying about the town ' for the souls of deceased brothers and sisters.

The chapel of the Holy Cross, rebuilt in the fifteenth century, the Gildhall, dating from 1417, and the buildings of the Grammar School, refounded by Edward VI, together form a remarkable group of buildings in the Stratford of to-day.

Amongst the duties required of chantry priests was often that of keeping a free school. It was common for schools to be held in an aisle of the parish church or in the chamber over the porch ; even in a chantry chapel when one existed of sufficient size. At Farthinghoe church, Northants, a chantry chapel south of the chancel was long used for the purpose. It was not unusual for wealthy benefactors to include in the provisions of a chantry endowment the founding of a grammar school. At Darlington a Robert Marshall founded a chantry ' for his soul and for all Christian souls and to keep a school of grammar for all manner of children thither resorting.' The office of schoolmaster usually devolved upon the priest, and the boys who profited by the munificence of the founder were required to take part in the periodical commemorations, when masses were said.

Margaret, Countess of Richmond, the mother of Henry VII and a great patroness of learning, founded a school at Wimborne Minster, Dorset ' to the intent that the incumbent should say mass for the souls of the founders and to be a schoolmaster to teach fairly all manner of children, grammar.' By a charter of Elizabeth's reign, the Lady Margaret School was constituted as the grammar school of the town.

In the *Calendar of Chantries* are recorded forty-two schools provided for by chantry endowments. They were all suppressed under the Act for the Dissolution of Chantries in 1547, though a number were refounded as Edward VI grammar schools.

Of the two thousand or more perpetual chantries that existed at the time of the Suppression, a considerable number were to be found in the cathedrals of the Old Foundation, such as Salisbury and York.

The cathedral priories, Winchester, Durham and so on, together with the Benedictine monastic establishments such as Westminster and Tewkesbury, had their share and there was a goodly number in the Augustinian houses and the collegiate churches. As might be expected, chantries were less common in the churches of the austere Cistercian monks and of the unworldly Carthusians.

Though not so general as in the great monastic churches, chantries were also founded in nuns' churches. In many a small nunnery the grateful sisters welcomed the endowment of a chantry by some wealthy patron, through whose munificence the rebuilding or enlargement of their church or conventual buildings had been made possible.

At S. Helen's Priory, Bishopsgate, a house of Benedictine nuns, Adam Franceys, mercer and mayor of London, left property in the city in 1371 for the founding and endowment of a perpetual chantry in the chapel of the Holy Ghost, which he had built in the south transept of the priory church.

The nuns of Holywell Priory, a Benedictine house at Shoreditch, were fortunate in having so wealthy and distinguished a patron as Sir Thomas Lovell (d. 1524). Leland states that he rebuilt the priory and according to Stow ' he endowed this house with fayre lands and was buried in the large chapel by him builded for that purpose.'

Lovell, who at one time was Speaker of the House of Commons, was a staunch adherent to the cause of Henry, Earl of Richmond, afterwards Henry VII, and he fought at Bosworth Field. He died at Elsing, near Enfield, in May 1524 and was buried in his chantry chapel in Holywell Priory church, of which he was regarded the second founder. Many of the painted windows there bore the inscription :

> All ye nunns of Haliwell
> Pray ye both day and night
> For the soul of Sir Thomas Lovell
> Whom Harry the Seventh made Knight.

The relatives of a nun who were desirous of founding a chantry might naturally be expected to do so in the church of the convent to which they were bound by personal ties. At Barking Abbey, Essex, a Benedictine nunnery of considerable repute, Dame Joan de Felton, the mother of the Abbess Sybil, founded a chantry in 1398 served by one priest, for the good estate of her daughter, of Margaret Sayham, one of the nuns, of Sir John Felton and other persons named, and for their souls after death. The masses were to be sung at the tomb (altar ?) of S. Ethelburga in the abbey church and licence was granted Dame Joan to alienate lands in London, Barking and Dagenham for the endowment. (V. C. H. Essex.)

At Lacock Abbey, Wilts., a house of Augustinian canonesses, a chantry was founded as part of a bargain made by the convent with Sir John Bluet, lord of the manor of Lackham. For long the good ladies had cast envious looks on the church at Lacock, the appropriation of which was a thing devoutly wished. From the time of its foundation the convent had held the advowson of the rectory conjointly with the manor of Lackham. This was never a satisfactory arrangement for there were constant disputes between rival patrons often leading to litigation. In 1312 licence was granted the abbess and convent to acquire Sir John's share and to appropriate Lacock church on condition that they founded a chantry in the abbey church for Sir John's soul. They were to find a priest to recite the mass daily in the Lady Chapel, which was to be built at the cost of both parties ; and on the occasion of the obit the nuns were to distribute a halfpenny to each of a thousand poor persons.*

The majority of nunneries were pitiably poor and in some houses the sisters were unable to provide the stipend for a priest to celebrate the daily mass in their choir. This was so at the little Benedictine nunnery of S. Sepulchre at Canterbury. To meet the situation Robert Vyntier of Maidstone founded a chantry in the nuns' church in 1369 and his executors granted a manor called ' La Mote ' to the priest for the endowment. This provided the sisters with their daily mass, from which the founder himself derived spiritual benefit.

Gifts of money made for prayers for the souls of the dead were of considerable benefit to the revenue of many a poorly endowed nunnery. In the account rolls of S. Michael's, Stamford, the names of the donors whose souls were to be prayed for were entered against the sums received.

One might not expect an abundance of chantries in the Charterhouses, of which there were nine in this country. The complete isolation of the fathers from the world and the exclusion of the laity from their precincts would seem to preclude chantry foundations in their churches, were it

*The appropriation of a parish church was a gift much appreciated by religious houses in times of poverty or financial stress, and the brethren readily reciprocated by establishing a chantry for their benefactors. When Sir John de l'Isle gave the church of Harewood, Yorks., to Bolton Priory in 1353, the prior and convent undertook to provide for the maintenance of six chantry priests at Bolton and Harewood.

not that the brethren were in a special degree under obligation of reciting prayers and masses for their founders. Much is known of the London Charterhouse, which originated in a burial ground known as Spital Croft. In the foundation deed, 1361, Sir Walter de Manny and Michael de Northburgh, Bishop of London, undertook to establish a Carthusian convent of thirteen priests ' to endure for all time, to celebrate daily for their two selves and for Dame Margaret Mareshall, wife of the said Walter, and for their children, etc., and for the souls of all their ancestors . . . as well as for all parents, friends and benefactors of both parties and for the souls of all those living and dead, for whom both parties are bound to pray or cause prayers and also for the souls of all whose bodies are or are to be buried there.'

The final clause in the foregoing definitely refers to the burial ground which preceded the Charterhouse and the obligations of the fathers in respect of the innumerable victims of the Black Death, who were there interred.

By his will, 1371, Sir Walter de Manny desired to be buried ' in the midst of the quire of the Carthusians called Our Lady near West Smithfield . . . of my foundation, but without any great pomp ; and I will that my executors cause twenty masses to be said for my soul and that every poor person coming to my funeral have a penny to pray for me and for the remission of my sins. Also I will that a tomb of alabaster with my image as a knight and my arms thereon shall be made for me like unto that of Sir John Beauchamp in S. Paul's, London.'

A memorandum *Concerning the Chantries of the Charterhouse*, dating *c.* 1431, gives a list of the benefactors for whom the brethren were bound to celebrate masses. The preamble of this document is not without interest : ' In the year 1431 the indented writings having been carefully examined, by which we and our successors are bound and held to certain definite chantries perpetually to be continued by our brethren-priests for certain of our great benefactors who at their costs built the cells in this cloister and bestowed other good things upon us . . . we have inserted them in this page as follows. . . .' Amongst those enumerated the following are worthy of note :

The chantry of Richard II. The king gave the advowson of Edlesburgh church to the brethren, for which they were under obligation to sing masses perpetually for the souls of Richard, Anne his queen, his father Edward (the Black Prince) and Joan his mother, his brother Edward, Edward III, etc.

Thomas Hatfield, Bishop of Durham (d. 1381) gave 600 marks by indenture for the building of two cells, stipulating that the two occupants of the same should recite masses for his soul and for the souls of his parents John and Margery, of his brother William, his sisters Joan and Margaret and of Edward III.

Another great benefactor whose chantry is recorded was William Symmes, a grocer (d. 1439), ' whose memory shall be blessed to a generation that is to come ' and who was specially received into the brotherhood of the Charterhouse in 1418. Besides founding a cell he did much to further the construction of a conduit and the paving of the cloister.

In general the brethren were bound by indenture to recite masses for their many benefactors. In two instances the absence of such an undertaking called for remark in the memorandum :

Adam Franceys, one-time mayor (d. 1374), ever active in good works, gave 1,000 marks for the founding of five cells ; and a more famous mayor, Sir William Walworth (d. 1385), did the same. ' And although neither of them by any writing has bound us, yet out of good conscience, those dwelling in the said cells which they built . . . are bound specially to pray for them as for their founders.'

Doubtful is it whether any chantry chapels were built in the Charterhouse, the soul-masses being celebrated at one or other of the altars in the church, such as the Holy Cross and S. Anne in the chapel at the west end.

The same stipulation that prayers be offered up for the founder and others, and post-mortem masses be said for their souls, occurs in the foundation charter of Mount Grace Priory, Yorks., also a Carthusian house. Many properties and privileges were conferred on the priory by Richard II, uncle of the founder, Thomas Holland, Duke of Surrey. After the execution in 1400 of the Duke, who had joined a conspiracy against Henry IV, his body was taken to Mount Grace for burial. Henry IV bore the convent no ill-will, for he made an endowment for five chaplains of the house to pray for his good estate and for his soul after death. In 1471 Edward IV founded a chantry in the priory church for the endowment of which he granted land in Yorkshire. The brethren were to sing the three masses of S. Erasmus, S. Mary and the Holy Trinity ' for the good estate of the king and for his soul after death and for the souls of the king's father, the late Duke of York, and the king's brothers and sisters, etc.'

In the churches of the Mendicants, who came to this country in the first half of the thirteenth century, chantry foundations were as common as in the churches of the older Orders. The high ideals, the self-sacrifice and the poverty of all orders of friars endeared them to the hearts of the people. This is shown by the generous gifts made by the prosperous citizens of the towns and cities. Royalty and nobles held them in high esteem and favoured them with many benefactions and endowments.

When Grey Friars, London, a Franciscan house, was rebuilt, 1306-27, the land and money were furnished by Queen Margaret, who was buried before the High Altar of the new choir. Generous gifts were also made by Isabella, Edward II's queen, and by Queen Philippa.

The Dominican establishments also attracted royal favour and beneficence. The Priory of King's Langley, Herts., was founded by Edward II in 1308 in pursuance of a vow he made to found a perpetual house of prayer there on behalf of the souls of his Plantagenet ancestors. The royal gifts were many. Tradition says that the priory church was built by the king as a burial chapel of his favourite, Piers Gaveston, after the execution of the latter by the barons in 1312. Edward II endowed the priory with 500 marks a year for the support of a hundred friars, who were to recite a daily mass for the soul of his lamented minion. Royal connection with the Black Friars of King's Langley did not end with the murder of Edward II. Edward III made generous gifts to the priory, and the remains of Richard II, after his death at Pontefract, were brought here for burial.

Prominent citizens and persons of high degree chose the churches of the London friaries as their last resting-place particularly in the fifteenth century. Nobles who were slain in battle or who perished on the scaffold were buried in one or other of the Mendicant churches. The lord-barons who fell at the battle of Barnet were taken to the church of Austin Friars, where also was buried Edward, Duke of Buckingham, executed on Tower Hill in 1541. In the church of Grey Friars, Newgate, which became as popular as Westminster Abbey, was a proud array of tombs. Stow gives the names of upwards of one hundred and twenty ' defaced monuments in this church, a remarkable list of queens, dukes and duchesses, earls and countesses, barons, etc.,' and he concludes, ' all these and five times so many more have been buried there ; for there were nine tombs of alabaster and marble environed with strikes (grilles) of iron in the choir, and one tomb in the body [nave] of the church, also coped with iron—all pulled down, besides seven score gravestones of marble.' If our historian is not guilty of exaggeration, the choir must have been crammed with tombs, leaving little space for the brethren to perform their offices. The many chantries and soul-masses were celebrated at one or other of the altars in the choir, which was reserved for the brethrens' own devotions and was structurally independent of the ' preaching nave.' Space seemed so limited at Black Friars that Lord Fanhope, in 1436, erected his chantry chapel in the churchyard. It was dedicated to the Blessed Virgin and was endowed with 40 marks a year. Other chantries at Black Friars included one valued at $4\frac{1}{2}$ marks for the soul of Henry VII ; and another, founded in 1504 by Henry Thabor, fishmonger, who made a bequest of 20s. and barrels of herrings to the brethren to the intent that they should say Dirige and a trental of masses for his soul.

Specially favoured by the gentry and the more prosperous citizens of London was the House of White Friars, or Carmelites, founded in 1241. By his will, dated February 1491, William, Marquis of Berkeley, made provision for the endowment of a perpetual chantry at the altar of S. Gasson in the church of White Friars, to be served by two of the brethren. He also granted a sum of £100 to the Austin Friars to found a perpetual chantry for the soul of his first wife, Joan. After the death of the Marquis, his widow married Sir Thomas Brandon, and in 1509 the latter made a bequest of £90 to the convent for the endowment of a chantry for the Marquis and his lady, who were buried side by side ' in the east wing ' as Stow calls it.

A famous monument in the church of the Crutched Friars, or Friars of the Holy Cross, at Aldgate, was that of Sir John Milborne, a London draper and mayor in 1521. He was the founder of the Drapers' Almshouse in the parish of S. Olave, close to the Friary. By his will he directed that thirteen bedesmen of the almshouse should attend the Friars' church every day to hear a mass sung for his soul at eight o'clock at the altar of Our Lady ' in the middle aisle.' Before the mass the bedesmen, standing on either side of Milborne's tomb, were severally, two and two together, required to say the De Profundis, a Paternoster, an Ave and the creed. Those who could not say the De Profundis had to recite a Paternoster, an Ave and a Credo for the souls of Sir John and Dame Johan, and Margaret, his first wife, and for the souls of their parents, children and friends, and for all Christian souls.

Milborne's almshouse was endowed with messuages and tenements in S. Olave's parish, the master and wardens of the Drapers' Company acting as trustees of the property.

The fashion of making pecuniary bequests to the Mendicant houses of London grew to a marked degree in the fourteenth century.

Preachers as they were, the friars poured forth warnings of the terrors of purgatory, and the wealthy opened their purses or made bequests to build and equip the Mendicants' churches, to found chantries therein or to make provision for soul-masses at the altars. The *Calendar of Wills* clearly demonstrates this. In the period 1324 to 1339 there were 13 bequests ; from 1339 to 1355 there were 50, and in the remaining years of the century the number rose to 135, an increase that was due doubtless to the horrors of the Black Death as well as to the popularity of the Preaching Friars.

As a rule the bequests were for building undertakings, for vestments and for priests to celebrate obits and soul-masses.

The Mendicant churches of London were not peculiar in this respect. Wherever the friars set up their establishments pious benefactors made liberal bequests to the brethren, founded chantries or endowed masses at the altars in their churches and sought burial within their precincts.

At Dartford Priory, Kent, a house of Dominican nuns, Richard II gave the sisters the manor of Massingham, together with other properties, to endow a daily mass in the chapel, then newly built, in the farmery or infirmary, for the relief and maintenance of the inmates and for the soul of the king and other benefactors. In 1526 Catherine, widow of Sir Maurice Berkeley, made provision for her burial in the Lady chapel of the same Priory, and in addition to other bequests she left £13. 6s. 8d. for the erection of her tomb, and made an endowment of £8 a year for four years for soul-masses at the altar of Our Lady in the conventual church.

John Garrington of Munton, Essex, was much attached to the Mendicant houses in the neighbourhood. By his will, dated 1516, he directed that Friar Symond Ward of White Friars, Maldon, should be given ' £8, good and lawful money of England, to sing for my soul, my fader's soul and all Christian souls two complete yeres at home in his cloister . . . and if he die within the said two yeres, another honest priest of the same house shall sing up his term after the discretion of my executors ; and they to be paid quarterly 20s., till the said two yeres be fully finished and ended,' and he bequeathed 10s. ' to the reparaciones ' of that house. He also left 10s. to be distributed amongst the convents of Maldon, one month after his death, to sing Dirige and mass for his soul, and the same amount to the Grey Friars of Colchester and the Black Friars of Chelmsford.

To be numbered amongst the *familiares* of the Mendicants was a privilege no less valued than that of spiritual fraternity with the convents of other Orders. In 1395 Prior Palmer of the London Black Friars undertook to admit one, Agnes Cumbe, to participation in all the ' masses, prayers, penances, fasts, vigils and all other benefits of his convent, and after her death to observe all the customary masses and prayers for the repose of her soul.'

VYING IN POPULARITY with the Mendicant houses were the hospitals, a designation which had a broader meaning than now, embracing as it did almshouses, bede-houses and asylums, as well as houses of healing.

Many almshouses that were founded in the fifteenth and early sixteenth centuries embodied what were to all intents chantry foundations in their constitution. Primarily the motive was the provision, as an act of piety, of a refuge for a few ' indigent faint souls past corporal toil,' but the founder also served himself by requiring the bedesmen or inmates to offer up intercessions unceasingly for his good estate whilst alive and for his soul after death. Ford's Hospital at Coventry furnishes an example. It was founded in 1529 for five poor men and one woman together with a priest, who were to celebrate a mass twice a week for William Ford and his family. In the normal chantry foundation the sole bene-ficiary was often the priest, who might or might not discharge his office faithfully ; but the bedesmen of a hospital, being several in number and bound by charter to fulfil their duties, there was less likelihood of negligence.

A picturesque survival, unspoilt by the passage of centuries, is the ' God's House ' or hospital of Ewelme, Oxon (page 177).

In their many pious benefactions, the laity, particularly in the crowded towns, were not unmindful of the hospitals in their midst, the institutions which—in the modern sense of the word—ministered to the sick, the blind, the paralysed and the insane. Many chantries were founded in the chapels of such establishments. At S. Margaret's Hospital, Wimborne, an asylum for the relief of lepers, John Redcoddes bequeathed property for the endowment of a chantry in the chapel there. Moreover, lazar-houses, which were mainly ' supported by voluntary contributions,' kept a bede-roll of their benefactors. In the will of Richard Cloudesley of Islington, dated 13 January 1517, occurs : ' Item, I bequeath to the poor lazars of Highgate to pray for me by name in their bede-roll 6s. 8d.' The poor lazars of Highgate were the inmates of a leper hospital which stood between Holloway and Highgate on the northern outskirts of London and which had been founded in 1473.*

In mediaeval London there were no less than twenty ' hospitals,' the greatest of which was S. Katherine's by the Tower. It was founded in 1148 by Matilda, Stephen's queen, and again by Henry III's queen, Eleanor, in 1273. Matilda's foundation was not a hospital or a charity in any sense of the word, but a religious house served by a master, brothers and sisters and a number of poor persons, whose sole duty was to offer up prayers and attend masses for the souls of the queen's two children, Baldwin and Matilda. The personnel of the hospital included three chantry priests, who recited a daily mass for the souls of Henry III and the past kings and queens of England. The endowment derived from lands and rents in Smithfield, Rainham and elsewhere. In 1350 Queen Philippa of Hainault founded a chantry in the chapel of the hospital, to be served by another priest at the stipend of £10 a year ; and in 1376 Edward III founded a chantry there for Philippa (d. 1369) with a charge of £10 a year upon the Hanaper office. Many other chantries were there at S. Katherine's. In 1381 Thomas of Hatfield, Bishop of Durham, alienated property in Bow Lane to the hospital, to endow a daily mass for his soul, and John Holland, Duke of Exeter (d. 1448), ordained that a chantry of four priests should be established in the little chapel of the hospital, where he was buried. He endowed it with his manor of Great Gaddesden, Herts.

*In addition to his gift to the Highgate lazars, Cloudesley made many further bequests for the welfare of his soul, as follows :
' I will that there be incontinently after my decease, as hastily as may be, a thousand masses for my soul and that every priest have for his labour, 4d.' This great number of masses was distributed amongst the parish churches of S. James, Clerkenwell, S. Pancras, Hornsey, Finchley and Hampstead, to the incumbents of which he left 20d. apiece that he might be numbered amongst the souls to be prayed for in their bede-rolls. At Islington church an obit was to be kept every month, the priest and clerk to ' have for their pains as they used to have afore this time,' and 6s. 8d. was then to be distributed to the poor to pray for the souls of himself and his wife.
Attached to the same church was a community of priests known as ' the Brotherhood of Jesus.' To this fraternity Cloudesley bequeathed £1. 6s. 8d. issuing from lands in Islington, for the keeping of an obit and for a trental of masses yearly for ever for his soul. Furthermore, he directed his executors within one month after his death to find ' an honest sadde preste to syng for my soule, my fader's and moder's soules and all Christian soules ' in the new chapel called the Hermitage at Islington towns-end. The said priest was to say three times weekly Placebo and Dirige and at every mass De Profundis.
To the Friars of Greenwich he left 40s. to sing a ' solemn Dirige and mass by note ' ; and to a priest to sing for his soul at Scala Celi at the Savoy by space of one year after his death he assigned a stipend of £6. 16s. 8d.
Richard Cloudesley of Islington died in 1518 and was buried in the parish churchyard.

Amongst the pious works of Henry VIII was the founding at S. Katherine's, *c.* 1518, of a religious fraternity known as ' the gild of Our Glorious Saviour Jesus Christ and of the Blessed Virgin and Martyr, S. Barbara.' The bede-roll runs :

First ye shall pray especially for the good estate of our sovereign lord and most Christian and excellent prince, King Henry VIII, and Queen Katherine, founders of the said gild and gracious brotherhood, and brother and sister of the same. And for the good estate of the French Queen's grace, Mary, sister to our said sovereign lord and sister of the said gild. Also ye shall pray for the good estate of Thomas Wolsey, priest, Cardinal Legate to our Holy Father the Pope, etc., brother of the said gild. Also for the good estate of the Duke of Buckingham and my lady, his wife ; also for the good estate of the Duke of Norfolk and my lady, his wife ; the Duke of Suffolk, also my Lord Marquis, the Earl of Shrewsbury, the Earl of Northumberland, the Earl of Surrey, my Lord Hastings and for all their ladies, brethren and sisters of the same.

Then follow the names of other distinguished brethren,

and for all their ladies, brethren and sisters of the same that be alive and for the souls of them that be dead. . . . Every man of your charity, say a paternoster and an ave. And God save the king, the master and the wardens and all the brethren and sisters of the same.

Here indeed was a chantry gild of distinction. No doubt royal interest in the gild ceased when some of the most illustrious brethren fell into disfavour with the founders and came to an unhappy end. ' The suppression of chantries by Edward VI not only deprived S. Katherine's of much of its property, but of the principal reason of its existence.' (V. C. H. London.)★

Another hospital much favoured by London citizens was S. Mary's within Cripplegate, known in the Middle Ages as the Elsing Spittle. It was founded by William Elsing, a London mercer, ' for the sustentation of an hundred poor men,' and a number of chantries were founded in the hospital during the fourteenth century, of which the following are typical : Robert Elsing, son of the founder, established a chantry served by three priests in the chapel of the hospital ; in 1337 Henry Frowyk founded another, for the endowment granting rents from certain tenements in three London parishes ; and John Northampton also bequeathed land in the parish of All Hallows the Great to support a chantry priest in the Spittle.

★S. Katherine's Hospital was demolished in 1825 to make room for the Docks and was rebuilt at Regent's Park. In the chapel of the new building is preserved the tomb of Holland, Duke of Exeter, with effigies of himself and his two wives.

In the church of the hospital of S. Thomas of Acons, Cheapside, later to become the Mercers' chapel, were buried many eminent Londoners and many chantries were founded there. That of Sir Edmund Sha, gold-smith, mayor in 1492, who 'caused the postern called Cripplegate to be newly built,' is of some interest by reason of the chapel the founder erected. By his will Sir Edmund ordained that he should be buried near a certain pillar in the church and a marble stone placed over his sepulchre. Against the pillar an altar was to be set up and around it an iron enclosure allowing sufficient room for the chantry priest and another as they celebrated the soul-masses. In the closure was to be an iron door which was to be kept locked after the office.

Almost identical in purpose with such hospitals were the so-called 'colleges' which were attached to parish churches. Several existed in London, a notable one being the college of the Holy Ghost and S. Mary, founded by the famous Richard Whittington at the church of S. Michael, Paternoster Royal, which he rebuilt. Licence for the foundation of Whittington's College was granted in 1410, and a year later the mayor and commonalty gave a plot of ground on which to build the college. It was not, however, until 1424, the year after his death, that the college really materialized, his executors applying the residue of his estate for that purpose and for the endowment. The college was served by five priests, one of whom, the master, was Rector of S. Michael's church. In 'the God's house,' as it was called, under the control of the Mercers' Company, were housed thirteen poor men, each receiving 14d. a week with other provisions. They were all bound to pray for the good estate of Richard Whittington and of his wife Alice, their founders ; for Sir William Whittington, knight, and Dame Joan, his wife; for the founders' parents and for Richard II and Thomas of Woodstock, Duke of Glouces-ter. Every day the five priests were to celebrate in the church and the almsmen were to assemble about the founders' tomb there and offer up prayers for the souls of their benefactors.

Richard Whittington was buried in S. Michael's Church, Paternoster Royal, under ' a fair monument' as Stow tells us in 1598, ' and the alms-houses with the poor men do remain.' To-day, the Whittington alms-houses in the Archway Road at Highgate house twenty-four poor spinsters and so perpetuate the memory of one of London's greatest citizens.

Chantries were sometimes founded in hermitages. In some instances the anchorite was a chantry priest living in a cell attached to a church. In the hermitage or chapel of S. James-in-the-Wall, Cripplegate, Mary, Countess of Pembroke, founded a chantry for herself and her husband. S. James's was a cell of Garendon Abbey, Leics., the convent of which held the presentation to the chantry. In Riley's *Memorials* the presentation, dated 1399, is given as follows :

To the venerable man, the mayor of the City of London, Brother John of the monastery of the Blessed Mary of Gerondon of the Cistercian Order in the diocese of Lincoln, greeting with honour. We do by these presents, present unto your reverence, our dearly beloved brother in Christ, John de Rither, our fellow monk and priest, for the chantry that was founded for the soul of Sir Aymer de Valence, Earl of Pembroke, by the most venerable Lady Mary de S. Pol, Countess of Pembroke, his wife, in the hermitage near to Cripulgate in London, and which unto our presentation belongs. In witness whereof we have to these presents set our Seal. Given in our monastery of Gerondon aforesaid, on the feast of S. Michael (29 Sept.) in the year of our Lord, 1399.

In virtue of which presentation the said John de Rither was admitted to the chantry aforesaid by Thomas Knolles, Mayor of London. . . .

In the churchyard of All Hallows Staining Fenchurch, are preserved fragments of the Norman crypt of S. James's chapel, which were transferred there in 1873.

Though not regularly constituted as chantries, the celebration of soul-masses in return for benefactions and bequests obtained in hermitages as in other religious establishments.

In 1354 Edward the Black Prince granted 16s. 8d. a year in addition to a stipend of 50s. to Sir William Pruit, a priest, on his undertaking to dwell for life in the hermitage of Restormel Park in the duchy of Cornwall, there to recite masses for the souls of the Prince's ancestors; and at Faversham in Kent, in 1519, a benefactor left the sum of 4d. ' to the ancres [anchoress] in the churchyard, to the intent that she shall pray for my soul and all Christian souls.'

At Whalley church, Lancs., two chantries were founded out of the suppression of a hermitage which stood within the churchyard. The hermitage had been founded in 1361 by Henry, Duke of Lancaster, but in 1444 the anchoress who dwelt there had fallen from grace and the cell was suppressed by order of Henry VI. The endowment was then conferred upon two chantries ; one, dedicated to S. Nicholas in the north aisle of Whalley church, the other, to S. Mary in the south aisle. Each was served by its own priest, who sang a daily mass at the altar for the soul of the Duke of Lancaster.

Bishops, deans, abbots and members of the royal and noble families were accustomed to found their chantries in the greater churches of this land ; wealthy citizens and merchants chose to be commemorated and buried in the large town churches, which they themselves had reared or rebuilt ; the landed gentry and families of repute often favoured their own rural parish churches. The wills of the Fitzherberts of Derbyshire and their alabaster tombs in Norbury church are witness of the affection

*Copyright Walter Scott, Bradford*

11. NORTH CHOIR AISLE, ELY CATHEDRAL, SHOWING ALCOCK CHAPEL AND BISHOP REDMAN'S CHANTRY TOMB

12. WILLIAM OF WYKEHAM'S CHAPEL, WINCHESTER CATHEDRAL

13. INTERIOR OF BISHOP FOX'S CHAPEL, WINCHESTER CATHEDRAL

15. BISHOP WAYNFLETE'S CHAPEL, WINCHESTER CATHEDRAL

14. FOX AND BEAUFORT CHAPELS, WINCHESTER CATHEDRAL

of that illustrious family for their parish church. When Elizabeth, the widow of Sir Ralph Fitzherbert, made her last testament in 1490 she directed that her body should be buried in the church of S. Barloke by the side of her late husband.

I bequeath to the abbot and convent of the abbey of Darley, for a trental to be said for my soul, 10 shillings. Also, I bequeath to the finding of a priest to pray for the soul of Ralph Fitzherbert, late my husband, and for my soul, £10 of money, beside the rent of Calton. Also I bequeath to seven priests, at the trust and disposition of mine executors, to pray for my soul, 46s. 8d. ; also that my said feoffees retain and keep in their hands, lands and tenements to the yearly value of 20 shillings, to find an obit yearly at Norbury, for my said husband's soul, my soul, our fathers' and mothers' and all Christian souls ; . . . and that, that remaineth over at any time to be laid out in purchase of bread and divided amongst the poor parishioners of Norbury, by the discretion of my son and heir and curate of the church for the time there being.

Two Fitzherbert chapels remain on the south side of the nave, separated by the low tower, but the family monuments, of rare splendour, are not within but stand in the chancel. So, in part at least, a parish church might become the mausoleum of a great family, and this can also be said of Stanton Harcourt church, where is a series of magnificent tombs of the Harcourts.

In times of dire need the appropriation of a parish church with its tithes and fruits was a godsend to a monastery. When a lay benefactor made the gift, the convent reciprocated by founding a chantry or singing masses for his soul in the newly-acquired church. They were also required to provide the vicarial stipend. Thus, in the late fourteenth century, when the abbey of Holme Cultram, Cumberland, was in a grievous plight from the inroads of the Scots, Margaret de Wigton came to their help by granting the convent the appropriation of the parish church of Wigton. In return they were to find four priest-monks of the Cistercian Order to perform divine office in the abbey church and two secular priests to serve a chantry in Wigton church for the souls of Margaret, her husband John and her progenitors.

In addition to ' personal ' chantries in parish churches there were those of the gilds and sodalities.

The majority of chantries were founded at altars already existing, as for example those which invariably stood at the east end of the aisles of the nave. Here, too, were recited the soul-masses for which many a humble parishioner bequeathed a small sum or gift in kind to the parish priest. The founding of the religious gilds gave a permanence to such offices.

Grim as it may seem, chantries were occasionally founded in the parochial charnel chapel, a detached building in the churchyard. At High Wycombe, Bucks., there were several in the chapel of the Trinity and

4

Our Lady, which was built over the repository for unearthed bones. In 1415 a special indulgence was granted the two chantry priests there to sing their masses in a low voice and with closed doors, should Wycombe ever be placed under an interdict.

In the churches of London and the suburbs there were nearly two hundred chantries, and there were forty-two in the city of York. At the large church at Newark, Notts., the *Calendar of Chantries* enumerates thirteen as follows : one at each of the altars dedicated to S. James, S. Nicholas, S. Katherine and All Saints ; two Trinity chantries, and another of the Gild of the Sacred Trinity, which was the most important of all the town gilds and had its own chapel in the south transept ; two chantries dedicated to Corpus Christi, the one of Alan Fleming, a merchant, and the other of Isabel Caldwell ; the Newark, Foster and Sawcendine chantries ; and finally one known as the ' chantry of Morrow-Mass,' dedicated to S. Mary Magdalene. This last-named was a very early celebration, even at four or five in the morning, to meet the convenience of travelling folk who wished to hear a mass before taking to the road. The popularity of morrow-mass is evident from the large number of entries in the chantry certificates of lands and tenements which were alienated to provide the endowment of a mass ' every morning before sonne rysing for such travellers by the way.'

One of the last chantries to be founded in a parish church was that of John Hammond, the last abbot of Battle, who had surrendered his house to the king's commissioners in 1539 and was granted a pension. By his will, dated December 1546, the ex-abbot provided a stipend for a priest who was to recite masses for his soul in S. Mary's Church, Battle, for *a period of six years*. The limited duration of the chantry is not without significance. Well the abbot knew that Henry VIII's Acts of 1529 and 1545 were an earnest of the complete suppression soon to follow. His chantry endured for one year, the priest being awarded a pension of £6 per annum.

Abbot Hammond's was not an isolated case. By virtue of the very generous pensions they were granted when they surrendered their houses to the Crown, ex-abbots possessed ample means to found chantries if they so desired, or to make bequests for soul-masses after death.

Robert Fuller, ex-abbot of Waltham and ex-prior *in commendam* of S. Bartholomew's, Smithfield, a ' yes-man ' after the king's own heart, was enjoying a princely income at the time of his death in 1540. As abbot of Waltham he was in receipt of a pension of £200, equivalent to at least £8,000 to-day, and as commendatory prior of Smithfield he held practically the whole of the possessions of that house for life. By his will, dated 1540, he desired to be buried in S. Sepulchre's Church,

Newgate, and ordained that two priests should sing masses there for his soul and for the souls of the founders and benefactors of the suppressed priory. The masses were to continue for a period of seven years and the priests had a stipend of £8 a year. To the parish church of Waltham, formerly part of the abbey church, Fuller bequeathed £8 a year for seven years for a priest to sing for his soul, etc., and his chaplains were granted liberal bequests for the same purpose. This willing tool also bequeathed ' to his most dear and dread sovereign lord, King Henry VIII,' the sum of £40.

In many churches a parchment scroll or a tablet of wood bearing the names of all persons who had founded chantries or for whom obits were to be kept was displayed near the High Altar or on the wall close by. There was a wooden tablet serving the purpose at old S. Paul's Cathedral.

The chantry movement was far more popular in London than it was in the country. There was no parish church in the city to which chantries were not attached.

During the fourteenth century, the heyday of the movement, about 280 chantries, not including those of the various fraternities, were founded in the innumerable churches of the crowded metropolis, but in the following century a rapid decline set in. From 1403 to 1502 the number of new foundations dropped to 120, and from 1503 up to the Suppression only 13 were founded. (V.C.H., London.)

Of those founded in London during the fourteenth and fifteenth centuries only about one-fifth were perpetual, excluding those of gilds and fraternities.

To these parochial chantries must be added a considerable number founded in S. Paul's Cathedral and in the churches of the monastic establishments as well as those which had been absorbed by other chantries ; for during the fifteenth century many which had decayed and were in danger of becoming defunct were united with others in the same church.

Large numbers had already ceased to exist by the end of the fifteenth century, and at the time of the Suppression, 1548, there were not more than two hundred in the parish churches of London.

To turn the pages of Stow and to glance through the lists of monuments, tombs and chantry chapels brings home to us what a wealth of Gothic art was lost to posterity by the Great Fire of 1666.

The following, from his account of the church of S. Michael, Bassishaw, are typical : ' Sir James Yarford, mercer, mayor, deceased 1526, buried under a fair tomb with his lady in a special chapel by him built on the north side of the choir ' ; and ' John Barton, mercer, and Agnes, his wife, were great benefactors, as appeareth by his mark placed throughout the whole roof of the choir and the middle aisle [nave] of the church.

He deceased in the year 1460 and was buried in the choir.' Barton directed his executors to maintain an obit in S. Michael's for ten years, and he also bequeathed seven chasubles wrought with gold to Wadworth church, Yorks.

The parish churches of the city provided a last resting-place for mayors, sheriffs, merchants and tradesmen of all kinds—goldsmiths, drapers, mercers, vintners, fishmongers and so on—many of whom founded chantries and erected monuments which, before Stow's day, had been ' destroyed by bad and greedy men of spoil.'

More than a hundred of London's mayors were buried in the city churches up to the time of the Suppression and many others found sepulchre in the churches of the monasteries and friaries. Their benefactions were considerable, and the poor of the parish were not forgotten. In the church of S. Michael, Cornhill, Robert Drope, draper and mayor (d. 1485), founded a chantry and was buried on the north side of the choir ' under a fair tomb of grey marble.' For marriage portions for poor maids of the parish he gave £20 ; to the poor of that ward £10, as well as 300 shirts and smocks and 100 gowns of broad cloth. At his burial the sum of £16 was distributed to the poor, to prisons and lazar-houses, and he left his house in Cornhill to be sold for the upkeep of highways. His widow, Joan, married Edward, Viscount L'Isle, and made large bequests including her dwelling-house, to the parish priest, ' to the intent that our souls be prayed for.' At the Suppression the parishioners surrendered her messuage as chantry property ' and wronged themselves.' (Stow.)

At one time and another there were upwards of seventy gilds and fraternities—co-operative chantries—attached to the city churches of London. Most of them came into being after the Black Death. Two are worthy of special note. At All Hallows' Barking, now a total ruin, was a religious gild dedicated to S. Mary, that could boast of royal patronage. In the church was a chapel of S. Mary, held in particular sanctity, which Henry VI granted to the gild. In 1465 Edward IV founded a chantry for himself in the chapel, the endowment of which included the manor of Tooting, and provided stipends of £10 and £8 a year for the two priests serving the royal chantry. Of equal interest is the gild that was attached to the church of S. Magnus the Martyr, London Bridge. It was founded in 1343 by the ' better folk of the parish. Of their great devotion and to the honour of God and Our Lady Mary the Virgin . . . they caused to be made a chauntry, to sing an anthem of Our Lady called *Salve Regina* every evening.' Five wax lights were to burn during the anthem in honour of the five principal Joys of the Virgin and ' for exciting the people to devotion . . . and thereupon many other good people of the same parish, seeing the great honesty of the said service and devotion, proferred to be aiders and partners to support the lights and the anthem, paying every person every week one halfpenny ; so that hereafter with the gift . . . there shall be found a chaplain singing in the said church for all the benefactors.' One of the members of the gild was Henry Yevele, the master-mason at Westminster Abbey during the rebuilding of the nave. He was a parishioner of S. Magnus's, and on his death in 1400 was buried in the chapel of S. Mary, in which he had founded a chantry for the souls of Margaret, his first wife, his parents, King Edward III and others. He left money to maintain a light at the image of the Salutation of the Virgin.

The chantry priests in London far outnumbered the parish priests, and when old age and infirmity overtook them their stipend was barely sufficient to support them. The plight of these unfortunates and that of parish clergy stricken by years and impotency led to the founding of the hospital or college of S. Augustine Papey, the only one of its kind amongst all the religious establishments in mediaeval England. It was founded *c.* 1440 by four London priests, William Barnby, who served a chantry in S. Paul's Cathedral, William Cleeve, a chantry priest of S. Mary Aldermary's, and two parish priests. The Papey, as it was called, stood within London wall in S. Mary Axe Street. ' The brethren of this house becoming lame or otherwise into great poverty, were here relieved, as to have chambers with certain allowance of bread, drink and coal, and one old man and his wife to see them served and to keep the house clean.' (Stow.) The hospital owned certain messuages in London but was never a wealthy establishment. Those brethren able to walk and sing used to attend the funerals of great personages as professional mourners and were often so represented on monuments.

Quite a number of chantry chapels were built to serve as chapels-at-ease at some distance from their mother churches. In many parts of the country the outlying districts of extensive parishes were separated from the parish church by bad roads or flooded areas, particularly in winter. The lord of the manor, who would make provision for divine worship in such remote spots, found it a much easier matter to erect a parochial or free chapel under the guise of a chantry foundation than to effect the legal subdivision of the parish. Thus it came about that under the convenient conditions of a chantry endowment, a number of chapels were founded which were virtually free, not being within the jurisdiction of the mother church of the parish. The chantry priest was at the same time responsible for the cure of souls, and the daily offices, matins, vespers and so on, which he was required to perform in addition to his other duties, were definitely laid down in the foundation deed.

In the wide parishes of Yorkshire there were many chapel-at-ease chantries, as for example at Macclesfield, where a chapel was erected by Archbishop Savage of York at a spot two miles distant from the parish church. At Kingston-on-Thames is to be seen the Lovekyn chapel that was technically a chantry foundation but served as a chapel-at-ease.

In 1305 licence was granted Edward and Richard Lovekyn to build a chapel there dedicated to S. Mary Magdalen and to endow it with thirteen acres of land for the maintenance of a chantry priest to sing masses for the souls of the founders and their family. In 1352 John Lovekyn, fishmonger and four times mayor of London, rebuilt the chapel, made it collegiate and augmented the endowment for the support of additional priests and a warden. Stow records that ' John Lofken gave thereunto, 9 tenements, 10 shops, 1 mill and 120 acres of pasture.' The priests were to dwell in a house provided for them and were to eat at a common table. The warden was to arrange the singing of the masses and to provide a clerk to wait upon the priests in their chambers. The grace after dinner was to conclude with ' May the souls of John, Edward and Richard Lovekyn, our founders, and of the Lord William [Edingdon], Bishop of Winchester, and of all the faithful deceased, rest in peace through the mercy of God.' The ordinance of the chantry college, 1355, specified the mass to be sung on each day of the week : on Monday, the founders' mass ; on Tuesday, a mass called ' Salus populi ' for the good estate of the king and queen and the bishop, and a mass of S. Thomas the Martyr for their souls after death, and so on. The endowment was further increased by William Walworth, the famous mayor. In 1534 the revenue of the Lovekyn foundation amounted to £34. 19s. 7d. The last warden, Charles Carew, was attainted in 1540 and the property was forfeit to the Crown. Twenty years later the chapel became the Grammar School of Kingston. It is an unaisled building some forty feet in length and was restored in 1882 when the school was transferred to another site.

An unusual instance of the suppression of a chantry chapel and its reconstitution as a free chapel occurred at Rainham, Essex. In the time of Edward III, Sir John Staunton founded a chantry in a chapel in Rainham churchyard for the souls of Isabel, the king's mother, and of himself and his wife. In course of time the endowment, which issued from lands, depreciated so much that it proved insufficient to support the priest. In 1521 the Bishop of London suppressed the chantry and the chapel became ' free.' The incumbent was, however, required to find a priest to sing a soul-mass once a quarter for the founder of the chantry.

The *Valor Ecclesiasticus* records a number of chantries which had been founded in the chapels within castles. An early one was the royal chantry in the chapel of Leeds Castle, Kent. In 1293 Edward I made a grant of 28 marks a year to the canons of Leeds Priory for the support of four of their number and a clerk, who were to recite a daily mass in the chapel of Leeds Castle for the soul of the late Queen Eleanor of Castile. The endowment was derived from the manor of Leeds, but in 1326 Edward II granted the priory the church of Old Romney in lieu of his father's endowment and provided for an additional canon, who was to sing masses in the priory church for the soul of Piers Gaveston. Later a further revision of the endowment was made and in place of Old Romney church the convent was granted a licence to acquire lands of the annual value of £10. However, the chantry was re-established by Edward III, for after 1341 the church of Leatherhead in Surrey was appropriated by the Priory, the number of canons attached to the chantry was increased to six, and provision was made for a daily mass in the chapel of Leeds Castle for the good estate of Edward III, of his mother Queen Isabel, and for their souls after death, as also for the souls of the king's brother, John of Eltham, and of Queen Eleanor of Castile. Thus, within a period of forty years the scope of the chantry had widened considerably.

Many founded in castle chapels were chantries by name only ; the endowment being from the first intended to provide the normal stipend for my lord's chaplain. It was, as with free chapels, very largely a matter of legal convenience. There are records of chantry foundations in castle chapels at Alnwick, Chester, Durham, Farleigh, Pontefract and elsewhere. In the same way though less frequently were chantries founded in the chapels of manor houses, mainly during the fifteenth century. Sir George de Breaute was granted licence by Robert, Dean of S. Paul's, with the consent of Walter Niger, Vicar of Navestock, Essex, to found a chapel and a chantry in his court at Navestock, ' provided that he and his heirs maintained a chaplain at their own charge, sworn to preserve the liberty of the mother [i.e. the parish] church.'

The modern chapel of Gray's Inn, London, is the descendant of the fourteenth-century ' chauntry of Portpoole.' The manor of Portpoole, which occupied the site of Gray's Inn, was the property of the Greys of Wilton, and in 1315 John, the son of Reginald, second Baron Grey, founded a chantry in the chapel of the manor, for the endowment of which he obtained licence to grant thirty acres of land, two acres of woodland and 10s. of rent in Kentish Town and Holborn to the priory of S. Bartholomew, Smithfield. The convent had to provide a priest to celebrate a mass every day in Portpoole chapel for the souls of the founder, etc. In 1505 ' the manor of Portpoole, 4 messuages, 4 gardens, the site of a windmill, 8 acres of land, 10s. of free rent and the advowson of the chantry of Portpoole ' were sold by Edmund,

Lord Grey, to Hugh Denny, and from him the property passed into the possession of the prior and convent of East Sheen, Surrey, who leased the manor house to certain students of law. At the Dissolution, the priory of Smithfield was deriving £10 per annum from the chantry property, out of which they paid the stipend of a priest who celebrated masses for the benchers of Gray's Inn in the chapel there.

In mediaeval England the only means of travel was by road, at all times difficult and perilous, especially in winter, when ways were foul and storms to be encountered. There were other dangers. In 1295 Matthew of Dunstable founded ' the chantry of Biddenham Bridge ' for the safety of travellers who were in danger of thieves. Very timely were masses that were sung for the well-being of travellers and for the souls of the victims of highway violence.

Public-spirited laymen and the religious fraternities often included road-making and bridge-building amongst their acts of beneficence. The building of a bridge was regarded as a pious undertaking before God, a charity for long-suffering travellers ; and the furtherance and patronage of such a project was accepted as an obligation by the Church. Richard of Kellawe, Bishop of Durham (1311–16), granted 'forty days' indulgence to all who will draw from the treasures that God has given them, towards the building and repair of Botyton bridge.'

At Stockbridge, Hants., the bridge spanning the river Test at one time bore a brass plate, probably of the fifteenth century, with an inscription which in modern English runs 'Say of your charity a Paternoster and an Ave for the souls of John Gylmyn otherwise Lokke, and Richard Gater and Margaret, the wife of the aforesaid John and Richard, founders and makers of this said bridge, on whose souls God have mercy.'

More obviously was the erection of a bridge an act of piety when the founder built a chapel thereon and endowed a chantry for himself and his family at the altar. As a rule the chapel was reared on a starling on one side of the bridge, though sometimes it stood at one end. Records are extant of many chantries in bridge chapels, notably at Wakefield, Rotherham, Rochester and Old London Bridge. In 1392 the gild of S. Mary at Stamford was granted licence to endow a chantry in the chapel of S. Mary-at-the-Bridge ; and the chapel of S. Mary on Wakefield Bridge was endowed by Edmund Langley, Duke of York, in 1398 'to the intent to pray for the sowle of the founder and of all Christian souls.'

One of the earliest and most important bridge chapels was that on London Bridge, founded in honour of S. Thomas Becket, by Peter de Colechurch in 1200, ' which chapel was then endowed for 2 priests, 4 clerks, etc., besides chantries since founded for John Hatfield and others.' (Stow.) Before the end of the thirteenth century the priests and clerks were formed into a fraternity known as ' Brothers of the Bridge ' and they dwelt together in a lodging known as the Bridge House. Ultimately they constituted what was virtually a chantry college. In 1270 Richard le Keu alienated certain tenements for the endowment of a chantry in S. Thomas's chapel and further chantries were founded there in the fourteenth century: in 1303, by Sir Robert Fitzwalter; in 1334, by John de Lindseye; in 1349, by Ralph de Linne; and one by the mayor and commonalty, the wardens of the bridge, under the will of John Hatfield, 1303. Towards the close of the century the old chapel was taken down and a new one, Perpendicular Gothic in character, took its place, a two-storied building with a five-sided apse at the east. In 1541 there were only one priest and a clerk serving S. Thomas's chapel, and a few years later, when chantries were suppressed, its goods and ornaments were surrendered to the bridge-master and the chapel was converted into a dwelling-house. It was finally demolished in 1553.

The finest remaining bridge chapel in the country is that at Wake-field, Yorks., on the bridge spanning the Calder. ' On the east side of this bridge,' wrote Leland, ' is a right goodly chapel of Our Lady and two cantuarie priests founded on it.' Though much restored it affords a good example of Decorated Gothic, dating *c.* 1360. Edward III by charter made a grant of £10 a year for perpetual masses there and in 1398 Edmund, Duke of York, founded chantries in the chapel. A further use is indicated in the chantry certificate of 1546, *viz.* ' to do divine service in the times of plague for the sick people thither to resort, that the rest of the parishioners may come to their parish church without danger of in-fection ' (Pl. 2).

4 The duplication of chantries—Presentation and stipend of the priests—Chantry houses—Constitution of colleges attached to parish churches—Chantry origin of some monastic houses.

BEQUESTS FOR A specified number of soul-masses to be sung within a limited period are of common occurrence in mediaeval wills. The number provided for sometimes runs into four figures. At Christ Church Priory, Hants, Thomas, Lord West (d. 1406), made a bequest for the recitation of 4,500 masses within six months of his death. This multiplication of soul-masses found increasing favour with those possessing deep purses ;

nor was it unusual for a wealthy benefactor, impelled by the same pious urge, to make assurance doubly sure, by founding two or more chantries, each in a different church or chapel. The following are not without interest. Two chantries were founded by John Drayton, citizen and gold-smith of London, as appears by his will, 1456.

> Two priests daily, one to say divine service at S. Paul's [Cathedral], London, and the other at the church of All Saints, Tottenham, at the altar of the Blessed Virgin and Martyr, S. Katherine ; and the same priest also on Wednesdays and Fridays to perform the like service in the chapel of S. Anne called the Hermitage in this parish near the king's highway ; for the souls of King Richard II, his queen and others, John Drayton's two wives, his parents and benefactors and all the faithful departed.

In atonement for his far from blameless life, Sir John de Moleyns (d. 1362) of the manor of Stoke Poges, Bucks., thought fit to found three chantries for himself and his kindred. One was in the chapel of S. Thomas the Martyr in Stoke Poges church, another in Ditton chapel and a third at S. Katherine's altar in Burnham Abbey church. For their endowment Sir John made a gift of the manor of Sylverton, Northants, and for the priest serving the chantry in the parish church he provided a dwelling-house.

Less usual than the duplication of chantries was the erection of two chapels by one person. This was done by Bishop Audley (1492–1502), who built a chantry chapel for himself in both Hereford and Salisbury Cathedrals ; by Abbot Lichfield of Evesham, who erected a chapel in each of two churches that stood within the abbey curia, and again by Bishop West of Ely. In the above instances, all the chapels are still *in situ* and doubtless there were other cases.

Frequently a chantry was endowed to be served by two or more priests. That of Edward the Black Prince, at Canterbury Cathedral, was of two priests, each of whom received a stipend of £12 a year ; and Henry IV's chantry in the same cathedral was likewise endowed for two priests.

Unusually ambitious was the chantry foundation which the wily Richard III planned for himself in York Cathedral. There were to be no less than a hundred priests ; six altars were installed for the masses and the building of a great house for the accommodation of the priests was commenced. However, Richard's death at Bosworth Field in 1485 put an end to this great project.

The most elaborate foundation of all, as regards its constitution and its chapel, was Henry VII's at Westminster Abbey. It was virtually a monastery within a monastery, for it had a separate establishment of its own, which included three additional monks beyond the normal personnel of the abbey. They were known as the king's chantry-monks, and there were also two conversi, three monk-scholars who were to have exhibitions at Oxford University, thirteen almsmen or king's bedesmen and three bedeswomen. Masses were to be sung in the royal chapel daily for the souls of Henry and his family, and a hundred wax candles, each twelve pounds in weight and nine feet long, were to burn during the offices. The royal endowment was generous in the extreme, and included the College of S. Martin-le-Grand, the Priory of Luffield and many manors and advowsons. In the title-deeds the provisions are particularized in the utmost detail.

In general, the right of presentation, *i.e.* the appointment of the chantry priest, was retained by the founder and his family. In the cathedrals the presentation was often in the gift of the dean and chapter, and went to one of the vicars-choral rather than to a canon. At Chichester at the time of the *Valor*, there were twelve vicars-choral serving the fourteen chantries in the cathedral, and they received stipends for that special office ranging from £3 to £13 a year. At Lincoln, at the same period, twenty-five vicars-choral served the thirty-six chantries.

The presentation in parish churches was often assigned by the founder to the parishioners or the incumbent. Sir Richard Towgall, priest, bequeathed his chalice to the church of Gateshead on condition that if 'there fall a chantry within this foresaid church, being *at the parishioners' gift*,' they should present his cousin, Sir John, and 'promote him before another.'

When Sir Reginald de Cobham founded a chantry in the parish church of Croydon in 1402, the presentation was vested in the 'twelve principal citizens of the place.' The endowment of £16. 1s. 2d. was derived from lands and tenements in Croydon, and when the chantry was suppressed, John Comporte, the priest, was awarded a pension of £6. 13s. 4d. In 1486 Rose Wrytell, of the parish of S. Mary-at-Hill, Eastcheap, bequeathed certain tenements in the city to provide a stipend for a chantry priest. The wardens were made the trustees of the property, but the parishioners held the presentation.

In Riley's *Memorials of London* is given an account of the presentation of the Pulteney chantry in S. Paul's Cathedral, 1352, which was in the gift of the mayor :

To the venerable and discreet men, the Dean and chapter of the church of S. Paul in London, Andrew Aubrey, mayor of the same city, greeting in the Lord. We do present unto you, by these presents, our dearly beloved in Christ, Sir William Mason, priest, to fill the perpetual chantry now vacant, with all the rights thereof, which has been founded for a fitting priest, in the church of S. Paul aforesaid, to celebrate Divine service for the soul of John de Pulteneye,

knight, and the souls of other persons in the will of him . . . and to our presentation, by reason of our holding the office of mayor of the city aforesaid, in virtue
of the will of the said John . . . we do beg of you that you will admit the said
William to the chantry aforesaid, and as the usage is, will canonically institute
him in the same, and will deign to do, in favour of us, the other things which
in this behalf, unto your office pertain. In witness whereof we have caused these
our letters patent, sealed with the seal of the mayoralty of the city to be made.
Given at London, on the Thursday next after the feast of the apostles, Peter
and Paul (29 June) in the twenty-sixth year of the reign of King Edward after
the Conquest the Third.

Not every chantry priest who was attached to a parish church was
*persona grata* to the incumbent, particularly where he was an outsider
presented by the founder. The goodwill of the parish priest was essential
in such case as the chantry of John Chamberlayn at Canterbury. In 1464
this gentleman bequeathed the sum of £100 a year to a ' fit chaplain '
of the Dominican Friary there. He was to celebrate masses for John's
soul—not in the Friary church but in the parish church of S. Paul beyond
the walls of the city.

Less welcome, no doubt, were secular priests in monastic churches.
In 1316 the canons of Hardham Priory, Sussex, in return for lands granted
them by William Paynel, undertook to find four secular priests to recite
a daily mass in the Priory church for the souls of William and Edward II.
The chantry priests, outsiders as they were, got along ill with the canons
owing to differences in their mode of life ; and as a result, Maud, the
heiress of the founder, agreed in 1352 that the chantry should be adminis-
tered by Augustinian canons in place of the imported seculars.

The countless wills of the fourteenth and fifteenth centuries shed much
light upon the duties of chantry priests and the payments they received
for their services. From these it appears that the normal stipend was about
£5 a year. The following is typical : ' Beatrice Hanley in 1389 left 20
marks and a silver cup to Thornton Abbey for soul-masses and £30 of
silver to six priests to celebrate for a year.'

The life of a chantry priest was, to say the least, less exacting than that
of the parish priest ; his daily mass sung, he had much time for indulging
in the pleasures of the world. Many priests with a cure of souls evaded
their responsibilities, forsook their parishes and sought to serve a chantry.
This gives meaning to Chaucer's lines on the poor parson who

> . . . left his sheepe accombred in the mire
> And ran unto London unto Saint Paules
> To seeken him a chantrie for souls.

To put an end to this evil, Archbishop Islip of Canterbury in
1362 fixed the stipend of the chantry priest at 5 marks a year.

In a letter to the Bishop of London, he expressed his views very definitely :

We are informed that modern priests, through covetousness and love of ease, not content with reasonable salaries, demand excessive pay for their labours and receive it ; and do so despise labour and study that they wholly refuse as parish priests to serve in churches and chapels or to attend the cure of souls, though fitting salaries are offered them ; and prefer to live in a leisurely manner by celebrating annuals for the quick and dead ; and so parish churches and chapels remain unofficiated . . . whereupon all unbeneficed chaplains, fitted for the cure of souls shall be required to put aside any private obsequies and officiate wherever the ordinary shall appoint them, at six marks of annual stipend, while priests without cure of souls shall be content with five marks.

But the Archbishop's measure was not easily enforced nor was a chantry priest always to be found who would be content with so small a stipend. This is clear from a document prepared in 1362 by Adam Franceys, to whom was entrusted the founding of a chantry for John Oxenford, deceased, one-time mayor of London. ' Whereas by common consent of the prelates and clergy of England, it is now ordered that no yearly chaplain shall make more by the year than 5 marks sterling for cele- brating masses for the soul of any person, under a certain penalty . . . and also in the Parliament of our Lord the King [Edward III] in the thirty-sixth year, etc., it is enjoined that no person shall give to any yearly chaplain more than 5 marks by the year, and that he shall be fined in a certain sum of money if he shall be convicted . . . and whereas Adam Franceys, citizen of London, is bound to dispose of a certain sum of money, the residue of £100, for the celebration of masses for the soul of John Oxenford, late citizen and pelterer . . . and whereas Adam *cannot get any chaplain for 5 marks only*, to celebrate for the soul of the said John, and does not dare to infringe the ordinance of our Lord the King, and yet desires to discharge his conscience thereof ' he faithfully expended the same in the repair of several churches in the city that had suffered gale damage, ' for the salvation of the soul of John Oxenford in such manner as was by him ordained.' Furthermore, the ' devisee,' Adam Franceys, on 17 October 1362, at the Guildhall, in the presence of the mayor and certain aldermen, distributed gifts of money to several of the religious houses of London on condition that they should celebrate masses for the soul of John Oxenford, their benefactor.

Thus the prior and convent of the hospital of S. Mary without Bishops- gate received £10 on their undertaking to find three canons to sing masses for one year ; the prior of the church of Holy Trinity was given 10 marks to find two canons for the same purpose ; the prior and convent of S. Bartholomew, Smithfield, receiving 10 marks, found two canons also ; the abbot of Stratford had 10 marks for two monks and the abbot of Lesnes a like sum for two canons. From the residue of Oxenford's bequest, on 20 February 1363, the sum of 40s. was granted on the same terms to each of the Mendicant houses in London.

In 1380 Archbishop Sudbury, ' taking into consideration the condition of the times,' saw fit to increase the stipends to 7 marks for chantry priests and 8 marks for parish priests. But there were always a few black sheep who found a means of evading episcopal edicts. In 1547 Richard Turner, the non-resident rector of Hillingdon, Middlesex, was in receipt of a stipend of £7. 13s. 6d. a year for his office as priest serving the chantry of Thomas Colney in S. Mary's Church, Reading. But not for long !

Thornbury speaks of the army of idle and often dissolute mass-priests attached to the many chantries in old S. Paul's ; and Bishop Vesey of Exeter (1519–51) after a diocesan visitation enjoined the chantry priests and others to avoid idleness by teaching the Paternoster, the Ave and the creed to the children in their respective parishes.*

Idle and dissolute they may have been, and according to the standards of such men as Erasmus and Colet even stupid and illiterate. In many village churches they had prescribed duties, but human nature being what it is, there were occasions when their relations with the parish priest became somewhat strained. At Ledbury, Hereford, the townsfolk were wont to spend much of the Sabbath forenoon in the taverns of the place ; they ignored High Mass in the parish church and chose to attend a chantry sung at an earlier hour in the chapel of S. Anne there. The parish priest appealed to the Bishop of Hereford in 1385, who ordered that the chantry was not to commence until the Gospel had been read in the High Mass.

The great army of chantry priests was further increased when the religious houses were suppressed, for numbers of the dispossessed monks and friars obtained appointments as mass-priests.

Frequently some provision was made in an endowment for a lodging for the priest. Masses were sung at a very early hour, morrow-mass as early as five o'clock. It was therefore necessary that the priest should reside near the church, especially if he was reciting a mass every morning. In towns and cities a lodging might not be difficult to find, but in remote

*In a monastic church, part of which was parochial, the cure of souls was sometimes entrusted to a chantry priest, an arrangement which enabled a poor convent to augment its scanty income. At Elstow Nunnery, Beds., where the nave was the parish church, the endowment of the rectory was worth 14 marks a year in 1343, but the incumbent received only one half, the remainder being appropriated by the nuns. Two years later, the abbess by letters patent from the Crown was granted the appropriation of the whole endowment and as a result a chantry priest was charged with the cure of souls in the parish.

or tiny villages a house often had to be built in the vicinity of the church to accommodate him. Bishop Hugh Northwold of Ely (1229–54) built a house on the Palace Green for the four chaplains who served his chantry in the cathedral. It was known as ' the Chantry on the Green ' and was perhaps the earliest of its kind.

A few chantry houses have survived. At Terrington S. John's, Norfolk, a two-storied dwelling is tucked in between the nave and the western tower of the church. Attached to the north side of the chancel of Cranfield church, Beds., is a square two-storied building which probably served as a dwelling for a chantry priest. It is entered from the chancel by a small doorway, and there is an outer door in the west wall of the house. In the south-western angle is a circular stairway leading to the upper chamber, which has a fireplace with an octagonal stone chimney.

At West Tanfield, in the North Riding, ' Chantry Cottage ' occupies the site of a house which was ' buylded ajoyned to the church yarde ' for the priests serving chantries founded in the church by Maud Marmion (d. 1360). Close to Newark parish church is a large house which bears the name ' The Chantry House.' It stands on the site of a house founded by Dame Alice Fleming by licence of Edward III. Each priest who served an altar in this big church had a chamber in the house, with the use of the common room, and was required to recite a daily mass for the souls of Dame Alice, her husband and others. A few years before the suppression, eleven were in residence ; they were amply provided with meat and drink and all other necessaries ' without needing to resort to alehouse, tavern or any other house, so that they were better disposed to their religious duties.' In spite of the statutes that had been enacted to promote order in the house, one of the priests, Robert Maune, failed to fulfil his obligations, for he would neither pay his dues nor discharge certain duties imposed on him. Furthermore, with a number of riotous companions he entered the chantry house, broke down doors, burst into the kitchen, buttery and cellar and carried away provisions. His brother-priests made complaint to the king, with what result is not known.

In the cathedrals and the large town churches, a goodly number of chantry priests were occupied almost wholly in reciting soul-masses, and it was deemed advisable by the bishops that such bodies of priests should be incorporated into colleges and live communally in their own buildings, rather than in lodgings here and there in the town. At Wells, Bishop Erghum (1388–1400) established a college for fourteen chantry priests, the memory of which survives in the thoroughfare known as College Lane. The seven chantry priests at S. James's, Garlickhithe, were formed into a college in 1481 ' because they associated with laymen and wandered about instead of dwelling among clerks as was fitting.' Their house was known as S. James's Commons. At Cobham, Kent, the almshouses ranged round a quadrangle to the south of the church were formerly the buildings of a chantry college founded in 1370 by John, third Lord Cobham. ' Inflamed with pious zeal and wishing to change earthly for heavenly things [he] had founded in the parish church, in which his ancestors had chosen their place of burial, a perpetual chantry in which there should be for ever five chaplains making a college there . . . of whom one was to be master, appointed by the prior of S. Saviour's, Bermondsey.' The endowment of the college issued from properties and manors in Kent. The abnormally wide and spacious chancel of Cobham church, now paved with brasses of the Cobham family, became the choir of the collegium. The small nave then proving inadequate to parochial needs, a new nave with aisles and a western tower were built. That done, the brethren of the college obtained licence from the convent of Bermondsey to whom the church belonged, ' to erect suitable houses and buildings equal in extent with the length of the church on the south side.'

On a grander scale is S. William's College at York, which constitutes one of the historic monuments of the city. In 1461 licence was granted by Edward IV to Bishop Neville of Exeter and his brother, Richard, Earl of Warwick, to found S. William's College for the community of twenty-four priests attached to the cathedral. By the end of the century thirty-six chantry priests, as a corporate body, were resident in the college. It is a quadrangular building to the south-east of the cathedral, and having undergone some changes now serves as a Church house for the northern province (Pl. 3).

The head of a chantry college was variously known as the master, the warden, the provost, the dean or the rector. The practice, begun by bishops and cathedral bodies, of establishing chantry colleges was followed by lay benefactors. The fellows were always under the obligation of offering up prayers unceasingly for the founders and their kin. Not only in town churches but often in comparatively small village churches were colleges founded. This often entailed the pulling down of the parochial chancel and the substitution of a spacious choir to accommodate stalls for the college. At Cotterstock church, Northants, the collegiate choir—now the chancel—entirely dwarfs the rest of the church. The statutes of the foundation, 1337, furnish interesting details of the common life of the chantry college there. The personnel consisted of a provost, twelve priests and two clerks, whose office was to sing a daily mass in the choir for Edward III, the royal family, John Gifford the founder, etc.

The provost and chaplains were to be clad in black or russet colour without red. When in church at divine offices they were to wear black tippets . . . and surplices and rochets after the manner of the vicars of the church of Lincoln. . . .

16. THE FROMOND CHAPEL, WINCHESTER COLLEGE

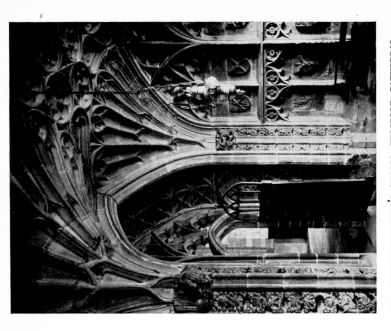

20. BISHOP STANBURY'S CHAPEL, HEREFORD CATHEDRAL

19. INTERIOR PRINCE ARTHUR'S CHAPEL, WORCESTER CATHEDRAL

21. THE CHAPEL OF PRINCE ARTHUR, WORCESTER CATHEDRAL

They were to have large, definite and uniform crowns to their tonsures, suitable for canons. They were to live in common and not to have more than two kinds of fish or flesh. On Sundays and festivals their meals were to be neither too slender nor too excessive. No chaplain was to play at tables (backgammon) either out of doors or in houses or elsewhere ; nor visit anywhere save for some special reason and with the leave of the provost or warden. Nevertheless he might once a year visit his friends by leave of the provost. (V. C. H. Northants.)

At Fotheringay church, but a mile or two distant from Cotterstock, was another college of chantry priests ; and here to a greater extent the church was enlarged and transformed to meet the needs of the college. Hard by was the castle of Fotheringay, which in 1377 was granted by Edward III to his son, Edmund of Langley. In 1411 Edmund's son, Edward of York, founded a college of chantry priests in the parish church there. The college consisted of a master, twelve chaplains, eight clerks and twelve choristers, whose office was to pray for the good estate of Henry IV and his queen, the Prince of Wales, the Duke of York and all the royal family, and for their souls after death.

The old parish church was far too modest for the purpose of the collegium, so the chancel was taken down and a large and stately choir took its place. In 1434 the present nave and western tower were erected, and to the south of the church collegiate buildings were grouped about a cloister. To the parishioners it must have appeared to all intents and purposes that their church was being converted into a monastic establishment. The church became in effect a grand chantry chapel and mausoleum for the York family. Therein were buried Edward, the founder, slain at Agincourt in 1415 ; Richard Duke of York, who built the nave, and his son Edmund, both of whom fell at Wakefield in 1460 ; and Ciceley, Duchess of York, who outlived her family and died at Fotheringay in 1495.

When the college was suppressed in 1548, the splendid choir was demolished, the college buildings swept away and the nave and western tower alone were spared for the use of the parishioners.

The church of Holy Trinity, Stratford-on-Avon, received its title ' Collegiate ' in 1415 from the college of chantry priests who served the altar of S. Thomas of Canterbury there. When Archbishop John of Stratford (1333–48) reconstructed the south aisle of the nave of Holy Trinity he established a chapel dedicated to S. Thomas in the aisle and later founded a chantry at the altar served by five priests to pray for the souls of the kings of England, the bishops of Winchester and himself. In 1415 the privileges of the college were confirmed by Henry V and the church was then made collegiate. A parallel case is that of Tattershall, Lincs., where a chantry college was established in 1439 by Ralph, Lord Treasurer Cromwell, who later raised the church to collegiate rank. It

5

should be borne in mind that a church was not necessarily collegiate by reason of a college of priests that might be attached to it. The patron, the incumbent and the parishioners had to be reckoned with and were jealous of their rights.

A rare instance of a college of chantry priests being founded to revive chantries which were well-nigh defunct occurs in the records of S. Michael's Church, Crooked Lane, London. In 1381 Richard II granted William Walworth, stock-fishmonger and mayor, licence to dissolve a number of chantries in S. Michael's Church owing to the depreciation of their endowments. In their place, Walworth was to establish a college, comprising a master and nine priests, who were to sing soul-masses for the founders of the suppressed chantries and for Walworth, his wife Joan, and John Lovekyn, an eminent citizen who was four times mayor. The endowment of the college consisted of property in Thames Street, Bridge Street and elsewhere which formerly belonged to the suppressed chantries, together with considerable benefactions made by Walworth himself. At the same time Walworth provided the priests with a dwelling-house near the church.

Still less usual was it for a chantry college to be established in order to maintain the divine offices in a parish church. From such a need arose the college of Thele, Herts. Early in the fourteenth century the rectory of Stanstead had become so impoverished that an incumbent was not to be found. That being so, the patron, Sir William Goldington, was granted royal licence in 1316 to alienate certain lands and rents in Herts. for the purpose of endowing a chantry in the church to be served by five priests, who formed a body known as the College of Thele. They were to sing masses for Sir William, his wife Margaret, Robert, Earl of Oxford, and Thomas his son, at the altar of S. Mary; they were to assist in celebrating the divine offices for the parishioners and were to dwell together in the college house.

It was a charitable and a noble gesture for the victors in a great battle to commemorate their success by founding chantries for the souls of those who had fallen, friend and foe.

More magnanimous was the establishing of a college of priests by Henry IV at Battlefield, Shropshire, the scene of the great battle of Shrewsbury, which the king fought with the Percys in July 1403. A few years later Henry built a chapel there, which was served by a col-legium of seven priests, to pray for the king, etc., and for the souls of all who had been slain on that fatal spot and were there buried. When the college was dissolved in 1547 the chapel fell into disuse and became derelict, to be rebuilt later as the parish church of S. Mary Magdalen, Battlefield.

Occasionally it will be found that a monastic establishment had its origin in a chantry foundation. This was the case at Maxstoke, Warwickshire. In 1331 Sir William de Clinton, admiral and warden of the Cinque Ports, founded a college of chantry priests in the church of S. Michael, Maxstoke. It consisted of five priests, one of whom was the warden. The college was suppressed in 1336 and reconstituted as a priory of Augustinian canons by Sir William, who incorporated the former foundation in the new house. A similar instance occurred at Kirby Bellars, Leics., which began as a chantry college and in the fourteenth century was refounded as an Augustinian priory.

Of particular interest in this respect is Edington, Wilts. The parish church there originally belonged to the nuns of Romsey, but in 1351 they surrendered it to Bishop Edingdon of Winchester for the use of the chantry college he was about to establish. Eight years afterwards the Bishop rebuilt the church, and, at the instance of the Black Prince, converted the college into a monastic house by introducing brethren of the Order of Bonshommes, a sort of Austin Friars. The nave of Edington church was, however, reserved for the parishioners' use.

5) The Statute of Mortmain—Granting of licences for chantries—Episcopal visitations—The Acts of Suppression.

TOWARDS THE END of the thirteenth century, the acquisition of lands by the religious foundations was increasing to such an extent that some form of control was deemed necessary. Landed property in the possession of the Church, whether bequeathed or purchased, deprived the Crown or the feudal lords of the services belonging to such lands, as well as of certain death dues.

Accordingly, in 1279 the Statute of Mortmain (*temp.* Edward I) was passed, which forbade the alienation of lands and rents in such wise that they should come into ' dead hand.' The endowment of chantries was necessarily affected by the statute, and henceforward before a chantry could be founded an inquiry was instituted to determine whether the king's revenue would suffer by the alienation of the property that was to provide the endowment. A commission was issued to the sheriff of the county directing him to summon a jury to hold the inquiry and to report their findings to the Crown. If proved that the benefaction could be made without harm to the royal revenue, *i.e.* that the founder would have sufficient property left to meet the Crown dues, a licence was duly granted under the Mortmain Act.

To quote an instance or two.

In 1347 an inquiry was instituted at Elstow, Beds., to decide whether Thomas atte Brugge of Elstow, the incumbent of Kempston, should be allowed to alienate four messuages, sixty-four acres of land and other property in Elstow, Kempston and Willshamstead for the support of a priest to say a daily mass for ever in the parish church of Elstow, for the souls of Thomas, his parents, etc. The alienation was allowed, as the land was held of the Abbess of Elstow and not of the Crown. In the following year John Message was regularly instituted as the chantry priest by the Bishop of London.

A century later an inquiry was held at the Guildhall, London, before John Norman, the mayor, respecting the alienation of Mackworth's Inn, Holborn, to the dean and chapter of Lincoln ' to find one sufficient chaplain to celebrate divine service in the chapel of S. George in the cathedral of Lincoln ' for the soul of Dean Mackworth.

' The jury said that it was not hurtful for the King (Henry VI) to license T. Atkins, citizen of London, and one of the executors, to give one messuage in Holborn . . . with the appurtenances called Mackworth's Inn to the dean and chapter of Lincoln . . . and to their successors for ever, etc.'

The licence granted to the executors of John Louth of Louth, Lincs., by Edward IV may be regarded as typical :

> Know ye that we have given licence to the executors of the will of John Louth to found, create and establish a chantry, lately erected by the said John Louth, of one chaplain who shall every day at the altar in the chapel of the Holy Trinity and all Saints on the north side of the parish church of S. James of Louth celebrate divine service for the healthy estate of us while we live and for our soul when we shall have departed from this life, and for the souls of the most dear prince our father, Richard late Duke of York deceased ; likewise for the souls of the said John Louth, of Simon Louth and Alice his parents, and also for the souls of Richard Argum and for the souls of all the faithful departed, to be called John Louthes Chauntrie. (R. W. Goulding, *Louth Records*.)

Once a licence was issued, with the leave of the bishop and the good-will of the ordinary or governing body of the church, the establishment of the chantry could be proceeded with.

The heads of religious houses, disposed as they frequently were to evade the statute, were sometimes required to produce their licences and their right to property which they held. Failure to do so might result in the seizure of the property by the Crown or the imposition of a substantial fine. In 1342 William of Erthyngton by his will had bequeathed some tenements in the parish of S. Martin Outwich to the prior and convent of S. Bartholomew, Smithfield, and ordained that he should be buried in the conventual church ' if so be that they undertake to provide a chantry there for the good of my soul.' But it was not so easy as that. Evidently the prior had ignored the statute, for more than thirty years later the convent was fined 40 marks for failure to produce the royal licence for the alienation. The fine was a heavy one, little less than £1,000 in the money of to-day.

However explicitly the conditions of a chantry endowment were stated in the foundation deed, the watchful eye of the bishop seemed to be necessary to ensure their exact observance.

The Chapter Acts of Canterbury and York, 1363, directed inquiries to be made on the occasion of episcopal visitations ' whether the monks fulfil completely as they are bound the masses and other peculiar prayers for their founders and other benefactors.' These inquiries relate to the *familiares* of the monastic houses rather than to the founders of chantries. That the latter suffered similar negligence is evident from the solemn warning issued by Bishop Goldwell of Norwich in 1493 after his visitation of the cathedral priory there.

Item, seeing that a man's last will hath the force of law we therefore, having it ever before our eyes that we are defenders of men's last wills, do strictly enjoin upon you that all foundations of obits and chantries for dead men be kept, in spite of all hindrances, according to the force, form and effect of the original foundation, even as ye wish to avoid the penalties imposed by canon law. Against all who contravene this, we will fulminate the severest penalties, specially reserving to ourselves the power of absolution therefrom or relaxation. (Vis. Dioc., Norwich.)

This was indeed straight talk from the titular head of the priory to his own brethren.

Other persons than bishops were aware that the religious communities did not always fulfil their obligations in this respect.

A letter to the Dean and Chapter of S. Paul's, bearing the mayoral seal and dated 1345, is extant, in which complaints are made that many tenements and rents in the City of London have been

devised for founding and maintaining divers chantries in the same church and for offering up prayers . . . perpetually for their souls . . . and we do see it daily with our eyes when we pass by your church of S. Paul's that there are but few chaplains to sing there in proportion to the chantries which in the said church have been founded, to the great peril of your souls, who ought to oversee such chantries, maintain and support the same. We do pray and request you, to the honour of God, and for the profit of the same church and of yourselves and your uccessors, that you will cause such defaults to be amended and redressed.

Furthermore, the letter suggested that no person who held a chantry at S. Paul's should hold one elsewhere, and then only a single chantry, at which he must be personally in attendance.

Such a document leaves no doubt that many abuses had crept into the chantry system two centuries before the Suppression.

In parochial chantries, the administration of the endowment was generally entrusted to the incumbent and the parishioners, but in towns and cities the mayor and corporation were found to be more reliable as trustees of chantry property and were more likely to enforce the exact observance of the founder's wishes. Sometimes the endowment provided a small fee to the mayor or some other official on condition that the recipient should attend the chantry and thus ensure that the testator's wishes were fulfilled. When William Cambridge, a London grocer, founded a chantry at S. Mary's-at-Hill in 1431 he willed that the mayor, the sheriffs and the City sword-bearer should be present at the obit and should receive 6s. 8d., 3s. 4d. and 1s. 8d. each respectively. According to the parish accounts this arrangement seemed to work well for some years, until the entry appears for 1478 : ' To Robert Harding and Robert Byfield, sheriffs, nothing payd, for they came not.' Maybe by this time the City sheriffs were personages of too exalted a rank to bother themselves about such things.

In many cases the patrons of chantry foundations accepted their obligations but lightly and made little effort to appoint suitable persons as priests.

Lax administration of the property by the trustees sometimes made it necessary for the chantry priest to resort to litigation to obtain his stipend, to which he had rightful claim, trustees or no trustees. In 1364 a priest at S. Michael's Church, Cornhill, seemingly left to his own devices, had to sue the tenant of a dwelling in the parish for the rent, which constituted the endowment of the chantry he served, and out of which he received his stipend.

The findings that were made on the occasion of episcopal visitations go to show that some chantry priests spent much of their time in pursuits not consonant with their sacred office. In 1501 Bishop Smyth of Lincoln discovered that the chantry priests attached to the cathedral were accustomed to resort to one of the chapels there to play dice, cards and bones in questionable company, often remaining until past midnight.

The founding of chantries continued unabated until the close of Henry VIII's reign, probably the last being one founded in 1547 at Welsh Newton, Herefordshire. Many had already died out through inadequate endowment or due to negligence on the part of the incumbent, especially in parish churches. Large numbers of obits and anniversaries had lapsed with the passage of time, from the indifference of the priest responsible for their observance. Moreover, a few patrons, shrewdly anticipating the measures of Suppression, dissolved chantries on their own account and enriched themselves by pocketing the endowments. In 1545 the Duke of Norfolk suppressed the Stonehouse chantry in East Tilbury church, the endowment of £12. 5s. 3d. being utilized for the making of a blockhouse for coastal defence.

The suppression of chantries was inevitable. The tide of the Reformation was to sweep them away as it did the monastic system, shrines, relics, pilgrimages, the cult of the Virgin and much else. The first move towards their dissolution was in 1529, 21 Henry VIII, when an Act was passed forbidding any person after Michaelmas of that year to accept any stipend for singing masses for the dead. This was followed in 1545 by another Act, transferring the properties of all chantry foundations to the royal exchequer 'for good and godly uses.' Henry VIII died before the purposes had been determined and the Suppression was not effected until 1547, 1 Edward VI, when a further measure ' whereby certain chantries, colleges, free chapels and the possessions of the same be given to the King's Majesty' was passed. The reason given was that ' the doctrine and vain opinion of purgatory and masses were upholden by the abuse of trentals and masses.'

The Act gave the Crown all the colleges, all free chapels and all chantries, all rents and annuities for the payment of stipendiary priests, and confiscated that part of the funds of gilds and fraternities assigned to superstitious objects.

And also be it ordained and enacted by the authority of this present Parliament, that our Sovereign Lord the King shall have and enjoy all such goods, chattels, jewels, plate, ornaments and other moveables as were or be the common goods of every such college, chantry, free chapel or stipendiary priest, belonging or annexed to the furniture or service of the several foundations. (1 Edward VI, c. 14.)

A preamble of the Act stated that the endowments thus confiscated were to be set aside for the relief of the poor, for the founding of grammar schools and the augmentation of the universities ; but large sums went into the royal purse ' for the relief of the King's Majesty's charges and expenses which do daily grow and increase by reason of the divers fortifications, garrisons, levying of men and soldiers.'

The Act empowered the king to appoint commissioners to survey corporations, gilds, fraternities and so on, ' thereby to know what money was bestowed to the founding or maintenance of any priest or priests, anniversary or obit or other like thing, light or lamp, by them or any of them.'

The commissioners were authorized to spare endowments for the maintenance of grammar schools and preachers, and they also granted pensions to the chantry priests on terms similar to those imposed on the dispossessed monks a few years before. In the returns made by the commissioners are given the amounts of the pensions thus awarded. To the priests who served the altars in Carlisle Cathedral the amounts varied from £2. 7s. 4d. for the priest attached to the chantry of S. Roch to £5. 10s. 6d. for the one serving the altar of Our Lady.

One of the clauses of the Act specifically excluded from its provisions the colleges of Oxford and Cambridge, the royal chapel of S. George at Windsor, Wykeham's College at Winchester, Eton College and the Chapel-on-the-Sea in Newton, within the Isle of Ely. This last-named was a chantry college which had been founded by Sir John Colvill in the reign of Henry IV, and its endowment was subsequently bestowed on the rectory of Newton. Chapels-at-ease for people dwelling at some distance from their parish church were also to be spared, as well as ' cathedrals or colleges where a bishop's see is . . . other than such chantries, obits, lights and lamps within the said churches.'

In all, 90 collegiate foundations, 110 hospitals and 2,374 gilds, chantries and free chapels were dissolved. A few of the chapels-at-ease fortunately survived the act of spoliation, for in some instances the local people purchased the endowment from the commissioners and provided the stipend for the priest.

The chantry commissioners failed not to seize so good an opportunity for enriching themselves. ' Now, all scruples removed, chantry land went down without any regret. Yea, such who mannerly expected till the King carved for them out of abbey lands, scrambled for themselves out of chantry revenues, as knowing this was the last dish of the last course, and after chantries, as after cheese, nothing to be expected.' (Fuller.)

Deprived of their office and of their means of livelihood, chantry priests in places like London were often subjected to insults and indignities from the populace. So much so that in November 1547 a proclamation was made against the evil behaviour of citizens and others towards priests. They complained that they could not walk freely in the streets nor attend the Court at Westminster without being reviled and having their tippets and caps violently pulled.

As many as could of the worthy and less indolent obtained a cure of souls and settled down to parochial duties.

Chantry chapels in the greater churches—Their various forms and positions—The founder's tomb—Two-storied chapels—Rood chantry altars—Chantry tombs—Chapels in parish churches.

THE CHIEF INTEREST in chantries to-day is that afforded by the splendid series of chapels that remain in our cathedrals and greater churches, despite the fact that many of them are sadly mutilated and nearly all are denuded of the fitments, statuary and colour that originally adorned them.

Large numbers of chantry chapels that must have crowded our churches great and small have been swept away, but a sufficient number survives to indicate their general form and architectural character. They vary considerably as regards their size, position, design and embellishment.

Generally speaking, the finest are those which are to be found in cathedral and Benedictine monastic churches. The memory of a bishop, an abbot or some noble founder or benefactor would be unfailingly perpetuated by a stone chapel such as that of Bishop Bubwith in the nave of Wells or of Richard Beauchamp in Tewkesbury choir. Moreover, in the popular mind, a church became of increasing importance by reason of its chantry chapels, objects of attraction to pilgrims and to the laity in general.

In Cistercian churches, from which the laity were wholly excluded, an array of chantry chapels might not be looked for. Benedictine abbots had their chapels and tombs, but the heads of Cistercian houses contented themselves with a slab in the pavement of cloister or chapter-house. That is not to say that soul-masses and obits were not sung in their churches ; chantries were founded and anniversaries of patrons and benefactors duly observed at their altars. At Waverley Abbey, Surrey, the earliest Cistercian house in this country, obits were kept of Bishops of Winchester who had been closely associated with the convent. It was William Gifford, Bishop of Winchester, who founded Waverley in 1128, and another great benefactor, Bishop Nicholas of Winchester, dedicated the newly-built church a century and a half later, and was buried there in 1280. He made a bequest of 200 marks to the abbey, but it was not until 1310 that a chantry was founded for his soul, and then, strangely enough, not by the monks but by two seculars. In that year Ralph de Staunford, priest of Alton church, and Hugh Tripacy, priest of Martyr Worthy, had licence to alienate the manor of Courage and seventy acres

of land to the abbot and convent of Waverley for the support of a priest
to celebrate a daily mass in the abbey for the soul of Bishop Nicholas
' of good memory.'

The masses were to be sung in the chapel of the Blessed Mary, which
stood at the abbey gate, or failing that, at an altar in the monastic church.
On the occasion of the Bishop's obit 5 marks were to be expended on
spicery for the monks and the sum of 20s. on shoes for aged widows
and the poor at the abbey gate. It is also on record that Bishops Edingdon
and Wykeham, both of whom built chantry chapels in Winchester
Cathedral, each bequeathed £10 to the convent at Waverley for the
recitation of masses for their souls in the abbey church.

The great eastern transept of the nine altars at Fountains and the range
of eight chapels flanking the nave of Melrose were built to meet the
need of more and more altars for soul-masses in those Cistercian
churches.

The prudent founder of a perpetual chantry would have his chapel
built and his tomb set up during his lifetime, knowing full well that if
left to his family or his executors it might never be done. The chapel
of William of Wykeham at Winchester Cathedral was completed some
years before his death in 1404. By his will, dated 23 July 1403, the good
Bishop desired that ' my body be buried in the middle of a certain chapel
by me newly erected on the south side of the nave of the cathedral church
of Winchester.'

Thomas Beckington, Bishop of Wells, was leaving nothing to chance,
for he himself consecrated a tomb which he had built for his remains,
saying a mass for his own soul and for the souls of his parents, etc., in
the presence of a large congregation. In the south choir arcade of Wells
Cathedral is the Bishop's chantry chapel within which stands his tomb.

At Great Malvern Priory is a fifteenth-century encaustic tile which
bears the following verse :

|  |  |
|---|---|
|  | Or in modern English : |
| THENKE · MON · YI · LIFFE | ' Consider, man, thy life |
| MAI · NOT · EU · ENDURE | May not endure for ever. |
| YAT · YOW · DOST · YI · SELF | What thou dost thyself |
| OF · YAT · YOW · ART · SURE | Of that, thou art sure. |
| BUT · YAT · YOW · KEPIST | But that thou entrusteth |
| UNTO · YI · SECTURE · CURE | To thy executors' care |
| AND · EU · HIT · AVAILE · YE | If it be of any avail |
| HIT · IS · BUT · AVENTURE | 'Tis but a matter of chance.' |

Such timely advice was not lost on such as Bishop Beckington.

Chantry chapels assume a variety of forms. The most splendid of all is
Henry VII's at Westminster, built as an eastern annexe to the royal abbey

church. Save that it is entered from the ambulatory it is structurally independent of the great church itself. Comparable with this in position is the Percy chapel at Tynemouth Priory occupying the normal site of a Lady chapel, at the east end of the choir.

In annexe chapels like the foregoing, the tomb of the founder was invariably placed in the middle, a few feet west of the altar. At S. Mary's Church, Warwick, the tomb of Richard Beauchamp stands in its original position, as do also the tombs in the Fitzalan chapel at Arundel. But with the passing of the Chantries Act, most chapels which could be incorporated into the church as aisles were dismantled and the tombs were then or subsequently relegated to a less prominent position against a wall or between the piers of the nave or choir. Few of those in the nave arcades at Salisbury Cathedral are in their original position ; some came from chantry chapels long since destroyed. In course of time many founders' tombs have been thrown out and broken up.

A most attractive form of chantry chapel is that which can best be described as ' a stone-cage ' chapel. This is a miniature building, generally rectangular on plan, erected between two piers of a choir or nave arcade, and consisting of an enclosure made by stone screens rising to a height of eight feet or more. The stately chapel of Prince Arthur at Worcester is this type at its best. Within the enclosure, at the east end, was placed an altar, and where space permitted, the tomb of the founder was set up in the middle with just enough room left for the priest to stand as he recited the mass. The entrance was near the west. Stone-cage chapels are almost without exception Perpendicular Gothic in character, with rectilinear panelling, open-traceried windows and cresting.* The finest examples are roofed with fan vaulting. In a few instances they are built with an upper story, e.g. the Ramryge chapel at S. Albans, the upper floor being used to accommodate the singers.

A few interesting examples of this form are extant which are constructed only partly of stone. At Salisbury Cathedral the Hungerford chantry chapel is in the main a grilled enclosure of wrought iron standing on low stone walls. The upper part of the Leschman chapel at Hexham Priory consists of timber screening reared on a panelled base of masonry, and at Oxford Cathedral is a two-storied chantry chapel, the lower stage of which is of a stone and the upper a wooden gallery.

The usual position for the stone-cage chapel was beneath one of the arches of the choir or nave, as for example the Bubwith and Sugar chapels at Wells ; but in those churches where there was a Saint's chapel, preference was for a site near the shrine. At Winchester Cathedral, adjacent to the shrine of S. Swithun are the chapels of Bishops Fox and Gardiner,

* Glass was not used in the window openings of screens enclosing chapels.

and in the retrochoir not many feet away are the tomb-chapels of Cardinal Beaufort and Bishop Waynflete.

Where there was no Saint's chapel, a position in the sanctuary near the High Altar was most favoured, as at Tewkesbury Abbey, where the sanctuary is encircled with chapels and tombs. At S. Albans, Abbot Ramryge built his chapel on the north side of the sanctuary, immediately adjoining the High Altar, the sites flanking S. Alban's shrine being already occupied.

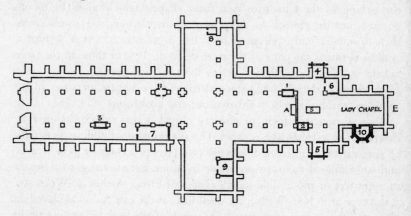

Fig. II  COMPOSITE PLAN SHOWING THE VARYING POSITIONS OF CHANTRY CHAPELS.  A *marks the position of the High Altar and* S *the shrine. 1. Abbot Ramryge's, S. Albans. 2. Bishop Fox's, Winchester. 3. William of Wykeham's, Winchester. 4. Bishop Stanbury's, Hereford. 5. Bishop Russell's, Lincoln. 6. Bishop Alcock's, Ely. 7. Neville Chapel, Durham. 8. Prior Sylke's, Exeter. 9. Archbishop Grey's, York. 10. Bishop Audley's, Hereford. 11. Bishop Bubwith's, Wells.*

Less costly maybe than the stone-cage type was the chapel that was formed by utilizing the space between a pair of deeply projecting buttresses of an aisle. The construction merely entailed the removal of the length of walling between the buttresses up to a height of six or eight feet, the building of an outer wall at the extremities of the buttresses, together with a covering vault or roof. There are three chapels of this kind in the Angel choir at Lincoln, the sites chosen being as near the shrine of S. Hugh as was possible. The royal chapel of King's College, Cambridge, is flanked on either side along its entire length by a series of low chantry chapels squeezed in between the huge buttresses.

Limitation of space often rendered a chapel so small that there was little or no room within for the tomb of the founder. The difficulty was solved quite effectively in the Fleming chapel at Lincoln, by placing the tomb at the side of the chapel, *i.e.* on the site formerly occupied by the aisle wall. The tomb with its canopy thus formed an enclosing screen. In other instances the tomb was set up outside the chapel at a place where it could be seen to advantage. At Canterbury that of Henry IV is between the columns of the Saint's chapel on the north side, only a few feet distant from the diminutive chapel built between the buttresses. At Hereford the chapel of Bishop Stanbury projects from the north choir aisle, whereas the tomb is in the north choir arcade close by ; and at Westminster, Henry V's tomb stands on a platform immediately beneath the King's bridge chapel which spans the ambulatory.

What may appear to have been an even simpler arrangement was to enclose the easternmost bay of an aisle of the choir with screening of timber or stone. At Ely Cathedral are two screened-off bays which were utilized as chantry chapels ; that of Bishop Alcock at the eastern extremity of the north aisle and Bishop West's in the south aisle. But the bays thus appropriated were transformed into Perpendicular chapels with rich tabernacling and elaborate vaulting ; and this was done at a cost which must have exceeded that of many a stone-cage chapel. A much less costly appropriation was the Langton chapel in the south aisle at Winchester, where the enclosing screen was a timber one.

Where no bays were available in the choir of a church the founder of a chapel might have to content himself with a bay or two of an aisle of the nave. This was done at Durham, where two bays of the south aisle of the great Norman nave were enclosed with screens to provide a chantry chapel for Ralph, Lord Neville, and a similar expedient was adopted at Norwich by Bishop Nix.

But chantry chapels took other forms and occupied many other positions. Here, an eastern chapel in a deep transept was made to serve the purpose ; at York Cathedral, Archbishop Walter de Gray appropriated a chapel in the south transept, the building of which he had undertaken ; there, an odd corner was utilized, as at Exeter Cathedral, where a screened enclosure in the north transept served as the chantry chapel of Sylke, the precentor. At Thetford Priory, the Howard family built a small square chapel in the angle of the nave and the north transept, and the Scrope chapel at Easby Abbey occupied a like position. At Hereford Cathedral, Bishop Audley's chapel, five-sided on plan, projects from the south side of the Lady chapel, and standing in a class by itself is Henry V's bridge chapel at the east end of Westminster Abbey.

Occasionally a chapel was constructed in the thickness of a wall or in some obscure corner of a church. At Canterbury Cathedral, Archbishop Warham's chapel was the narrow passage or chamber between the north transept and the chapter-house. Bishop Grandisson of Exeter made use of the small space between the west wall of his cathedral and the screen which masks it. At S. Mary's Church, Warwick, a diminutive chapel nestles between the walls of the choir and the Beauchamp chapel ; and when Bishop Skirlaw of Durham built the chapter-house at the collegiate church of Howden, he ingeniously utilized the odd space to the east of the vestibule for his chantry chapel.

On a far larger scale is the Fromond chapel at Winchester College, which stands in the middle of the cloister garth.

Amongst the decorative enrichments carved in the masonry or wood-work of chantry chapels will often be found a rebus, a punning device on the name of the founder. This was commonly employed by ecclesi-astics and the heads of religious houses. Thus at Wells Cathedral the sugar-loaf occurs on the stonework of the Sugar chapel ; in the Alcock chapel at Ely, the Bishop's rebus, a cock on a globe, appears in the glass as well as on the masonry ; and two versions of a rebus occur at Abbot Islip's chapel at Westminster.

For chapels and tombs of noble families and often of bishops, the rather more dignified heraldic shields were employed as a means of identification.*

Occasionally chantries were founded at an altar standing against the rood screen, which in the greater churches was a stone structure spanning the nave at the east end and was of sufficient depth to render it suitable for the placing of altars on either side of the door opening into the choir.

At the two rood altars in Chichester Cathedral were chantries for the souls of the bishops who had installed them; and at S. David's Cathedral there still remains the Gower chantry chapel within the southern half of the rood screen.

Rare instances of chantries founded at an altar in the loft of a rood screen occurred at York Cathedral, where were two at the altar of S. Saviour ' in the little rood loft,' at Grantham parish church in 1349 and at Lichfield Cathedral.

Sometimes, a vault was excavated beneath a chantry chapel of the annexe or excrescent type to receive the leaden coffins of the founder and members of his family.

In 1869 the vault beneath the tomb of Henry VII in his chapel at West-minster was opened and the leaden coffins of the king and Elizabeth of York were brought to light. Beneath the Kirkham chapel in Paignton church, Devon, is a small vault and there is one beneath Duke Humphrey's chapel at S. Albans.

---

*A chapel on the north side of Ampton church, Suffolk, bears the inscription ' *Capella perpetua cantarie Johannis Coket, 1483* ' but this is rather exceptional.

The particular form that a chantry chapel assumed was necessarily subject to considerations of cost, site and goodwill. It might be that the cost alone precluded the erection of a chapel at all. The next best thing was a chantry tomb. Such a monument occupied less space and yet could be so designed that its chantry purpose would be adequately met. Where there was no effigy the slab of a table-tomb served as an altar ; or in any case a small portable altar could be used for the mass. At the western end of the tomb sufficient room was left for the priest to perform the office. Many splendid chantry tombs with ornate canopies remain in our churches, notably that of Bishop Redman at Ely Cathedral. A small but charming example is the monument to the poet Chaucer in Westminster Abbey.

No less plentiful than in the greater churches were the chantry foundations in parish churches, within whose walls countless soul-masses were recited—in the main for the humble villagers and townsfolk who could make but modest bequests. The local gentry, the prosperous trader and the gilds and sodalities could do more, and accordingly established their own chantry chapels. Most commonly, part of an aisle in the church was appropriated for the purpose ; it was enclosed with timber screens and an altar set up within. There were large numbers of parclose chapels in the churches up and down the land, but when the Suppression came zealous reforming bishops issued injunctions for the dismantling of them, and the screens being mostly of timber were easily torn down. A few parclose chapels remain, as for example the Yonge chantry chapel at the east end of the north aisle of Axminster church, Devon.

Often the whole of an aisle flanking the chancel was enclosed with screens to serve as a chantry chapel, as at Colebrooke church, Devon, where the north aisle of the sanctuary became the Copplestone chapel. Here and elsewhere the screens have fortunately escaped destruction.

In many churches where the chancel was aisleless a chantry chapel was built flanking it on the north or south. A small but charming example remains at Berkeley church, Gloucester, where the Berkeley chapel adjoins the chancel on the south. It is shut off from the church by the eastern wall of the south aisle of the nave and is entered by an outer doorway on the south. Occupying a similar position is the chapel of the De la Poles at Wingfield church, Suffolk. The arches which divide this chapel from the chancel are studded with the Suffolk fetterlock and the knot of the Staffords.

There was no normal position for the chantry chapel in the parish church. As in cathedral and monastic churches, the tendency was for chapels to gather themselves about the sanctuary ; but they are to be found in varying positions as circumstances dictated. At S. Botolph's,

Boston, a short aisle to the west of the south porch was built as a chantry chapel ; at Bere Regis, Dorset, the Turberville chapel lies to the east of the porch ; and the Kirkham chapel at Paignton church, Devon, occupied the south transept. The most convenient site for a chantry altar was undoubtedly at the east end of an aisle of the nave, particularly where the chancel was without aisles. An indication of this is often provided by a piscina in the aisle wall.

In the wall flanking the chancel arch of some churches will often be found an oblique opening or slit known as a squint, the purpose of which was related to chantries and soul-masses. It frequently happened that a chantry priest would be reciting his office at an aisle altar before High Mass for the parishioners had commenced. The parish priest, needless to say, disapproved and appealed to the bishop, who ordained that chantry masses should not begin until High Mass was in progress. The chantry priest claimed that, standing before his altar, he was unable to see when the parochial mass had begun. So the difficulty was overcome by the provision of a squint. Henceforth, a chantry priest at a side altar could not feign ignorance of what was taking place in the chancel, as the squint afforded him a direct view of the high altar from his station in the aisle. At Holy Trinity Church, Bradford-on-Avon, commanding a view of the altar from the Horton chapel in the north aisle, is a squint nearly twenty feet long—an inordinate length, due to its being cut through the walls of both nave and chancel, which are not in alignment.

When a parish church had become fully aisled and no space was available for more altars, chantry chapels were erected as excrescences from the main structure. The small rectangular Hall chapel at Grantham church, Lincs., projects from the north aisle of the choir ; and at Evesham, Abbot Lichfield built himself two small chantry chapels projecting from the south side of the naves of S. Lawrence and All Saints respectively.

It was not unusual for a chantry altar or sometimes two to be set up against the western face of the rood screen in a parish church, the altar being enclosed with timber screens so as to form a chantry chapel. At Shelsley Walsh, Worcs., is a parclose chapel built against the southern half of the rood screen (Pl. 5) ; and two chapels of this kind, dating from the fifteenth century, remain *in situ* at Wootton Wawen church, Warwickshire, though the screen to which they are attached was not a rood screen but stood, as at present, beneath the western arch of the central tower.

Chapels of the stone-cage type were far less common in parish churches. It may have been due to the limited space between the piers of a nave or choir arcade, the span of which was far less than in a cathedral church. Nor was this form suitable for the religious and craft gilds, who would

22. THE CHAPEL AND TOMB OF BISHOP FLEMING, LINCOLN CATHEDRAL

23. BISHOP BUBWITH'S CHAPEL IN THE NORTH NAVE ARCADE, WELLS CATHEDRAL

**24. THE BUBWITH CHAPEL, WELLS CATHEDRAL**

25. THE LONGLAND AND RUSSELL CHAPELS FLANKING THE JUDGMENT PORCH, LINCOLN CATHEDRAL

need a chapel large enough to accommodate all their brethren on the occasion of important festivals and commemorations.

In the larger churches of the towns there were undoubtedly many. Two stone-cage chapels are still to be seen in the choir arcades of the large church at Newark, Notts. ; at Ludlow church, Shropshire, there were at one time three of this kind in the nave. It is reasonable to assume that chapels of this form constructed of wood, and therefore less costly than stone, were by no means uncommon, but, being easily removed and broken up when chantries were no more, few remain to-day. On the north side of the nave of Burford church, Oxon., is a roomy little timber chapel with a panelled base, but there is no screenwork above. The roof is supported by slender buttresses at the angles (Pl. 4).

Occasionally a chantry chapel was erected as a detached building in the parish churchyard. The Sylvester chapel, which now forms a south-western aisle at Burford church, Oxon., was originally an independent building, the chantry chapel of the Merchants' Gild. In the fifteenth century it was extended eastwards and joined on to the body of the church.

6

## PART TWO

# FOREWORD

'I desire my tombe be made of marble . . . and also a chapel of timber surrounding it, with an altar for masses to be daily celebrated thereat for the health of my soul.' (Will of Thomas Montacute, 4th Earl of Salisbury (d. 1428), buried in Bisham Priory, Berks.)

IN THE FOLLOWING chapters the more important chantry chapels which remain in the churches of this country are described, together with the founders' tombs where they exist. Here and there an historical note is added and reference is made, in the respective churches, to chapels which have been swept away and to chantries of interest for which no chapel was built. The author makes no apology for the account of the chantries in Chichester Cathedral, now devoid of the chapels and altars which served the purpose, nor for the enumeration of the chantries in Old S. Paul's, in which vast cathedral more soul-masses were sung than in any other church in the kingdom.

The Puritan Revolution and the drastic and ill-conceived 'restorations' of the nineteenth century wrought irreparable damage to fabric, fittings and monuments of many cathedrals and churches ; so much so that a number of them are entirely denuded of the screens, stalls, monuments and chantry chapels that formerly graced their interiors. At Peterborough Cathedral, the church of one of the proudest Benedictine monasteries in the Middle Ages, there are neither chantry chapels nor stately tombs of warriors or statesmen. With a few exceptions the monuments there are those of abbots or post-Reformation ecclesiastics. Its bareness in this respect must be attributed mainly to the wanton destruction during the Civil War. Chester Cathedral, on the other hand, fell a victim to the ruthless 'restorers' of the nineteenth century, when 'every vestige of antiquity that could be removed was cleared off.'

Of the seventy or more chantry chapels which are in a fairly complete state in the greater churches, thirty are to be found in what were originally Benedictine establishments, including the cathedral priories; eighteen are in the secular cathedrals and the remainder in Augustinian priories and collegiate churches. These figures do not include aisle chapels long since dismantled and shorn of their altars and screens. Of stone-cage chapels there are three dozen or so, of chapels of the annexe and excrescent type about twenty, and the rest are those of unusual form or position.

More than one-half of the seventy surviving chapels are those of bishops, abbots and priors. Fortunately, not all post-Reformation ecclesiastics were obsessed with a ' purging ' zeal. To make a clean sweep of chantry chapels and such ' monuments of superstition ' must have been abhorrent to those prelates who cherished a regard for their predecessors. Moreover, chapels which stood in long naves or spacious retrochoirs, as at Winchester Cathedral, were certainly not ' in the way,' nor did they interfere with the offices or ritual of the reformed faith. Many chantry chapels which survived the upheaval of the sixteenth century were destroyed subsequently.

It is significant that approximately three-quarters of the chapels of which records exist in the cathedral and monastic churches occupied sites in or near the sanctuary or the Saint's chapel.

---

7  Chantry chapels in the monastic cathedrals : Canterbury, Carlisle, Durham, Ely, Norwich, Rochester, Winchester, Worcester.

---

OUR SURVEY BEGINS with the monastic cathedrals, *i.e.* the bishops' churches which before the Reformation were also served by monks.*

## CANTERBURY CATHEDRAL

A noble array of chantry chapels might be expected at Canterbury Cathedral, the mother church of the Christian faith in this country, the seat of the archbishop and withal a famous resort of pilgrims. Few, however, remain in this great church, a number having been destroyed since the Reformation. Two are of outstanding interest, *viz.* those of the Black Prince and of Henry IV. It might appear that the bays of S. Thomas's chapel to the east of the choir would have afforded attractive sites for chantry chapels of the stone-cage form, though the plan was not wholly suited to such a purpose.† The prior and convent, anxious as they were to cater for sight-seeing pilgrims, were at pains to keep the

---

*These establishments were known as cathedral priories and, with the exception of Carlisle, the monks attached to them were of the Benedictine order. At the Dissolution the priories were suppressed and the churches were reconstituted as cathedrals of the New Foundation.

†A comparison of the choir arm of Winchester Cathedral with this at Canterbury leaves no doubt as to the superiority of the squared retrochoir over the peri-apsidal plan when sites were needed for chantry chapels.

bays of the Saint's chapel unencumbered with chantry chapels, which would have blocked the view of the shrine from the ambulatory. The tombs of the Black Prince and Henry IV occupy bays on the south and north sides respectively, but their chantry chapels are elsewhere.

Edward of Woodstock, popularly known as the Black Prince, son of Edward III, was from his earliest association much attached to Canterbury, probably due to his having been entrusted in his youth to the care of Prior Hathbrand. In 1363 he married his cousin Joan, the 'Fair Maid of Kent,' but as the union came within the prohibited degrees of the Church a papal dispensation was sought, in pious acknowledgment of which the

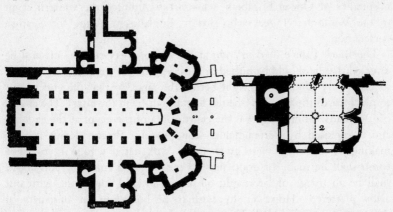

FIG. III  PLAN OF CANTERBURY CRYPT SHOWING CHAPELS OF THE BLACK PRINCE. *1. S. Trinitas.*
*2. Blessed Virgin.*

Prince founded two chantries in the crypt of Canterbury Cathedral. The ordinance, dated 4 August 1363, is preserved in the Treasury.

There were to be two chapels, one dedicated to S. Trinitas and the other to the Blessed Virgin, and each was to be served by 'a priest, proper, sober, honest and not quarrelsome,' whose presentation was in the gift of the archbishop. A daily mass was to be sung for the Prince and Duchess Joan and for their souls after death by each of the priests at his own altar ; and a lodging was provided for them in a common hall near the almonry of the priory. For the endowment of his chantries Prince Edward made a grant of the manor of Fawkes' Hall—the modern Vauxhall—at Lambeth, to the prior and convent.

Unusual was the site chosen for the chapels, for they occupy that part of the Norman crypt beneath the south transept of the choir. They consist of a pair of apsidal chapels, the Norman masonry of which was clothed in Perpendicular garb.

The walls of the apses were opened up with three-light windows to make the interior lighter, the central piers and the responds were refaced with clustered shafts, and lierne vaults enriched with sculptured bosses replaced the Norman vaults. In the northern chapel, S. Trinitas', are the earliest heraldic bosses in the cathedral, including the arms of the Black Prince and of Edward III. One of the bosses, a female head, is said to be that of the Fair Maid. Another boss is a lively rendering of Samson, a nude figure with the head of an ass or a lion beneath his right arm. The altars were placed against the walls of the apses (Pl. 6). Every Sunday a French Protestant service is held in these chapels to commemorate the hospitality of Queen Elizabeth, who in 1575 granted the western crypt to the Walloon refugees who fled to England to escape the Spanish persecution.

The Black Prince died in 1376 at the age of forty-six. By his will he directed that he should be buried in the crypt ' in the middle of our chapel of Our Lady Undercroft, right before the altar, so that the end of our tomb towards the foot may be ten feet distant from the altar.' The chapel of Our Lady Undercroft was the central area of the crypt at the east end and is enclosed by Perpendicular stone screens. Precise details for the making of the tomb were given in his will, dated 7 June 1376. ' The tomb shall be made of good marble and of good masonry and above shall be an image of laton gilt, all armed in steel for battle, with our arms quartered.' However, his wish to be buried in the obscurity of the crypt was disregarded. The convent decided otherwise ; the tomb of so illustrious a prince should be set up in the most hallowed spot possible, namely near the shrine of Becket, where it would be an additional attraction for the pilgrims. So it was erected between the coupled columns on the south side of the Saint's chapel, and, having no canopy or tabernacling above, it in no way obstructed the view of the shrine.

The tomb, which was cleaned and restored to its pristine condition and splendour by Professor Tristram in 1935, is an outstanding example of fourteenth-century craftsmanship. It is constructed of Purbeck marble and the sides are adorned with sixteen enamelled shields of arms, each set within a traceried panel. Eight of them are the arms of England and France, the Prince's ' arms for war,' and the remainder are his ' arms for peace,' represented by three silver ostrich plumes on a sable field, beneath which a scroll bears the motto ' *Ich dien.*' The familiar Prince of Wales's feathers were derived from the family of Philippa of Hainault, the Prince's mother. (Woodruff and Danks, *Canterbury Cathedral.*)

On a slab of gilt bronze lies the life-size effigy clad in armour, his helmet with the visor up, so that his features should be visible. The head rests on a helmet, a cap of maintenance and a crowned leopard. The surcoat is enriched with lions and fleurs-de-lis in relief and the fingers of the prince meet in the act of prayer. At the feet is a little French bulldog and on the verge of the slab is a lengthy inscription in Norman-French as ordained by the Prince's will.

Professor Lethaby was of opinion that this noble effigy was the work of John Orchard, 'latoner,' who made the bronze effigy of Edward III in Westminster Abbey.

The tomb stands within an iron grille which dates c. 1400 and above is a wooden tester, on the underside of which is a large painting of the Trinity surrounded by the symbols of the Evangelists.

Lady Joan of Kent, who survived the Prince by nine years, was not buried at Canterbury. By her will, dated 7 August 1385, she directed that she should be buried ' in her chapel ' in the church of the Grey Friars at Stamford, near the tomb of her first husband, Sir Thomas Holland (d. 1360).

The only other royal chantry chapel at Canterbury is that of Henry IV (d. 1413). Though he died in the abbot's house at Westminster, Henry had no love for the monks of S. Peter's, to whom Richard II had been so deeply attached ; but he made generous gifts towards the rebuilding of the nave of Canterbury and by his will, 1409, ordained that his body should be buried in the cathedral ' at the discretion of my cousin, the Archbishop ' (Arundel). Henry left definite instructions for the building of a chantry chapel near to his tomb, where was to be ' a chauntrie per-petuell with twey prestis for to sing and pray for my soul.' The erection of both tomb and chapel was delayed until some years after his death.*

The tomb of Henry IV and his queen, Joan of Navarre (d. 1437), stands in a bay on the north side of the Saint's chapel, immediately flanking the site of Becket's shrine and the tiny chantry chapel is built off the north ambulatory between two buttresses.

The altar within the chapel was dedicated to Edward the Confessor in 1437 and above was a reredos, now destroyed. Scratched on the wall is an item referring to the cost of a figure of the reredos : ' Ye middel image was 19s. 11d.' The chapel has a fan vault, the first of its kind in the cathedral, and is lighted by two Perpendicular windows in the outer wall (Pl. 9).

*In a manuscript preserved at S. Benet's College, Cambridge, a curious story is told of the body of Henry IV. It affirms that the boatmen conveying the body by water to Canterbury were overtaken by a storm of wind and rain off Gravesend and so alarmed were they that they threw the body overboard and the next morning substituted a corpse from the graveyard at Gravesend. This was buried in the Cathedral on Trinity Sunday 1413 in the presence of Henry V. and many nobles and ecclesiastics. In 1832 the tomb of the king was opened and the story disproved for the perfectly preserved body of Henry with a thick beard of deep russet colour was exposed to view.

The tomb of Henry IV was thoroughly cleaned by Professor Tristram in 1937 and much of its former beauty thereby revealed. The sides are adorned with canopied niches now tenantless, alternating with traceried panels and on the slab are alabaster effigies of Henry and his queen, Joan, both attired in coronation robes. Their crowned heads rest on pillows supported by angels and the queen wears the SS collar. These effigies were the work of the Nottingham School of ' alablaster-men ' which flourished in the fourteenth and fifteenth centuries. Enclosing the tomb is an iron grille similar to that around the Black Prince's monument, and above is a wooden tester with coats of arms in colour.

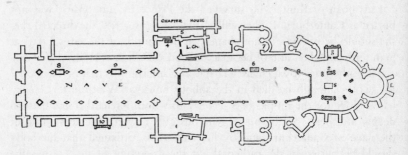

Fig. IV CANTERBURY CATHEDRAL. *1. Tomb of the Black Prince. 2. Tomb of Henry IV and Joan. 3. Henry IV's Chapel. 4. Archbishop Warham's Tomb. 5. Archbishop Warham's Chapel. 6. Archbishop Chicheley's Tomb. 7. S. Stephen's Chapel. 8. Buckingham Chapel. 9. Arundel Chapel. 10. Brenchley Chapel. S. Shrine of S. Thomas.*

Of the chantry chapels founded by archbishops, none was more curiously situated than was that of William Warham (1503–22). In April 1507 the prior and convent of Christ Church by deed granted the Archbishop a site for his tomb near the new Lady chapel in the transept of the Martyrdom ' together with a certain oratory or chapel ' close by. Squeezed in between the wall of the chapter-house and the north wall of the transept is a long, narrow chamber in which were kept the book-presses of the monks. At no great cost this chamber was reconditioned and converted into a chapel for the Archbishop's chantry. Very little structural alterations were needed, for in September 1507 the chapel was dedicated to the Blessed Virgin and S. Margaret. It was served by two priests. Warham's tomb, for which there was no room in his gloomy little chapel, was placed in a recess in the north wall of the transept. Originally a small doorway to the east of the tomb opened into the chapel, but it was blocked up about a century ago and the tomb, on which lies the recumbent effigy of the Archbishop, was moved to the centre of the recess. The Warham monument is noteworthy for the tall Perpendicular canopy of three ogee arches and for the panelling on the walls of the recess.

In the wide bay of the north choir arcade, opposite the choir transept, is the tomb of Archbishop Henry Chicheley, who occupied the See from 1414 to 1443. Chicheley was a close friend and advisor of Henry V, and was prominent in inducing the king to embark on the war with France. In 1438, long after Agincourt, he founded All Souls College, Oxford, it is said from feelings of remorse and to commemorate his friends and countrymen who had perished in the French wars. All Souls was a chantry foundation as well as a college and was established in order that the Fellows might pray not only for the souls of the founders, the Archbishop and Henry V, but also for ' the illustrious Prince Henry, late King of England . . . and of the dukes, earls, barons, knights and others who fell in the wars for the crown of France.'

The endowment of the college was derived mainly from a number of alien priories that had been suppressed by Henry V.

The tomb of Archbishop Chicheley was erected during his lifetime, and by an agreement made with the prior and convent of Christ Church, masses were to be sung for his soul at the altar of S. Stephen in the southern of the apsidal chapels of the north choir transept. Licence had been granted the Archbishop to alienate land in mortmain to the value of £20 a year to the convent for this purpose.

His college of All Souls provided the sum of £7 a year for the maintenance of the tomb, and to this day the Fellows make it the object of their care. The resplendent colour and gilding is as fresh to-day as it was in the fifteenth century. On the slab of the tomb rests the alabaster effigy of the Archbishop wearing the Eucharistic vestments, his head supported by angels, and at his feet are two monks. Below, through three open arches, is to be seen an emaciated figure in a shroud, a grim reminder of mortal decay that occurs in the monuments of bishops elsewhere. At each end of the tomb is an octagonal standard or pier on the faces of which are two tiers of tabernacled niches containing modern figures. The standards support a canopy enriched with angels bearing heraldic shields.

Archbishop Chicheley was a native of Higham Ferrers, Northants, where his family was one of note. In 1425 he founded a chantry college there, consisting of eight chaplains, four clerks and six choristers, whose particular office was to pray for Henry V, his queen and the Archbishop during their lives, and for their souls after death. They were granted a dwelling in the town, still called ' the College,' and the front of the quadrangle remains to-day.

In the chancel of Higham Ferrers church are the rich stalls, formerly used by the members of Chicheley's college, and beneath the shadow of the western tower is the Archbishop's little chantry chapel.

Less than twenty years after the death of the Black Prince a chantry was founded at the altar of Our Lady Undercroft, always held in special veneration, by Lady Mohun, widow of the eighth Baron Mohun of Dunster. Somner gives the terms of her agreement with the convent :

For the sum of 350 marks sterling (and certain utensils convenient for the chantry), with which money the Manor of Selgrave was purchased and amortized to the convent, with licence of the King . . . a perpetual chantry is granted unto her by them, who covenant with her besides, that when she died, her corpse should be laid in the tomb which she of her own cost had prepared and caused to be set up near the altar of our Lady in the undercroft ; and being there so entombed should never be removed, nor the name of the tomb ever altered, but be honourably kept. Five shillings per annum is to be given to the clerk that kept the Lady chapel for the keeping clean of her tomb, with many other clauses in the same indenture, which in order that the chantry might not vanish out of memory with their successors, the monks caused to be enrolled in their martyrology, that upon her obit-day it might be annually recited.

Her tomb, with effigy, now sorely mutilated, was erected on the south side of the chapel during her lifetime. Round the tomb is an inscription set in latten which runs : ' *par Dieu pries par l'arme johane de borwaschs* [Burwash] *ke fuit dame de mohun*.'

There were several other chantry chapels in the cathedral, of which only the records survive. Of these, three which stood in the nave call for some notice.

In the seventh bay of the north arcade from the east was the chapel of John Buckingham (1363–97). He had been Keeper of the Privy Seal to Edward III and was successively Bishop of Lincoln and of Lichfield. In 1397 he resigned his See and retired to Christ Church Priory, where he ended his days about six months later. He made many gifts, mainly of copes and vestments, to the prior and convent. By his will he provided for the erection of a chantry chapel, where masses should be recited for his own soul and the souls of Edward III, Thomas de Beauchamp, Earl of Warwick, and others. His chantry was to be served by two priests, who were given a house in the precincts and 10 marks a year each as a stipend. Further, each of them was to receive ' 6 yards of good cloth with a sufficient trimmings of fur, a candle from Michaelmas to Whitsuntide and one load of firewood.' In 1399 his executors paid some 1200 marks to the prior and convent of Canterbury for the endowment of Buckingham's chantry chapel, which was probably of the stone-cage type. It was evidently quite small, for the tomb of the Bishop stood outside it in the nave.

Also of the stone-cage form was the chantry chapel of Archbishop Thomas Arundel (1396–1414), who was translated to Canterbury from the See of York.

Arundel was a cousin of Henry IV. As far as can be determined, his chantry chapel stood in the north arcade of the nave in the third bay from the crossing, a site that was chosen in order that the chapel could be used by the laity for their private devotions. It was served by two priests, who received a stipend of £10 a year each and a house in the south of the precincts. The endowment was provided out of the rectory of North Fleete. Within the chapel the Archbishop was 'fairly entombed,' but both chapel and tomb were destroyed at the time of the Suppression.

Between the deep buttresses of the south aisle of the nave in the fourth bay from the east was built the chantry chapel of Dame Joan Brenchley, daughter of William Batisford. It was founded in 1447 and therein a daily mass was to be said for the well-being of Henry VI and Margaret of Anjou and for the soul of the founder's husband, Sir William Brenchley. It was dedicated to S. John Baptist, and the chantry priest had a stipend of £10 a year and was given a lodging in Canterbury. In the seventeenth century the Brenchley chapel, which resembled that of Bishop Fleming at Lincoln, was made the mortuary chapel of Dean Neville and his family, but unfortunately it was taken down in 1787. From the engraving of the cathedral made by Wenceslas Hollar, it appears to have been a very small structure. By her will, 1453, Dame Joan also founded a chantry in Bexhill church, Sussex. It was known as the Batisford chantry, and the presentation was in the gift of the Archbishop of Canterbury. In 1548 the endowment was valued at £8. 6s. 8d. (V. C. H., Sussex.)

In the bay to the east of the tomb of the Black Prince stands the monument or cenotaph of Archbishop William Courtenay (1381–96). It assumes the form of an altar tomb, on which lies the effigy of the Archbishop, with his hands raised in prayer. A year before his death Courtenay founded a chantry in the cathedral, at which altar is not known. He had been very active in promoting the building of the new nave of the cathedral, a fact which may account for the privileged position of his cenotaph, within a few feet of S. Thomas's shrine. The Archbishop died at Maidstone, and by his will decreed that he should be buried in All Saints church, which by Papal permission he had made collegiate the previous year. His tomb-slab there is still to be seen.

One of the most imposing monuments in Canterbury Cathedral is the tomb of Archbishop Thomas Bourchier, 1454–86, which adjoins the High Altar on the north. Bourchier was a staunch adherent to the Yorkist cause and during his thirty-two years at Christ Church he crowned Edward IV, Richard III and Henry VII. In 1473 he founded a chantry in the cathedral, to endow which he made a grant of the manor of Panfield, in Essex. His tomb is enriched with canopied niches and above is a tabernacled canopy adorned with flowers and the Bourchier knot.

## CARLISLE CATHEDRAL

The number of chantries in the diocese of Carlisle is given as nineteen in the *Valor Ecclesiasticus, temp*. Henry VIII, of which, according to the returns made in Edward VI's reign, four had been founded in the cathedral, then the church of an Augustinian priory. One of these was the chantry of S. Cross, of which little is known except that it was valued at £3. 19s. per annum. Another, ' the chantry of S. Roch,' was probably that founded by Bishop Roger Whelpdale (d. 1422) who be- queathed the sum of £200 for the endowment of a chantry for the souls of two dear friends, Sir Thomas Skelton and John Glaston, both of whom were buried in the cathedral. These chantries were founded at altars already existing.

The sole remaining chantry chapel in Carlisle Cathedral stands to the east of the south transept. It was dedicated to S. Catherine, and was founded in the closing years of the thirteenth century by John de Capella, a wealthy citizen, who endowed it with lands, houses and rents. The chapel, square on plan, is enclosed from the transept and choir by timber screens bearing the initials of Prior Thomas Gondiber (1484-1507).

## DURHAM CATHEDRAL

As early as the middle of the thirteenth century the monks of Durham Cathedral priory were under the obligation of celebrating more than seven thousand soul-masses every year. (*Rites of Durham*.) In succeeding centuries that number was increased by the many chantries that were founded at altars in that great church. One chantry chapel alone remains though records of others equal in historic interest have been preserved.

On the south side of the choir of the cathedral, occupying the whole of the third arch from the west, is the striking monument erected by Bishop Thomas Hatfield (1345-81). It comprises a small chantry chapel and an episcopal throne in one, and is thus described in the *Rites of Durham* : ' Thomas Hatfield, Bishop of Durham, lyeth buried over against the Revestorye doore in the south allye of the quire, betwixt two pillars, under the bishopp's seate which hee did make before hee died, his tombe being all of alabaster, whereunto was adjoyned a little altar, which hee prepared for a monke to say masse for his soule after his death, the altar beinge invironed with an iron grate ' (Pl. 7).

In 1362 the prior and convent granted Bishop Hatfield the right to choose his place of burial between the High Altar and the choir, and this gives the date after which he began the erection of the chapel and throne.

The monument is a lofty structure of stone, designed in two stories, the lower stage forming a small chapel in which is the founder's tomb ; the upper, reached by a straight stairway at the east, consists of a gallery with a bishop's throne, flanked on either side by two seats for his chaplains. The chapel is opened up with a wide cusped arch on both sides and is roofed with a lierne vault, which has a number of foliage bosses. The tomb, on which is the effigy of alabaster, has a range of ogee-arched panels, and was originally a blaze of colour. At the south-west of the chapel stood the ' little altar ' and there were paintings of angels on the walls at each end. The arms of the Bishop occur on many parts of the structure. The throne and the chaplains' sedilia are crowned with tabernacled canopies, once richly coloured, which rise almost up to the choir arch. Originally the gallery and stairway had a traceried or panelled front, but this was replaced in the nineteenth century by the present balustrading. In 1937 the monument underwent a colour-restoration.

In some way or other Bishop Hatfield was connected with the convent of Lesnes Abbey, Kent. Amongst the muniments at Westminster Abbey is a document, dated 1380, by which the abbot and convent of Lesnes founded a chantry in their church for the souls of Edward III and Queen Philippa, and for the good estate of Thomas Hatfield, Bishop of Durham, in gratitude for his gifts and in soul-alms for his parents John and Margery, his brother Miles, and Joan and Margery, his sisters.

The same year, in recognition of some benefit conferred upon them by Hatfield, the brethren of Stratford Langthorne, a Cistercian house in distant Essex, founded a chantry for the Bishop in their conventual church. They undertook to sing a mass daily at the altar of the Holy Ghost, except in times of ' pestilence, war or the burning of their house.'

Closely associated with Durham over a long period was the great Neville family, whose benefactions were considerable. They were laid to rest in the cathedral, they founded chantries there, and the convent granted them a site for a chapel. In return for gifts of rich vestments to the convent in 1355 the prior granted Ralph, Lord Neville, and his lady, Alice, the right of burial in the church before the Jesus altar against the rood screen ; and Lord Ralph besought the prior that he would grant him and his wife a soul mass every day at that altar, for which the convent were to receive an annual rent of £10. Lord Ralph (d. 1367) was the first layman to be buried in the cathedral. His widow presented a sum of £120 (equal to £5,000 to-day) to the sacrist to pay for repairs to the fabric of the church, and on her death she bequeathed wax and money to the convent. She was buried in the nave near her husband. Still more generous was their son John, Lord Neville, who provided the base of marble and alabaster for S. Cuthbert's shrine and contributed £500 towards the cost of the magnificent reredos, ' the Neville screen,' which backs the High Altar. In 1378 he founded a chantry at the Jesus altar for the souls of his parents, and on his death in 1389 was buried in the south aisle of the nave, where his first wife, Matilda, lay. It was not until 1416 that a chantry

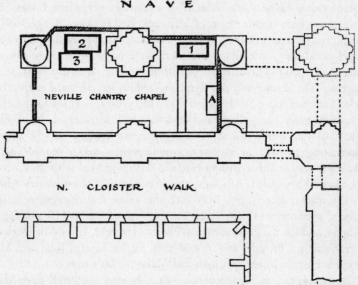

FIG. V  NEVILLE CHANTRY CHAPEL, DURHAM CATHEDRAL. *Screens conjectural. 1. Tomb of Ralph Lord Neville. 2. Tomb of John Lord Neville. 3. Tomb of Bishop Robert.*

chapel was founded for the Nevilles at Durham. In that year Bishop Langley granted a licence for the removal of the remains of Lord Ralph and his wife from the nave to the south aisle, and it was then that the Neville chapel was fitted up.

It was not a separate structure but was made by enclosing two bays of the south aisle of the nave at the east end. The easternmost bay of the aisle was left open, for there the main door from the cloister led into the church. In the *Rites of Durham*, written in 1593, are given details of the Neville chapel. At the east end, where the altar stood, it was closed with a stone wall somewhat higher than the altar, with an oak screen above. Behind the altar was a sculptured reredos of alabaster. The western end of the chapel was closed by a low stone wall surmounted with a grate of iron and the north side was similarly shut off from the nave by iron grilles set between the Norman piers. To the north of the altar was a ' seat or pew where the Prior was accustomed to sit to here Jesus messe.' The entrance to the chapel was probably in the western wall. Traces of colour decoration remain on the wall of the aisle, and a Perpendicular five-light window, now ' restored ' away, was inserted in the wall to light the chapel more adequately.

When the remains of Lord Ralph and his lady were transferred to the chapel a tomb with their effigies was erected on the north side adjacent to the altar, but it suffered mutilation at the hands of the Scottish prisoners who were confined within the cathedral after the battle of Dunbar, 1650. On the sides of the tomb a part of the panelling enclosing shields remains, but the effigies are little more than shapeless lumps of alabaster.

In the next bay westwards is the tomb of Lord John Neville and Matilda in a less mutilated condition. The sides are adorned with canopied niches, alternating with panels containing Neville and Percy devices. Of the eighteen niches, sixteen retain their ' weepers.' In its original glory the tomb and the effigies were resplendent in gold and colour, faint traces of which still remain.

Adjacent to Lord John's tomb is the blue marble slab of Bishop Robert Neville (1437–57), grandson of Lord John, and the last of the family to be connected with the priory.*

One of the greatest building bishops of Durham was Walter de Skirlaw (1388–1405). He was responsible for the greater part of the cloisters and the monastic dormitory. He also built a beautiful little chapel at Skirlaw, his native place, as well as bridges at Shincliffe, Auckland and Yarm. At the collegiate church of Howden, Yorks, where he was at one time a canon, part of the central tower and the charming octagonal chapter-house were his work. In the north choir arcade at Durham,

---

*The Nevilles also had a chapel at Staindrop, hard by their castle at Raby. In the church of S. Mary the Virgin, Staindrop, they founded chantries, built a great aisle, established a college of priests and erected their tombs. The glory of the church is its almost unrivalled collection of monuments, all of them of the great Nevilles of Raby. In 1343 the convent of Durham, to whom Staindrop had been given by Canute, granted licence to Lord Ralph to found three chantries at the altar of Our Lady in S. Mary's church, ' for the souls of his parents.' Each was to be served by one priest. Apparently a new altar of Our Lady was needed, for almost at once the south aisle of the church was taken down and a new aisle built, four feet wider than the nave. The Decorated windows of this chantry aisle have reticulated tracery, and in the south wall are two tomb recesses and sedilia. At the south-east is a curious little vestry built for the use of the chantry priests. The founder was, however, buried in Durham Cathedral.

opposite the Hatfield monument, Bishop Skirlaw founded an altar, dedicated to S. Blaise and S. John of Beverley, in front of which he erected his tomb. By his will he ordained that his executors should find a monk-priest to sing a mass daily at the altar. Tomb and altar were enclosed within an iron grille *curiose compositum* and the tomb was ' sumptuously beset with many brasse pictures, having his own picture portrayed in brasse in the midst thereof.' Along the wall of the north

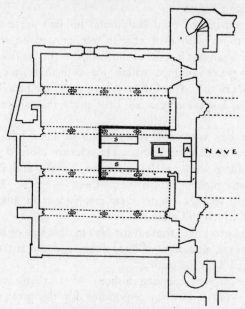

FIG. VI LANGLEY'S CHAPEL IN THE
GALILEE, DURHAM. A. *Altar of Our Lady.*
L. *Cardinal Langley's Tomb.* S. *Stalls.*

aisle runs a stone bench, part of which bears Skirlaw's arms and was assigned to the Bishop's bedesmen.

The year before his death Skirlaw founded a chantry at Howden, where he had built the chapter-house to the south of the choir. It is entered from the choir by a vestibule, on the eastern side of which is a unique little chapel, built by the Bishop for his chantry. His arms appear on the gable.

Skirlaw's successor at Durham was Cardinal Thomas Langley, who was elected to the See in 1406. During his thirty-one years as Bishop he spent enormous sums of money on the fabric of the cathedral, mainly on the cloisters and the Galilee chapel at the western end of the nave. On various works in the Galilee, then in a ruinous state, he spent nearly £500, a sum equal to £20,000 to-day. To each of the Norman piers there

26. BISHOP AUDLEY'S CHAPEL, SALISBURY CATHEDRAL

27. CANOPY OF THE BECKINGTON CHAPEL, WELLS CATHEDRAL

*Copyright N.I.P.S.*

28. THE BRONZE GRILLE, HENRY VII'S CHAPEL, WESTMINSTER ABBEY

29. HENRY V'S BRIDGE CHAPEL, WESTMINSTER ABBEY

30. PART OF THE REREDOS AND A LOCKER (UNDER), HENRY V'S CHAPEL, WESTMINSTER
ABBEY. LEFT TO RIGHT: FIGURES OF THE VIRGIN MARY, S. EDWARD AND S. DENIS

two stone shafts were added, a new timber roof was put up and the lighting improved by the insertion of Perpendicular windows. In 1414, before these extensive reparations were begun, the Cardinal founded a perpetual chantry served by two priests in the chapel. It was dedicated to the Virgin Mary and S. Cuthbert, and the deed of foundation, dated 18 June 1414, is preserved amongst the archives at Durham. While the work was in progress Langley planned and began a chapel for his chantry within the Galilee. The original western door of the nave was walled up, and against the wall was placed an altar dedicated to Our Lady, with a magnificent wooden reredos.

The eastern bays of the middle aisle were enclosed with timber screens and stalls were put up in the enclosure at the western end. In 1435, two years before his death, Cardinal Langley erected his tomb of blue Eggleston marble, in front of Our Lady's altar. To-day nothing remains of altar, reredos, screens, stalls or tomb.

At the nine altars of the great transept, built athwart the east end of Durham Cathedral (1242–80), innumerable obits and anniversaries were kept, and there, according to the *Rites of Durham*, ' founders and benefactors were prayed for every day and had in remembrance in the time of masse.'

## ELY CATHEDRAL

When the *Valor Ecclesiasticus* was compiled there were twenty-nine chantries in the diocese of Ely. In the cathedral two chantry chapels are left, together with one of the largest and most ornate chantry tombs in the country. They are all to be found in the eastern arm of the cathedral.

The earliest is the chapel of Bishop John Alcock (1486–1500), who appropriated the easternmost bay of the north choir aisle and transformed it into a Perpendicular structure. Alcock was a patron of learning and bore a great reputation for sanctity ; he was comptroller of the Royal Works and Buildings for Henry VII and he founded Jesus College, Cambridge, in 1497, out of the possessions of S. Radegund's nunnery. The scholars of the college were ' to be instructed in grammar and to celebrate divine service daily for the King, the Queen, etc.' Alcock's chapel is remarkable for the extraordinary richness of its architectural make-up, though now mutilated and deprived of the many figures which formerly tenanted the niches. To enclose the chapel on the west and south, stone screens were built, laden with a mass of tabernacled canopies. The principal doorway of the chapel is in the western screen, but there is a portal on the south. Recurring again and again in the carved stone-work is the Bishop's rebus, a cock on a globe, a device which appears also in the two small windows flanking the doorway. Inside the chapel is

7

more tabernacling and on the north side stands the tomb, a door at the foot leading to a small recess. The tomb and the ogee-arched canopy above it are covered with a mass of carved ornament. To complete the chapel, larger windows were inserted in the outer walls and a fan vault with a central pendant was put up. (Pl. 8.)

The corresponding bay at the end of the south choir aisle is the chantry chapel of Bishop Nicholas West (1515–34), who was the son of a baker at Putney. Bishop West had a distinguished career as a diplomat. In 1506 he was made one of the commissioners to negotiate a commercial treaty with the Netherlands, and in 1514 he concluded an alliance with Francis I, in recognition of which Cardinal Wolsey advanced him to the bishopric of Ely.

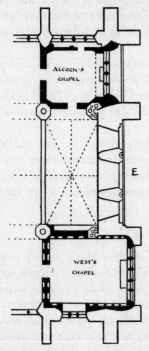

For the making of his chantry chapel in the cathedral, *c.* 1533, the eastern bay of the south choir aisle was subjected to the same process of 'Perpendicularizing' as had been employed for Alcock's chapel. Less ornate than the latter, West's chapel is rather larger, for the original east wall was torn down and a new wall built farther to the east, thus adding about five feet to the length of the new chapel. Enclosing screens of stone were erected at the west and north and rectilinear windows lighted the interior. The wrought iron gates of the western entrance afford a good specimen of contemporary smithery.

FIG. VII  EAST END OF ELY CATHEDRAL

The chapel, a rich piece of Perpendicular Gothic, is particularly noteworthy for the tiers of canopied niches with which the walls are covered. The niches vary considerably in size, form and decoration, and would house some 200 figures or more. The vault is overlaid with traceried panels and retains much of its colour ; on the surfaces are painted the arms of Bishop West and of the See. Above the entrance are panels enriched with antique ornament in low relief, heralding the advent of Renaissance art which was destined to overwhelm Gothic. Beneath the panels is an inscription :

*Gracia Dei sum id quod sum,* A.D. 1534
(' *By the grace of God I am what I am.*')

On his death in 1534 Bishop West was buried in his chapel ; but, not unmindful of the place of his birth, he had also built a chantry chapel in Putney church. When the church was rebuilt in 1836 his chapel, which originally stood on the south side of the chancel, was transferred to the north side. It is about fifteen feet in length and is planned in two bays. The south wall is opened up with two four-centred arches, and the west wall with one. The fan vault is original ; in the spandrels are quatrefoils containing the arms of the See and rosettes bearing the initial W (Pl. 10).

In the north arcade of Ely choir, four bays from the east, stands the chantry tomb of Bishop Richard Redman (1501–5), a sumptuous example of Perpendicular Gothic. The Bishop had been Abbot of Shap, a house of Premonstratensian canons in Westmorland, also Bishop of S. Asaph, and later of Exeter before he came to Ely. He gained a reputation for kindliness and hospitality and it was said of him that when in his journeyings he halted for but an hour he would have a bell rung that the poor might be summoned to partake of his charity. The recumbent figure of the Bishop lies on the tomb, the sides of which are enriched with traceried panels containing shields. The tomb is set within a Perpendicular ' frame ' above which is a tall canopy of three ogee gables richly cusped and surmounted by tiers of rectilinear panelling. The cresting above reaches the full height of the choir piers. At the foot of the tomb is a space for the priest in front of the altar, which stood against a narrow wall attached to a pier (Pl. 11).

There were other chantries at Ely, notably an early one founded by Bishop Hugh de Northwold (1229–54), who built the Early English bays of the choir. His chantry provided for the recitation of masses for his soul and for the souls of Henry III and Queen Eleanor ; and he built a dwelling on the Palace Green for the four priests who sang the masses. The southernmost chapel in the north transept is said to have been the chapel, dedicated to S. Edmund, specially endowed by Bishop Northwold for these priests. He was buried in the centre of the choir which he had built, but his tomb, with a Purbeck marble effigy clad in episcopal robes, stands in the bay north of the High Altar.

## NORWICH CATHEDRAL

In the great Norman cathedral at Norwich are to be seen two chantry chapels, both founded by bishops. On the south side of the choir in the second bay from the west stands the chapel of Bishop James Goldwell (1472–99) who was at one time Edward IV's ambassador at Rome. During his episcopate, the new clerestory and the amazing lierne vault of the choir were put up ; the Bishop's rebus—a well and a golden bucket—

appears in the carved bosses. At the same time Goldwell remodelled the choir arcade, transforming the Norman round arches into the four-centred arches of Perpendicular Gothic. His chapel is noteworthy mainly for the canopy carried by four-centred arches and faced with rectilinear panelling. At the western end of the chapel is the founder's tomb, its sides adorned with traceried panels ; and on the tomb-slab is an effigy of the Bishop in full canonicals. An altar once stood against the east wall of the chapel. The good works of Goldwell were not restricted to his diocese. In 1487 when the brethren of Leeds Priory, Kent, found themselves burdened with heavy debts the Bishop came to their aid, and in return they undertook that a canon should recite a daily mass for the souls of their benefactor and his parents at the altar of S. Mary in the conventual church.

Entirely differing in character from the Goldwell chapel is that of Bishop Richard Nykke or Nix (1521–36) who was responsible for the tangled vaulting of the cathedral transepts. He gained an evil reputation at Norwich and was notoriously harsh with the Reformers, some of whom he sent to the stake. His chapel, which was set up during his life-time, occupies two bays of the south aisle of the nave, which were trans-formed into Perpendicular for the purpose. The Norman nave arches of these bays were converted into four-centred arches like those in the choir ; the groined vaults were taken down and a Perpendicular vault covered with a lattice work of ribs took their place. The chapel was enclosed with screens, now removed. The making of Nix's chapel was a much more costly work than the Neville aisle at Durham (Pl. 17).

Projecting from the south aisle of Norwich choir is a square chapel, dedicated to S. Mary the Less, which is now used as a consistory court. It was commonly spoken of as the Beauchamp chapel, a local corruption of Bauchon, and was built in the fourteenth century for chantry uses. It has a later vault in which are a number of carved bosses representing incidents in the life of the Virgin.

## ROCHESTER CATHEDRAL

No chantry chapels have survived at Rochester Cathedral but the tombs of two bishops remain, to each of which a chantry was attached. Built in the wall dividing the north aisle from the choir is the tomb of Bishop Hamo de Hythe (1319–52), a former prior of the house. His chantry in the cathedral was founded through the agency of the canons of Lesnes Abbey, Kent, to whom he paid a sum of £106. 13s. for the purpose. In 1344 licence was granted the abbot of Lesnes to make over 6 marks a year, issuing from the manors of Lesnes and Acol, to the prior and convent of Rochester, who were required to find a priest to celebrate a mass every day in the cathedral for the soul of Bishop Hamo. The Bishop's tomb, much mutilated, is surmounted by one large cusped arch contained within a crocketed gable. There is no effigy.

Hamo's successor, John de Sheppey (1352–60), founded a chantry in 1360 at the altar of S. John Baptist in the north choir transept. The priest received a stipend of 16 marks a year but was not allowed to hold any other office ; the prior and convent of Rochester were pledged to maintain the chantry and to distribute 10 marks to the poor on the occasion of the obit.

The Bishop's tomb, which was discovered buried beneath a mass of masonry in 1825, is the most important monument in the cathedral. It stands in the north choir aisle flanking the chapel of S. John Baptist and resembles the tomb of his predecessor. On the tomb, which has panelled sides, lies the coloured effigy of Bishop Sheppey in his episcopal robes and wearing a mitre. Above is a canopy carried by a segmental arch with large cuspings, the outer order of the arch being carried up as an ogee arch into a quatrefoiled parapet in the Decorated manner.

Amongst other chantries in Rochester Cathedral was one founded in 1395 by Thomas, Earl of Nottingham, who granted the appropriation of Findon church, Sussex, to the convent, they on their part undertaking to recite masses for their benefactor's soul in perpetuity at the altars of S. Andrew and S. Ithamar, which stood east of the sanctuary.

## WINCHESTER CATHEDRAL

In no church in this country is so fine a series of chantry chapels to be found as in Winchester Cathedral. Here are no less than six chapels of the stone-cage form, three of them of exceptional beauty and size. It will be observed that of the nine shown on the plan below, six occupy positions east of the sanctuary and near the site of S. Swithun's shrine. The Fox and Gardiner chapels flank the Saint's chapel beyond the High Altar ; farther east, in the retrochoir, are the Beaufort and Waynflete chapels ; on either side of the Lady chapel are the Orleton and Langton chapels ; in the nave arcade, those of Edingdon and William of Wykeham ; and Prior Silkstede's chapel is in the south transept. With the exception of the last-named, the founders of all these chapels were bishops of Winchester.

Very fitting was it that the chapels of William Edingdon and of William of Wykeham should stand in the nave which through their energy was transformed into a Perpendicular building. The remodelling of the old Norman nave, begun c. 1346, though carried out very largely by Wykeham, was the conception of Edingdon, who died before much had been done. Edingdon was successively Treasurer and Chancellor of England, and in 1366 was offered the Primacy by Edward III, but on account of his age and infirmity he chose to remain at Winchester. ' If Canterbury is the higher rank, Winchester is the better manger.' His chapel stands in the second bay from the crossing on the south side and is the earliest of its kind in the cathedral. It is comparatively small and low, and the screen-walls enclosing it are quite simple in design. Above a low plinth are two tiers of Perpendicular windows surmounted with cresting. As in the majority of chantry chapels, the entrance is at the west. Inside is the tomb of the Bishop with his effigy in pontificalibus,

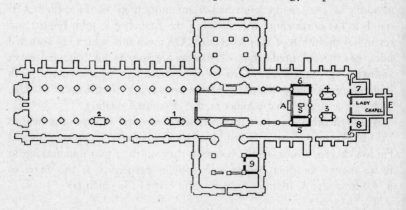

Fig. VIII WINCHESTER CATHEDRAL. *1. Edingdon Chapel. 2. Wykeham Chapel. 3. Beaufort Chapel. 4. Waynflete Chapel. 5. Fox Chapel. 6. Gardiner Chapel. 7. Orleton Chapel. 8. Langton Chapel. 9. Silkstede Chapel.*

the stole which he wears bearing the curious fylfot cross. On the verge of the tomb is a strip of enamelled brass with a Latin epitaph. There is no trace of the altar other than the raised step at the east end.

On a more imposing scale is the elegant chantry chapel of Edingdon's successor, William of Wykeham. It occupies the fifth bay from the west on the south side of the nave, where previously had been an altar of the Virgin Mary. The career of the founder—statesman, ecclesiastic and builder—is remarkable in many respects. He is best remembered for the founding of New College, Oxford, and of Winchester School, as well as for the reconstruction of the cathedral nave, all of which undertakings were crowded into the last twenty-five years of his busy life. Bishop Wykeham died on 27 September 1404, ten years after he had resumed the work in the nave begun by Edingdon. A clause in his will, 1403, shows that his chapel was built in his lifetime : ' Item, I desire my body to be buried in the middle of a certain chapel by me erected on the south side of the nave of the cathedral church of Winchester.' It is almost certain that it was built by William Wynford, the master-mason employed by Wykeham for the reconstruction of the nave. The good Bishop had no intention that he should be forgotten after his death, for he directed that three chantry monks should recite masses in his chapel thrice daily, each of whom was to receive one penny a day, and the boy choristers who sang there nightly were to be paid 6s. 8d. a year (Pl. 12).

Wykeham's chapel is a rectangular enclosure, but as the long sides project into the nave and the aisle the angles are chamfered to meet the nave piers. In elevation it fills the whole of one bay from the pavement to the balustrading of the clerestory. It is thus half the height of the nave. In scale and design the screen-walls of the chapel are admirably suited to their position and purpose ; they are conceived as large three-light windows divided by slender mullions. The heads of the lights are ogee-arched with rectilinear panelling in the spandrels. The lower half of the screen-walls on each side consist of two tiers of Perpendicular lights above a range of blind panels. The treatment of the whole is delicate in the extreme. Within the chapel is the altar (restored), which is backed by a reredos of two tiers of canopied niches, now tenanted by modern figures. There is also a range of five niches in the wall at the west, and the lierne vault has a number of gilt bosses. In the middle of the chapel is the tomb of Bishop Wykeham, on which reposes his effigy wearing episcopal vestments with mitre and crozier. Two angels support his head, and at his feet are three seated figures, their hands together in prayer. These figures are said to represent Master William Wynford, Simon Membury, clerk of the works, and John Wayte, ' monk of my said church and controller of the work (i.e. the rebuilding of the nave) on the part of the prior and convent.' On the sides of the tomb are gabled niches in which appear heraldic shields, including the arms of the See of Winchester and those of Wykeham with his famous motto, ' Manners makyth man.' Few chantry chapels are at once so complete and so graceful as this of William of Wykeham.

Resembling late Gothic tombs on a grand scale are the chapels of Cardinal Beaufort and Bishop Waynflete, which flank the retrochoir. The former stands in the second bay east of the Saint's chapel on the south side and the latter occupies the corresponding bay on the north. They are alike in their general form and reach the full height of the arches of the retrochoir.

Cardinal Henry de Beaufort, the natural son of John of Gaunt by Katherine Swynford, succeeded William of Wykeham in 1405 and held the See for forty-two years. He was nominated Cardinal and Papal Legate in 1417, though he did not obtain royal licence for these preferments until 1426. The scheming Cardinal who, rightly or wrongly, figures rather badly in Shakespeare's *Henry VI*, Parts I and II, acquired immense wealth, much of which he devoted to charitable uses. He enlarged the hospital of S. Cross at Winchester, by founding the ' Almshouse of Noble Poverty,' and the large gatehouse known as the Beaufort Tower at the entrance to the inner courtyard of S. Cross is witness of his interest in the hospital.

The Beaufort chantry chapel consists of an enclosure made by four grouped piers at each end, supporting a complex mass of tabernacling, niches and pinnacles. The central space, which is quite open, is spanned by a large four-centred arch above which is a canopy piled up with niches and buttresses. The tomb, on which lies the coloured effigy of the founder in cardinal's robes and tasselled hat, is thus open to view on either side (Pl. 14). There was originally no effigy, the present figure being placed there in Charles II's reign. The chapel is covered with a fan vault.

The chantry chapel of Bishop William Waynflete (1447–86), the illustrious founder of Magdalen College, Oxford, pairs with the Beaufort chapel, standing in the second bay east of the Saint's chapel to the north of the retrochoir. Waynflete, who succeeded the Cardinal at Winchester, was a great patron of learning. Besides founding Magdalen he established a free grammar school at Waynflete, his native place, and he was a considerable benefactor to Eton College, where he had been provost.

His chapel is similar in design and arrangement to his predecessor's. The canopy of crowded buttresses and niches is carried by four clusters of buttresses at each end, enriched with large niches for figures. The three arched openings of the chapel are of equal span and are enclosed by Perpendicular screens in the lower part, which somewhat obscure the tomb within. The much-restored effigy of the bishop has the hands closed as in prayer, with a heart between them, in allusion to the *sursum corda* of the liturgy. There are traces of colour in many parts of the chapel, which is kept in a state of repair by the Fellows of Magdalen College ★ (Pl. 15).

*Bishop Waynflete also built a small chantry chapel at Magdalen, but in 1830 it was transplanted to the new church of the Holy Trinity then in course of erection at Tilehurst, Berks, where it was rebuilt to the north of the chancel. In the statutes for Magdalen College, the Bishop provided for his anniversary and ordained that ' every year on the day of the burial service, four pence for his trouble be paid to the common bellman, who is accustomed to make public proclamation, after the Oxford practice, for Master John Bowyke and myself as benefactors.'

The most coveted site for a chapel in the cathedral was that flanking the Saint's chapel, within a few feet of the shrine of S. Swithun.

The Saint's chapel, immediately behind the High Altar, was bounded on the east by a low wall and on the west, before the erection of Fox's great reredos, by an altar screen similar to that now to be seen in Westminster Abbey.

Until the early years of the sixteenth century the bays flanking S. Swithun's chapel had been kept free of monuments in order that the crowds of pilgrims who visited the cathedral would have an unobstructed view of the shrine as they passed round the east end. However, Bishops Fox and Gardiner, with little consideration for sight-seers, effectively enclosed the Saint's chapel by erecting their chantry chapels in the bays flanking the shrine. On the south side is Bishop Fox's and on the north the Gardiner chapel.

Bishop Richard Fox (1500–28) successively occupied the Sees of Exeter, Bath and Wells, and Durham before he came to Winchester. He was Lord Privy Seal in the reigns of Henry VII and Henry VIII, and he negotiated the marriage of Prince Arthur and Katherine of Aragon. Himself a scholar, Fox was a patron of learning, a benefactor of Magdalen College, Oxford, the founder of Corpus Christi at Oxford and of grammar schools at Taunton and Grantham. He also carried out the wishes of Margaret, Countess of Richmond, in founding S. John's College, Oxford. During his rule at Winchester he rebuilt the aisles of the choir, put up the stone screens enclosing the choir from its aisles and was very largely responsible for the magnificent reredos of the High Altar. His chantry chapel is the most splendid in the cathedral. The aisle front is composed of four ' bays ' divided by octagonal shafts carried up above the parapet. Intermediate pedestals in the parapet support the Bishop's emblem, the pelican feeding her young. The elevation is of two stories, the lower of solid masonry enriched with canopied niches and panels; the upper stage consists of ranges of four-light Perpendicular windows with rich tracery. This front has no less than fifty-five niches. The north front of the chapel is open to the Saint's chapel. There is no tomb within, but in the second compartment from the east is an arched recess containing an emaciated figure of the Bishop. Behind the altar and reredos is a small chamber which was used as a vestry or an oratory. The scale of the chapel, the exuberant detail in every part and the exquisite craftsmanship displayed in the wealth of carved ornament render it one of the most imposing in the country (Pl. 13, 14).

Contrasting in architectural character with the above is the chantry chapel of Bishop Stephen Gardiner (1531–55) who left Norwich, where he had been archdeacon, to occupy the See of Winchester. He was deprived in Edward VI's reign, but was reinstated by Mary Tudor, whom he had crowned at Westminster. In July 1554 he performed the marriage ceremony of Mary and Philip of Spain in Winchester Cathedral. Intolerant and ruthless, his measures to stamp out Protestantism in England earned for him the title ' the hammer of the heretics.' Gardiner's chantry chapel was the last one to be erected in Winchester Cathedral. It was probably built *c.* 1540, but it served its purpose only a few years. It was indeed a bitter pill for the Bishop to witness the suppression of his own chantry. Albeit he wrote to Sir William Paget, 1546, ' I understand it hath pleased Parliament to give into the King's majesty's hands the disposition of all hospitals, chantries and other houses, whereof I am very glad.' It was politic to say so at the time. His chapel was built at the moment when Renaissance details were trickling across the Channel and the result is a curious mixture of Gothic construction and classic ornament. It is of the stone-cage type, its front being divided into three bays by octagonal shafts. The walls in the lower part are panelled in the Renaissance mode, but above are four-light Perpendicular windows, and the whole is surmounted with a classic cornice. In the western face of the chapel is a narrow entrance doorway at the top of a short flight of steps in the north aisle.

As in the Fox chapel, there is a small chamber or vestry at the east end. The tomb of the Bishop has gone, though a headless figure reposes in a small recess on the aisle side of the chapel.

The earliest chantry chapel at Winchester is one flanking the Lady chapel on the north. With the corresponding chapel on the south it formed part of the reconstruction of the east end of the cathedral in the early years of the thirteenth century. From the roundels of seraphim painted on the vault surfaces it is known as the Guardian Angels' chapel, but it was acquired by Bishop Adam de Orleton (1333–45) for his chantry. Orleton, who is said to have been involved in the murder of Edward II, was translated to Winchester from Worcester. He was buried in his chapel but nothing of his tomb remains.

Nearly two centuries later the chapel on the south side of the Lady chapel was remodelled for the chantry of Bishop Thomas Langton (1493–1500). He came to Winchester from Salisbury and was Archbishop-elect of Canterbury but died of the plague before he could be translated. A complete transformation was effected in the architectural character of this chapel; a large three-light Perpendicular window was inserted in the east wall and an elaborate lierne vault was put up. In the carved bosses of the vault appear many rebuses, a ' long ' (musical note) in a tun, for Langton ; a vine and tun for the See and a hen sitting on a tun for the prior, Hunton. The walls are lined with oak panelling with rich tabernacling and canopies above, and a carved oak screen encloses the chapel from the retrochoir. Though mutilated, the woodwork affords a magnificent display of late Gothic craftsmanship. In the centre of the chapel stands the tomb of the Bishop.

Here and there in monastic churches will chantry chapels be seen which were founded by abbots and priors. Strict observance of their Rule precluded the acquisition by the ' religious ' of sufficient means to found and endow a chantry and build a chapel ; moreover, the celebration of obits of deceased brethren was a normal office in the monastic day, and that being so, there was not the need for individual chantries. But in the later Middle Ages the Rule enjoining poverty was greatly relaxed and some wealthy abbots took to building chantry chapels in their conventual churches.

In cathedral priories like Winchester and Ely the head of the monastery was the prior, always an important personage by reason of his authority ; and at Winchester one of the last priors, Thomas Silkstede (1498–1524), who held office during the enlargement of the Lady chapel, made a chapel for his chantry in the south transept of the cathedral. The middle bay of the eastern aisle of the transept was adapted by the Prior for the purpose and was enclosed at the west by a Perpendicular stone screen. The upper part of the screen consists of traceried windows and within the chapel is much tabernacling and canopy work.   Amongst the sculptured ornament occurs the founder's rebus, a skein of silk.

As ' Seinte Marie College of Wynchestre,' founded in 1382 by William of Wykeham, is directly connected with the cathedral, it is fitting to mention here the chantry chapel which was erected in the college afterWykeham's death. To the south of the college chapel lies a small square cloister ' for the retired walk of the studious in wet weather, and for processions and ceremonies and memorials of the dead.' Originally planned by Wykeham, the cloister was built at the expense of John Fromond, the Bishop's steward. At the same time Fromond built the chantry chapel which stands free in the middle of the cloister garth.

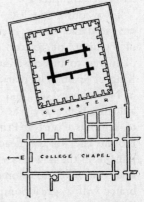

FIG. IX  THE FROMOND CHAPEL AT WINCHESTER COLLEGE

The cloister, together with the chapel, was completed by 1430.

Fromond's chapel, which occupies a large area of the garth, is rectangular on plan and was built of stone from Beer, in Devon, brought by sea and thence carted over the Downs to Winchester. It is a two-storied building, the upper floor being reached by a stairway in the south-west angle. The upper chamber was provided as a lodging for Master William Clyffe, the chantry priest, and his successors. It is ceiled in oak with angel corbels, and after the Suppression was used as a muniment room. It is now the library. In Edward VI's reign the chapel below was converted into a library, but it is now fitted up again as a chapel for the junior boys of the college. With its Perpendicular windows and its lierne vault, enriched with a number of bosses bearing the arms of John of Gaunt and Henry VI, Fromond's chapel is very similar to the Lady chapel of Christ Church Priory, Hants, which likewise has an upper story. The latter, which dates c. 1395–1405, may have served as a model for the chantry chapel at Winchester (Pl. 16).

## WORCESTER CATHEDRAL

The most stately chapel of the stone-cage type in this country is that of Prince Arthur, the eldest son of Henry VII, in Worcester Cathedral. In its architectural character and its Tudor ornament this royal chapel bears close relationship to Henry VII's chapel at Westminster, with which it is contemporary. It is probable that it was the work of masons from Westminster.

To a consuming love of money and power the first of the Tudors sacrificed everything, even the happiness of his children. In consideration of a jointure of 200,000 crowns his son Arthur was married at the age of fifteen to Princess Katherine of Aragon, the fourth daughter of the King of Spain. The marriage took place in S. Paul's Cathedral, London, in November 1501, and was celebrated with great pomp. Immediately after the pageantry was over the young Prince and his bride were sent to keep his Court as Prince of Wales at Ludlow Castle. Less than five months later he was dead. Henry VII would find no place for his son's remains in the new chapel he was planning at Westminster ; instead, the body was taken to Worcester Cathedral, where his obsequies were cele-brated with as great pomp as had been his marriage a few months before. A chantry was founded for the soul of the Prince, and the chapel, a rich example of Tudor Gothic, was begun in 1504. It stands on the south side of the choir in the bay adjoining the High Altar, and is seen to advantage from the open area of the choir transept.

The pavement of the choir being at a higher level than that of the aisles, the south front of the chapel is loftier than the other, and a small chamber is thus formed beneath. Within the chamber are the tombs of Bishop Giffard (d. 1301) and Audela, wife of John de Warren. These monuments were in their present position before the chapel was erected and were incorporated in the structure, being still visible through the panelling of the basement. Above the open panelling is a range of blind rectilinear panels, each embellished with a Tudor badge—the rose, the portcullis, the falcon and open fetterlock, the *rose-en-soleil* and the sheaf of arrows, a device borne by Prince Arthur in compliment to his bride. The chapel is entered at the west by a door on the sanctuary side (Pl. 21).

The screen-walls are divided into compartments by slender buttresses in pairs, faced with tiers of niches containing figures. The space between each pair of buttresses is filled with Perpendicular panels, which are blind at the angles of the chapel. The whole is surmounted with a parapet with open panels and with pinnacles rising from the buttresses. The interior is also richly overlaid with panelling. The whole of the eastern wall forms a reredos to the altar ; four large niches retain their figures, somewhat mutilated. At the western end is a small seated figure of Henry VII. The vaulting of the chapel is almost flat and is covered with traceried panelling, into which a flying arch cuts at the east and west (Pl. 19). In the centre stands the granite tomb of the Prince, with no other ornament than the arms of England and France in the panels on its sides.

There is no effigy, but a painted inscription round the tomb, in place of the brass formerly there. The western of the two tombs in the basement of the chapel is that of Bishop Godfrey de Giffard (1268–1301) whose effigy in vestments and mitre lies thereon. This tomb caused some differences between Archbishop Winchelsea and the Prior of Worcester. It appears that Giffard had erected the tomb in its present position before his death ; but when the Archbishop saw it he wrote to the Prior in January 1301 expressing his disapproval. ' The tall and costly structure like a tabernacle ' shut out light from the High Altar, and it occupied the rightful position of sedilia. Moreover, to make room for his tomb, Giffard had removed the remains of another Bishop, John of Coutances. That being so, the Archbishop ordered the Prior to remove Giffard's monument without delay. But shortly afterwards the offending Bishop died, and the Prior, resentful at archiepiscopal interference, respected the wishes of the late prelate, who was accordingly buried in the tomb he had prepared. There is no record to show whether the lofty tabernacling or canopy remained until Prince Arthur's chapel was erected two centuries later.

IN THIS CHAPTER some account is given of the chantry chapels in the cathedrals of the Old Foundation, *i.e.* the cathedrals which throughout the Middle Ages were served by secular canons and not by monks.

Though the Reformation effected little change in the constitution of the secular cathedrals, it stripped many of them of their chantry chapels, altars and screens.

## CHICHESTER CATHEDRAL

At the time of the Suppression there were twenty or more chantries in the cathedral of Chichester. Save for the outer aisles of the nave there is little evidence of the existence of any chapels there.

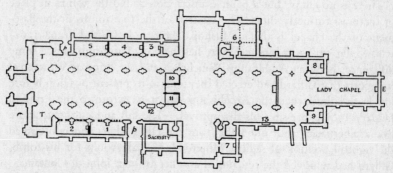

FIG. X CHICHESTER CATHEDRAL. *1. S. Clement Chapel. 2. S. George Chapel. 3. S. Thomas Chapel. 4. S. Theobald Chapel. 5. S. Anne Chapel. 6. Chapel of the Virgins. 7. S. Pantaleon Chapel. 8. S. John Baptist Chapel. 9. S. Mary Magdalen Chapel. 10. Altar of Holy Cross. 11. Altar of S. Mary-at-Stok. 12. Arundel Tomb. 13. Tomb of Bishop Sherburn.*

The reconstruction of Chichester nave after the fire of 1186 was hardly completed when it was decided to add more chapels to the cathedral, the altars being needed for soul-masses and obits. About 1250 the wall of the south aisle between the porch and the western tower was opened up in four bays to permit of the erection of external chapels. The bays then put up were subdivided so as to make two chapels, which were dedicated to S. Clement and S. George.

So satisfactory was this, that shortly afterwards the process was repeated on the other side of the nave. The outer wall of the north aisle, in the second bay from the east, was taken down and a small projecting chapel, square on plan, was erected and dedicated to S. Thomas and S. Edmund.

Towards the close of the thirteenth century the remaining north wall of the aisle, between the new chapel and the porch, was also cut through, and an outer aisle four bays in length was built, thus providing another two chapels, which were dedicated to S. Theobald and S. Anne. All these outer chapels were divided from each other by cross-walls of stone, and timber screens were set up in the arcade dividing them from the aisles. The wall-buttresses of the old aisles were incorporated in the cross-walls, and when first built the chapels were separately gabled. The dividing walls, with reredoses on their western faces, were destroyed when the chapels were dismantled in Edward VI's reign, but parts of the original buttresses or cross-walls are still attached to the piers.

These aisles were not chantry chapels built and endowed by individual benefactors but were erected by the cathedral chapter to house altars at which soul-masses and obits for all and sundry should be celebrated ; and, as the records show, when chantries came into fashion the altars were used for that purpose. The chantry of Dean Closs (1481–1500) was kept in S. Clement's chapel ; a religious gild celebrated its obits in the chapel of S. George. In 1446 William Hoore and other persons were granted a licence to establish a gild of S. George for the purpose of maintaining a priest in the chapel of that dedication or elsewhere in Chichester, to recite masses for the good estate of Edward IV and for the souls of the gild members. The fraternity was also to support its poor brethren and sisters. At the same altar a chantry was founded in 1481 for the soul of James, one-time mayor of Chichester, but most important of all was the Okehurst chantry. This was founded in 1467 for the well-being of Edward IV and of Elizabeth, his queen, and of John Goring, Humphrey Heuster and Thomas Best, joint founders, and for the souls of William Okehurst, John Okehurst and Cicely, his wife.

At the altar in the chapel of S. Thomas and S. Edmund were three chantries—of Bishop John Clymping (d. 1262), Thomas Berksted, Dean (d. 1296), and ' William the Dean.'

In the chapel of S. Anne in the north outer aisle a chantry was founded to pray for the soul of Walter de Gloucester, Dean of Chichester (1262–76).

Between the north transept and the chapel of S. Thomas and S. Edmund a lodging for the chantry priests was erected at some time, but was demolished at the Suppression.

Remarkable is the number of chantries in the cathedral for bishops and deans of the thirteenth century which were founded long after their death. The Fellows of Magdalen College, Oxford, founded one in 1482 for the soul of Thomas de Lichfield, Dean of Chichester (d. 1247), at the altar of S. Augustine and the Holy Cross ; this nearly two and a half centuries after the Dean's death.   There were several at the altar in the Lady chapel, notably two known as the Mortimer chantries, which were founded by Henry V and were re-endowed by Edward IV in 1461. The two priests, known as ' the king's chaplains,' recited masses for the good estate of Edward and his mother and for the souls of his father, Richard, Duke of York, Henry V and Nicholas Mortimer. The ' king's chaplains ' were given a lodging which stood at the south-east of the cathedral cloisters. Bishop Gilbert de Sancto Leophardo (1288–1305) who made many additions to the Lady chapel, had two chantries at the altar there, and in 1321 Dean Henry de Garland transferred to the same altar a chantry he had founded in Little Hadley church about eighteen years before.

To the east of the north transept is a large square chapel, two bays in depth, which was dedicated to ' The Four Virgins,' viz. S. Katherine, S. Agatha, S. Margaret and S. Winifred. It is almost as large as the transept itself, and was part of the rebuilding which followed the dis-astrous fire of 1186. In this chapel, now used as the cathedral library, two chantries were founded for the soul of Bishop John de Clymping (1253–62).

Of the same period as the Four Virgins chapel is the small square chapel dedicated to S. Pantaleon, now the vestry, which lies to the east of the south transept. At the altar was celebrated a chantry for the soul of Bishop Ralph Neville (1224–44) for whom masses were to be sung twice weekly. The piscina is to be seen in the south wall. Bishop Neville died in London at his house in Chancellor's Lane, now Chancery Lane, and property in Lincoln's Inn owned by the See is known as ' the Chi-chester Rents.' The Bishop's remains were taken to Chichester and buried in the choir, not far from the High Altar.

Both aisles of the cathedral choir terminated at the east in chapels which flanked the Lady chapel. On the north was the chapel of S. John Baptist and on the south that of S. Mary Magdalen. In the former were founded two chantries—for William, first Earl of Arundel (d. 1176), and for ' William the Dean.' As the east window is of the fifteenth century, it is most probable that the chapel was then remodelled. The chapel of S. Mary Magdalen, which has been restored, was the repository of a much-prized relic, the head of S. Richard, for an aumbry in which the treasure was kept remains in the north wall.

31. HENRY VII'S CHAPEL, WESTMINSTER ABBEY

32. INTERIOR OF THE ISLIP CHAPEL, WESTMINSTER ABBEY

33. DUKE HUMPHREY'S CHAPEL, S. ALBANS CATHEDRAL

34. ABBOT ISLIP'S CHAPEL, WESTMINSTER ABBEY

35. ABBOT RAMRYGE'S CHAPEL, S. ALBANS CATHEDRAL

Prior to the fall of the central tower of Chichester Cathedral in 1861, a very beautiful rood screen, dating *c.* 1477, stood at the east end of the nave between the piers of the crossing. It was erected by Bishop John Arundel (1459–78).

The front of the screen was opened up with a vaulted arcade of three bays and behind were stairways leading to the rood-loft. The central arch was the entrance to the choir, and, the screen being of some depth, there was ample space in the lateral bays for an altar with room for the celebrant. In the northern bay was the altar of S. Augustine and the Holy Cross, ' *Subter crucem in majori ecclesia,*' and south of the choir entry was the altar of S. Mary at Stok. Altars bearing the same dedications which stood against an earlier rood screen had been founded by Dean Thomas Lichfield (1232–47) for whose soul masses were celebrated at each. At the new altar of S. Mary at Stok was founded ' the chantry of John Arundel, Bishop, at the choir door,' and the anthem of the

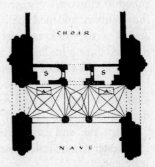

FIG. XI CHICHESTER
*Arundel Rood Screen.*
S. *Stairway to loft.*

Virgin was sung there every evening. The Bishop's tomb stands close by on the south side of the nave.

In 1859 Arundel's rood screen and the two chapels attached to it were swept away, to be replaced thirty years afterwards by the present oak screen. Other chantries were founded in the cathedral for bishops and ecclesiastics. Licence was granted William de Langeton in 1344 to alienate lands in North Mundham to Boxgrove Priory, not far distant, the prior and convent undertaking to find a priest to sing a mass every morn at the altar of S. Lawrence and S. Mary Magdalen in the cathedral for the soul of John de Langeton, the late Bishop (1305–37), a kinsman of William. The tomb of the Bishop is now in the south transept.

Against the wall of the south aisle of the choir is the alabaster tomb of Bishop Robert Sherbourne, of New College, Oxford (1508–36). A chantry was founded at the tomb in 1530. It was served by a prebendary who was to pray for the souls of the Bishop, of William of Wykeham and others. A curious rite was to be observed at the obit. The eight singing boys of the cathedral were to proceed to the tomb, each holding in one hand a glass cup of egg and milk coloured with saffron and in the other a silver spoon and a loaf. After consuming the bread and drink they were to say, ' May the soul of Bishop Robert, our benefactor, and the souls of all the faithful dead, by the mercy of God, rest in peace.' Furthermore

8

the chantry prebendary was to ensure that the tomb and the effigy were 'kept free from cobwebs, dust and filth, and that the curtains hanging over the image should be drawn or folded back according to the state of the weather,' an injunction that indicates the neglect which some tombs suffered in pre-Reformation days. Bishop Sherbourne's monument is the best preserved in the cathedral. Within a canopied recess lies the effigy, robed in episcopal vestments with two angels at the head. The front of the tomb is adorned with panels containing shields and two carved angels at the back support the Bishop's coat of arms. The tomb was installed during his lifetime and is kept in repair by New College, Oxford.

At the east end of the south walk of the cloisters at Chichester are the remains of the chapel of S. Faith, now used as a dwelling-house. At the altar there Dean Garland founded a chantry in 1332 for Master Roger de la Grave.

When the end came there were fifteen chantry priests attached to Chichester Cathedral, most of whom were vicars-choral of the establishment.

# EXETER CATHEDRAL

The *Valor Ecclesiasticus* records a total of thirty-six chantries in the diocese of Exeter, of which, according to the returns of Edward VI, there were sixteen in the cathedral, mostly for bishops and ecclesiastics. The chantry chapels that remain are noteworthy for the stone screens enclosing them.

The reconstruction of the eastern arm of Exeter Cathedral, begun towards the end of the thirteenth century, primarily undertaken to provide the canons with a more commodious choir, incidentally furnished additional chapels for the ever-increasing soul-masses. What more fitting for the purpose than altars in the choir transepts and retrochoir?

Bishop Peter Quivil (1280–92) to whose munificence and energy the project was largely due, was held in so high esteem by the chapter that he was referred to as ' the first founder of the new work.' In the roll of the departed for whose souls prayers were to be offered during mass, his name was to be spoken ' first and foremost.' Quivil was buried in front of the altar in the Lady chapel and there his obit was observed by the canons.

By 1305 the choir was well advanced, for in that year Quivil's successor, Bishop Thomas de Bytton (1292–1307) ordained that the chantry of Dean Andrew of Kilkenny and other persons, including Canon Henry of Kilkenny, should be celebrated at one of the two altars, S. Andrew and S. Katherine, in the north choir transept.

The piscinas of both altars remain. Beneath the window in the north wall is a triple-gabled canopy of the early fourteenth century, rich with crockets and finials. The carved stops represent angels bearing open books. The canopy is said to have served as a reredos of one of the altars.

Bishop Bytton, together with William Bodham, archdeacon of Totnes and Cornwall, founded two chantries in the cathedral, the priests serving them receiving £8 a year which issued from the parsonage of Unele. At which altars the masses were sung is not known.*

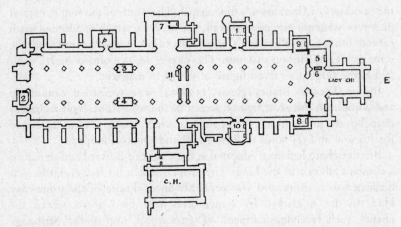

Fig. XII EXETER CATHEDRAL. *1. S. Andrew's Chapel. 2. Grandisson's Chapel. 3. Brantyngham's Chapel. 4. Courtenay Chapel. 5. S. John Evangelist Chapel. 6. Bishop Stafford's Tomb. 7. Sylke's Chapel. 8. Oldham's Chapel. 9. Speke's Chapel. 10. S. Mary's Chapel. 11. Bratton's Altar.*

As curiously placed as Archbishop Warham's chapel at Canterbury is the chantry chapel of Bishop John Grandisson (1327–69). Grandisson has been described as the most magnificent prelate who ever occupied the See of Exeter, though his election had been opposed by the chapter. With great energy he pushed on with the rebuilding of the cathedral, and at his death it was all but completed. He also rebuilt the church of Ottery S. Mary when he made it collegiate in 1337. At Exeter his chantry chapel, always referred to in the records as 'John de Grandisson's chapel,' is a cavernous recess on the south side of the central portal in the great western screen and occupies part of the space between the screen and the

*A more lasting memorial to the Bishop is seen at Bitton in Gloucestershire, his native place. There he built the north aisle of the parish church as a chantry chapel for his parents, c. 1300. The Bitton aisle, dedicated to S. Katherine, retains its early Decorated windows and sedilia.

west wall of the cathedral. The dedication of the chapel is unknown though it is mistakenly called S. Radegund's (Bishop and Prideaux). There certainly was a chapel of that dedication at Exeter, for in 1283 the advowson of the church of Widdicombe-on-the-Moor was granted the dean and chapter on their undertaking to maintain an obit for the soul of Roger de Thorey, late Dean of Exeter, ' in the chapel of S. Radegund, where the body of the deceased is buried.' However, all evidence goes to show that the chapel stood at some distance from the cathedral.

In the Fabric Rolls for the year 1350 is a reference to the glazing of the windows of Grandisson's tiny chapel. The tomb of the founder stood in a recess against the eastern wall, the arch of which is adorned with carved foliage. In Elizabeth's reign the tomb was destroyed and the remains of the Bishop cast out. The chapel has a pointed barrel vault and at the ridge is a carved figure of Christ in majesty.

Bishop Thomas Brantyngham (1370–94) who succeeded Grandisson and completed the great figured screen of the west front, built a chantry chapel in the north arcade of the nave wherein masses were to be recited for his soul and the souls of Edward III and Queen Philippa.

Brantyngham had been educated at the Court of Edward and remained a constant advisor to the king. The chapel, which no longer exists, was dedicated to S. Anne and was probably an enclosure of the stone-cage kind. Its site is marked by a memorial slab. Two priests served the chapel, each receiving a stipend of £10 a year ' out of the parsonage of Morthe.'

Opposite Brantyngham's chapel, in the corresponding bay of the south nave arcade, was another chantry chapel whose destruction is to be deplored. It was that of the Courtenay family, erected in 1375 by Hugh Courtenay, second Earl of Devon, for himself and his wife Margaret (d. 1391). It was a screened enclosure resembling the Brantyngham chapel and was dedicated to S. Agatha. Within was the tomb with effigies of the Earl and the Countess, which was removed when the chapel was demolished in the seventeenth century. Much restored, it now stands in the south transept.

Brantyngham's successor to the See was Edmund Stafford (1398–1419), a kinsman of Richard II. The year following his election to the bishopric he became Keeper of the Great Seal. He founded a chantry in the cathedral for himself and for the souls of Henry IV and his queen and all benefactors. The ordinance decreed that two priests were to recite the masses ' at the altar of S. John Evangelist by the Lady chapel.' This has now been identified as the altar in the chapel which flanks the Lady chapel on the north (Bishop and Prideaux.) The two chantry priests received stipends of £10 a year, issuing from the manors of Winterbournewaste, Swanage and Bockhampton. The Stafford chapel is enclosed from the retrochoir by a stone screen which was built during the Bishop's lifetime. Beneath the arch in the south wall is his tomb, on which rests an alabaster effigy in episcopal robes.

The tomb is surmounted by a large canopy carried by a four-centred arch, richly cusped, and above is a carved cornice with cresting. Both tomb and canopy are much later than the effigy. In the pavement of the chapel is a brass dated 1413 of Canon Langton, a cousin of the Bishop.

In the north transept of the cathedral is a screened enclosure which was built as the chantry chapel of William Sylke, precentor from 1499 until his death in 1508. It occupies a small area in the north-east angle of the transept, stone Perpendicular screens enclosing it at the south and west. The southern screen is designed in two bays, each with a four-centred arch. In the lower part is the founder's tomb beneath an arch which breaks into the mullions of the screen. On the tomb lies an emaciated figure of the precentor with the inscription, ' *Sum quod eris, fueram quod es, pro me, precor, ora* ' (I am what you will be, I was what you are, pray for me I beseech you). At the angles of the chapel the masonry is enriched with niches and above is a carved cornice. Much of the ornament has been destroyed or mutilated, but in the niche above the tomb are the remains of a Virgin and Child. There is no altar in the chapel. Sylke was a man of some importance in the diocese. Evidently the abbot and convent of Cleeve Abbey, a Cistercian house in Somerset, were under some obligation to him for they made a gift of £6. 13s. 4d. to the dean and chapter of Exeter, that the obits of Sylke and one of the canons might be kept in the cathedral.

Of particular interest and beauty are the two chantry chapels which project from the north and south sides of the retrochoir. Each is built between two buttresses, the upper part of the aisle-walling being taken down and an outer wall built from buttress to buttress.

That on the south side was the Oldham chapel and on the north was the Speke chapel. Both were erected and fitted up by Bishop Hugh Oldham (1504-19). He was a native of Manchester and founded the famous Grammar School there. Together with Bishop Fox of Winchester he also founded Corpus Christi College, Oxford, in 1516. The Oldham chapel, dedicated to S. Saviour, is a splendid example of Perpendicular Gothic, the panelled walls, the vault and the screen being of especial beauty. The surface of the barrel vault is covered with quatrefoils enclosing heraldic and other devices, including the Bishop's rebus, ' the owl dom.' In an ogee-arched recess in the south wall is the Bishop's tomb, with his effigy in full canonicals. He is buried in a small vault beneath the chapel. Though much mutilated, the three relief panels of the altar retable can still be made out, the subjects being the Annunciation, the Nativity and the Vision of S. Gregory.

The screen enclosing the chapel on the aisle side, save for the absence of a vaulted canopy, is a stone version of a Devon rood screen, with a loft front of solid panelling. Much figure sculpture was employed to adorn the screen ; set within niches are small but mutilated figures of Fathers of the Church and other saints, and heraldic devices abound— the arms of the Confessor, of England and France, the portcullis and other Tudor ornaments.

The chapel on the north side of the retrochoir, of the same size and form as Oldham's, was founded for Sir John Speke (d. 1518) of White Lackington. It was dedicated to S. George and was endowed with lands, tenements and hereditaments in Langford, Frehead and Ashill in Somerset, which provided a stipend of £7 a year for the priest. Internally, the lower parts of the walls of the chapel are overlaid with rectilinear panelling, above which is a range of niches occupied by figures of angels. From the traceried vault drop a number of pendants. In a recess in the north wall is the tomb of Sir John, with his effigy clad in armour. The screen, like that of the Oldham chapel, bears niches, figures of the Evangelists, as well as many heraldic devices.

Obits and chantries were founded at other altars that were set up from time to time. In 1301 W. de Puntyngdon made a gift of certain rents for his obit ' at the altar of the Blessed Mary and S. Thomas the Martyr by the vestry of the church.' This may have been in the south transept.

Against the western face of the choir screen stood two altars. The northern, known as ' Bratton's altar,' was dedicated to Our Lady. Here was founded a chantry by Sir Henry de Bratton, a legal luminary of the day. The altar was enclosed with screens for there is mention of a latch-key to the chapel in the Fabric Roll of 1380–1.

About this time one of the canons, Henry Blakeborne, was excommunicated by the archbishop. In expiation of his offence, the nature of which is not known, he made many gifts of money to the fabric fund of the cathedral. Furthermore, in 1386, he gave £50 for the recitation of masses for the soul of Edward, the Black Prince, Duke of Cornwall, of which duchy Exeter had been part since 1337. One pound per annum was to be expended for the purpose.

In the bishop's palace, to the south of the cathedral, is a chapel dedicated to S. Mary, founded in the thirteenth century for the recitation of masses for the souls of all the deceased bishops of the See. Bishop Brantyngham speaks of it in 1381 as the chapel ' beneath our palace at Exeter for the souls of our predecessors in this foundation.' The priest who served the altar received a stipend of 6 marks a year, derived from the churches of Harberton and Alwyngton.

## HEREFORD CATHEDRAL

In the much-restored cathedral of Hereford are two chantry chapels, both founded by bishops of the See. They afford charming examples of late fifteenth-century Gothic art and are in good preservation.

Projecting from the eastern bay of the north choir aisle is the diminutive chapel of Bishop John Stanbury, who held the See from 1458 to 1474. Stanbury was a Carmelite friar at Oxford and was appointed by Henry VI to be the first provost of the new college at Eton. In the service and retinue of the king, he was taken prisoner at the Battle of Northampton in 1460, and was confined to Warwick Castle for a time. On his release he retired to the Carmelite house at Ludlow, where he died in 1474, his remains being brought to Hereford for burial.

The Stanbury chapel, which was built during the lifetime of the Bishop, is rectangular on plan and measures seventeen feet by eight feet (Pl. 20).

The eastern and western walls are covered with panelling. In the panels are a variety of sculptured shields displaying the arms of the Bishop and of the See, emblems of the Apostles and of the Passion. In the south wall is a low arched recess containing the tomb with effigy of an unidentified bishop. The most arresting feature of this little chapel is the beautiful fan vault. As there was no room within, the alabaster tomb of Bishop Stanbury, dating c. 1476, was placed beneath the first arch of the north arcade of the choir in close proximity to his chapel. The effigy is damaged and the Perpendicular canopy which originally surmounted the tomb has been destroyed. The ends and the north face of the tomb are enriched with a number of panels, each containing a weeper. The figures include S. Ethelbert, S. Edward the Confessor, the Virgin and Child, and angels holding shields.

On a grander scale is the chantry chapel of Edmund Audley, Bishop of Hereford from 1492 to 1502. Semi-octagonal on plan, it projects from the south side of the Lady chapel and is built in two stories, the upper floor being reached by a small turret stairway at the west end. Beneath a wide four-centred arch is a stone screen, enclosing it from the Lady chapel and carried up to a height sufficient to provide a parapet wall for the upper floor. The screen is faced with two tiers of rectilinear panelling and retains much of its original colouring. Both stories of the chapel have fan vaults, that of the upper floor having a central boss of the Virgin.

Bishop Audley was not to be buried in this splendid chapel at Hereford, for in 1502, soon after its completion, he was translated to Salisbury, and in the choir of that cathedral he erected another chantry chapel, in which he was interred on his death in 1524.

In Edward VI's returns, Audley's foundation at Hereford is described as ' the chantry of Our Lady within Our Lady chapel, called Bishop Audley's chapel.' Of others mentioned in the returns little remains save the names, *e.g.* Burcott's chantry in S. Katherine's chapel and another in the chapel of S. George, called Lochard's.

Amongst the obits was that of Joanna de Bohun, Countess of Hereford, ' the Lady Kilpeck ' (d. 1327). In the north wall of the Lady chapel is a recess containing the effigy of the Countess, who had been an especial benefactress of the Lady chapel. She founded a chantry at the altar there, and just before her death she granted one acre of land at Lugwardine and the appropriation of the church there together with certain chapels to the dean and chapter of Hereford. Out of her gifts forty pence per year was to be paid for her obit. Later, the revenues issuing from Lady Joanna's benefactions were set aside for the maintenance of the divine office in the Lady chapel ' because in other churches in England the Mother of God has better and more serious service ; but in the church of Hereford the Lady's sustenance for her priest was so small, that out of their respect they add this, by their deeds, dated in the chapter at Hereford, April 10, 1333.'

The chapel was to be served by eight priests and two deacons.

Beneath the arch of the recess containing the effigy is a painting representing a kneeling lady offering a church to the Virgin Mary crowned, and behind the donor are the priests and deacons serving the chapel.

The *Valor Ecclesiasticus* records fifty-seven chantry foundations in the diocese of Hereford.

## LICHFIELD CATHEDRAL

No traces remain to-day of any chantry chapels in the cathedral of Lichfield. During the Civil War the Roundhead troopers wrought grievous damage to the fabric, the furniture and fittings. Screens were torn down, tombs broken open, brasses ripped from their settings and glass wantonly smashed. Small wonder then that no chantry chapels have survived. Nevertheless the scanty records are of some interest.

Of the hundred and seven chantries in the diocese of Lichfield and Coventry in 1534 about twenty had been founded in the cathedral. In addition sixty-seven obits, valued at sums ranging from 6s. 8d. to 7s. 6d., were sung by the vicars-choral.

Bishop Walter de Langton (1296–1321) who commenced the building of the Lady chapel, founded two chantries, one at the altar of S. Nicholas and the other, known as the King's (Edward I's) chantry, in the Lady chapel. Langton's tomb, which originally stood to the south of the High Altar, has been moved farther west. The canopy has gone and the Purbeck marble effigy in episcopal vestments is terribly mutilated. The so-called Byrmyngham chantry in S. Andrew's chapel was founded by Thomas Stretton, Dean (1390–1426). John Byrmyngham was chancellor of the diocese in 1349. As his chantry was founded thirty or more years after his death, he must have been a man worthy of remembrance. It was served by one priest, who was granted a stipend of 10s. 4d. by licence of Richard II.

Other deans founded chantries at Lichfield. Dean Thomas Heywood (1457–92) had two, one at the altar of S. Katherine and the other in S. Blaise's chapel.

The mass priest who served the chantry of Dean Yotton (1492–1512) was required to be a graduate in Divinity or else in Civil Law ; and as a civilian he was to help poor men solely with their causes in the Consistory Court.

As the chantry priests attached to the cathedral were 'destitute of mansions,' Bishop John Cattarick (1415–19) founded a common dwelling called 'the Chantry House' for their accommodation. The stipends of the sixteen priests, according to their several rates, amounted to £10. 1s. 8d., and an allowance of £6. 3s. 4d. was made for the board and wages of two cooks and of 'the laundrese.'

An entry in another record reads as follows : 'In 1424, I [John] de Odenbie, archdeacon of Derby and executor of the will of Bishop John Burghill (d. 1414) built a house for chantry priests in the close [of Lichfield].' This would hardly be another dwelling, but probably implies the completion of Cattarick's chantry house.

## LINCOLN CATHEDRAL

The Act of 1547 put an end to thirty-six chantry foundations in Lincoln Cathedral. Three noteworthy chapels remain.

In the returns of 1 Edward VI a chantry called King Edward's is named. It was founded by Edward II for the recitation of perpetual masses at the altar of the Blessed Virgin for the soul of Queen Eleanor of Castile, who died at Hardeby, Notts., in 1290. Part of her remains were buried in Lincoln Cathedral and a monument was erected in the choir. On it was placed a bronze effigy of Eleanor, cast by William Torel, the London goldsmith who made the effigy on her tomb in Westminster

Abbey. A modern reproduction, cast in 1891, is to be seen near the east window of the Angel choir. Winkles states that a chantry originally founded at Hardeby for Eleanor was transferred to Lincoln Cathedral in 1310, and the masses were recited at an altar beneath the east window.

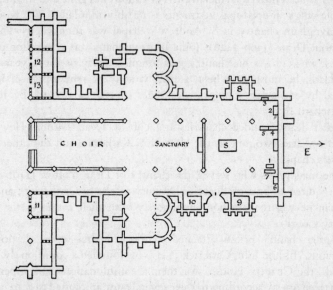

FIG. XIII    LINCOLN CATHEDRAL.    *1. Eleanor Monument. 2. Burghersh Chapel. 3. Tomb of Bartholomew, Lord Burghersh. 4. Tomb of Robert, Lord Burghersh. 5. Tomb of Bishop Henry Burghersh. 6. Altar of S. Nicholas. 7. Tomb of Nicholas Cantelupe. 8. Fleming Chapel. 9. Russell Chapel. 10. Longland Chapel. 11. 'Works'' Chapel. 12. Stretton and Wolfe Chapel. 13. Buckingham Chapel.*

In the easternmost bay of the north aisle of the Angel choir, which was nearing completion early in the fourteenth century, an altar dedicated to S. Katherine was erected and a chantry founded there by Bartholomew, Lord Burghersh, *c.* 1355, for the souls of his father, Robert (d. 1306), and Henry, Bishop of Lincoln, his brother. The family derived from Burwash in Sussex and the bay in the north aisle was made their mortuary chapel, where their tombs are still to be seen. The chantry was served by five priests, and out of the endowment of £57 a year six poor scholars were to be maintained at a grammar school in Lincoln until they attained the age of sixteen, and certain sums were to be disbursed at the obits of the founder and of Edward III. The sums included 20s. to be paid the custodian of S. Peter's altar, 4s. 6d. to the priests and vicars-choral, 15d. to twelve poor scholars, 6d. to the chapter clerk, 12d. to the bell-ringers, 12d. to the almoner and 41s. 8d. to fifty poor persons. The five priests occupied a dwelling in James Street known as the Burghersh chantry-house, part of which remains to-day.

The canopied tomb of Bartholomew Burghersh, the founder, a warrior of renown who had fought with the Black Prince at Crécy and died in 1355, is built into the wall of the aisle beneath the first window from the east. On the tomb-slab is the effigy of Bartholomew in plate armour. At his head two angels support shields, while two at the foot bear his soul. The canopy has three ogee arches set beneath crocketed gables. Shields in the spandrels of the canopy display the arms of Edward III and his sons. The tombs of Robert, the father, and of Bishop Henry stand in the Angel choir a little to the south of the Burghersh chapel, but they have lost their canopies. Statesman as well as ecclesiastic, Bishop Henry (d. 1340) was Chancellor of England in Edward III's reign. On the north face of his tomb are five panels, each containing two weepers, amongst which are figures of Edward III and his four sons. On the slab lies the recumbent effigy of the bishop, his mitre supported on each side by an angel.

At the altar of S. Nicholas, which stood at the east end of the south aisle of the Angel choir, a chantry was founded in 1355 by Nicholas, the third Baron Cantelupe. It was served by three priests, for whom the founder's widow built a chantry house still standing in the cathedral close next to the sub-deanery. The baron was a famous warrior in the campaigns of Edward II and Edward III, and on his death he was buried in the cathedral. His tomb is close by the monument of Queen Eleanor ; a mutilated effigy, without head or legs, rests on the slab.

Of greater interest are the three chantry chapels which project from the choir on the north and south. They were all founded by bishops of the diocese and are built between the buttresses of the aisle walls. The most desirable site for a chapel was one near the shrine of S. Hugh, which from the end of the thirteenth century had stood in the retrochoir to the east of the High Altar. Thus it was that the chapels of three bishops were built in proximity to the shrine but in positions that did not in any way interfere with the circulation of the countless pilgrims who flocked hither.

The earliest is the chapel of Bishop Richard Fleming (1420–31) on the north side of the choir. It was founded by Dean Fleming *c.* 1425 on behalf of his uncle the bishop and himself. In his early days the Bishop had been in sympathy with the Lollards, but, forsaking their heresies, he founded Lincoln College, Oxford, ' to defend the mysteries of the sacred page against these ignorant laics who profane with swinish snouts its most holy pearls.'*

The Fleming chapel is a low structure built between the buttresses of the second bay from the east. Its erection entailed the destruction of part of the aisle wall and its exquisite Geometrical arcading. The front, facing the choir, has three pendant arches, below which is the Bishop's tomb and a small portal at the west. Above the doorway and the arches are tabernacled canopies. On the tomb is the effigy of the Bishop holding a pastoral staff, and at his feet is a dragon. Angels support his mitre. Through three open arches below is visible the emaciated figure of the Bishop, a grim *memento mori* (Pl. 22). The wooden roof of the chapel is enriched with carvings of the vine and of oak foliage. Externally the Perpendicular windows are divided by niched buttresses and the parapet is panelled. The Fleming chapel, which was dedicated to the Holy Trinity, served as a model for the chapels on the opposite side of the choir, one on each side of the Last Judgment portal.

Between the buttresses of the second bay on the south side is the chapel of Bishop John Russell, who held the See from 1480 to 1495. Russell was translated to Lincoln from Rochester and gained some reputation as a scholar. He was Chancellor of England in the reign of Richard III. His chantry chapel was dedicated to S. Blaise, and the endowment provided for a priest to serve the altar and for a custodian, the latter to receive £3. 6s. 8d. a year. Its ornaments included a pax, a chalice, basins of silver and seven bells. The chapel is a small rectangular building similar to Fleming's and has an oaken roof. Formerly it had two portals, the western one retaining its oak door, surmounted by the Bishop's arms. The eastern portal is now blocked up. Within is a double piscina and close by, two brackets for figures. The railed-in tomb of the Bishop has no effigy, but a brass heraldic shield and a punning inscription, ' *Le Ruscellin je suis.*'

The chapel to the west of the Judgment porch was that of Bishop John Longland (1521–47). Longland was the confessor to Henry VIII, whom he entertained at Lincoln in 1541. The chapel, dedicated to S. Catherine, is more ornate than Russell's. The front, facing the choir, consists of a deep stone screen reaching to the sill-level of the aisle windows and furnishes a rich example of late Gothic. Centrally placed in the screen is the tomb, which bears heraldic shields in the panels of the front, but is without an effigy. The door is at the west and there is a panelled recess of the same size at the east. The stonework is overlaid with

*'. . . As the heresies that men do leave
Are hated most of those they did deceive.'
MIDSUMMER NIGHT'S DREAM

ogee arches rich with crockets and finials and much traceried panelling. In the frieze is the inscription : ' *Longa terra mensuram ejus Dominus dedit.*' The walls of the interior are adorned with a range of canopied niches. In common with the other chapels, the Longland chapel is covered with a panelled roof of oak.

It is doubtful whether this chantry chapel was ever utilized as such. The Bishop's intention was that he should be buried here ; but after his death his body was taken to the chapel of Eton College and his heart deposited at Lincoln.

Of so low an elevation are these two southern chapels that they neither bury nor dwarf the Last Judgment portal. Though two centuries later than the Angel choir, their scale and symmetry produce no inharmonious effect (Pl. 25).

A less familiar chantry chapel in the cathedral is that spoken of as the ' Works' ' chapel. It occupies the most northerly bay of the eastern aisle in the south transept and was founded *c.* 1342. The endowment provided for the singing of a mass every day on behalf of all the benefactors of the cathedral, both living and dead.

The chapel is enclosed from the transept by a stone screen and round the entrance arch is an inscription in Gothic lettering : ' *Oremus p. bene-factorib. istius ecclesie.*' On either side is the kneeling figure of a chantry priest, and above is a seated figure of a bishop in a canopy, together with the royal arms of England.

The priests serving this chantry dwelt together in a house, now destroyed, which stood west of the deanery.

For a century or more prior to the founding of the Works' chantry, an unusual expedient was resorted to in order that benefactors of the great church might derive the spiritual benefits of intercessory prayers. In the Consuetudinary of Lincoln Cathedral it is recorded that ' it is an ancient usage of the church of Lincoln to say one mass and the whole psalter daily on behalf of the living and deceased benefactors of the church.' This office, somewhat akin to a chantry, was to be recited by the dean and canons, each of whom was required to say some portion of the psalter as he sat in his stall in the choir. Hanging from the backs of the choir stalls are still to be seen a number of wooden tablets on which are inscribed in Latin the titles of the psalms to be recited by the respective occupants at this daily mass ; and to-day every newly-installed prebend is reminded of his obligation.*

---

* From 1265 an observance similar to this obtained at Salisbury Cathedral. Every Sunday morning a mass for ' all the souls that have done any good to this church' was sung at the altar of the Holy Cross, which stood against the western side of the rood screen. The altar came to be known as the Works' altar or the altar of the fabric.

There were chantries in other of the transept chapels. In the middle bay of the north transept a chantry called 'Stratton and Wolfe' was endowed by Richard de Stratton and William Wolfe for one priest. Stratton was prebendary of Thorngate in 1312.

In the southernmost chapel of the same transept John Buckingham, Bishop of Lincoln (1363–97), founded a chantry for two priests to celebrate at the altar of S. Hugo and S. Katherine for his soul, and the endowment also maintained two poor scholars from the age of seven to sixteen. One of the scholars received 33s. 4d. half-yearly for his commons and living. Bishop Buckingham was translated to Lichfield in 1397, but retired to Christ Church, Canterbury, the same year.

At the altar of S. George in the cathedral, the site of which is not known, was founded the chantry of Dr. John Mackworth, Dean of Lincoln (d. 1452). The dean's choleric disposition brought him into conflict with the canons. He used to keep the choir waiting if he was late ; he would not keep his proper place in the processions, and in chapter he enforced his wishes upon the canons by bringing a number of armed men with him. His executors obtained royal licence to alienate Mackworth's Inn, Holborn (later known as Barnard's Inn), to the dean and chapter as an endowment for his chantry.

## OLD S. PAUL'S CATHEDRAL

In his *Survey of London*, 1598, John Stow gives a lengthy list of the tombs and monuments in Old S. Paul's, and he makes mention of not a few chantry chapels that stood in that great church. They had been founded by kings—Henry IV and Edward IV—by bishops, deans and canons, by members of noble families, by judges and by wealthy citizens of the metropolis ; and they varied in character and endowment according to the wealth and munificence of the founders.

At the Suppression there were thirty-five and they were served by fifty-four priests. One of the most richly endowed was that founded by Henry IV for the souls of his parents, John of Gaunt, 'time-honoured Lancaster' and Blanche of Lancaster. Commemoration masses were to be sung on February 4 for Gaunt and on September 12 for Blanche. The ordinance assigned stipends to the dean, the canons and others, down to the vergers and bell-ringers, and payments were to be made to the mayor and sheriffs of London for their attendance. Amongst other provisions was one for eighty wax tapers to burn on the anniversaries and on special festivals for ever.

By his will John of Gaunt (d. 1399) made bequests for soul-masses for himself and Blanche. His executors built a chapel at his tomb in the cathedral and in 1403 a college of chantry priests was founded to serve the chapel. Bishop Braybrook granted a piece of land formerly belonging to his palace for the erection of a chantry-house which became known as ' Lancaster College.' No description of Gaunt's chapel is extant, but an engraving by Wenceslas Hollar gives a fair idea of the tomb which stood in the north arcade of the choir of S. Paul's. On the tomb lay alabaster effigies of the Duke and his lady, surmounted by a canopy of Perpendicular tabernacling like that of Beaufort's chapel at Winchester.

Of the chantry chapels founded by bishops of London in the cathedral, the most splendid was Bishop Thomas Kempe's. He held the See for nearly forty years and died in 1489. A licence was granted him by Edward IV to found a chantry for the good estate of the King, his consort Elizabeth, and Kempe, and for the souls of the King's progenitors and the founder's parents. The endowment consisted of 170 acres of land, forests and meadow, in the county of Essex. Bishop Kempe's chapel, dedicated to the Holy Trinity, stood ' in the body of S. Paul's church on the north side,' probably between two of the massive piers of the Norman nave. In Allen's *History and Antiquities of London*, 1837, is given a description of Kempe's chapel, which is worth quoting :

> The screen consisted of three open arches decorated with trefoils, the buttresses with pinnacles and foliage. Above was a frieze with angels, shields of arms, badges, etc., furnished with a cornice formed of lozenges pierced into quatrefoils. The basement had delicate arched panels. At the east end of the screen was a circular arched niche with a pointed moulding over it, on each side of which were small statues. The effigy of the Bishop arrayed in pontificalibus lay on an altar tomb within.

The plan of Old S. Paul's, 1645, shows the chapel set between the second and third piers of the north nave arcade from the crossing.

A little later was the chantry chapel of the fanatical Bishop, Robert Fitz-James (d. 1521). This stood at the north-west pier of the crossing. It was built in two stories, in the lower of which was the Bishop's tomb of grey marble, probably Purbeck. The upper story was constructed of timber ' with stairs mounting thereunto.' In June 1561 the wooden spire of the central tower of the cathedral was fired by lightning and the Bishop's chapel was wrecked by the mass of burning timbers that crashed into the crossing.

Another notable chantry in the old cathedral was that of Dean Thomas Moore, who obtained a licence from Henry V c. 1418 to erect a chapel dedicated to S. Anne and S. Thomas of Canterbury. In the chapel, which was not completed until after the Dean's death, a daily mass was sung for the good estate of Henry V and the founder and for their souls and the souls of Edward III, Richard II, Henry IV and others. Above the altar in the chapel was displayed a tablet on which were inscribed the names of all those for whom prayers were to be offered. The site of Moore's chapel is unknown ; probably it was one of the two built between the buttresses on the south side of the choir which the old plans of the cathedral seem to indicate.

Near the north door of S. Paul's was ' a fair chapel ' dedicated to S. John Baptist, which had been built in 1348 by Sir John Pulteney (or Poultney), a wealthy draper and four times mayor. It was known as Pulteney's chapel and was served by three chantry priests, who said masses therein for his mother and other kindred and friends, for John Stratford, Archbishop of Canterbury, and for the souls of the Archbishop's parents and of other benefactors. Pulteney had also endowed and founded chantries in other churches in the city ; in 1330 he bestowed a messuage and four shops on the prior and convent of S. Bartholomew, Smithfield, to maintain two chantries—one in the priory church and another in the church of S. Thomas the Apostle in Knightrider Street. A few years later he established a college of chantry priests in the church of S. Lawrence, Candlewick Street.

Of no less interest was the ' chapel at the north door of Paules, founded by Walter Sherington, by licence of Henry VI, for two, three or four chaplains, endowed with £40 by the year. This chapel was pulled down in the reign of Edward VI.' The founder was the chancellor of the Duchy of Lancaster, temp. Henry VI, and was a prebendary of Lincoln and a canon of S. Paul's. Withal he was a very rich man ; at his death in 1446 his money chest at the cathedral was found to contain over £3,000 in gold. However, he used his wealth to good purpose during his lifetime. He built a library above the east walk of the cloister enclosing Pardon churchyard, which stood within the precincts of the cathedral to the north-west, and he also commenced to build the chapel near the north door mentioned by Stow. In this chapel Sherington founded a perpetual chantry shortly before his death. These buildings were completed by 1448.

There were a number of co-operative chantries in the old cathedral, of which the following are typical. In 1352 a gild of S. Katherine was formed to maintain one wax light burning in S. Katherine's chapel. Ten years later the members of the gild undertook to support a chaplain, who was to say masses for all the faithful departed and in 1389 the gild had two wardens who were London citizens.

In 1379 the Fraternity of All Souls was established to maintain the chapel of the Virgin above the charnel house in S. Paul's churchyard. A century earlier a chantry served by one priest had been founded in the chapel by Roger Beyvin, but during the first quarter of the fourteenth century the revenues had so declined that the masses had ceased. In

36. THE TRINITY CHAPEL, TEWKESBURY ABBEY

37. THE FITZHAMON CHAPEL, TEWKESBURY ABBEY

38. THE WARWICK CHAPEL, TEWKESBURY ABBEY

39. THE CHAPEL OF THOMAS DE LA WARR, BOXGROVE PRIORY

1430 the chapel was re-endowed by Jenkyn Carpenter, one of Richard Whittington's executors, and here he founded a chantry for one priest for the souls of Beyvin and Whittington.

In 1453 the Armourers' Company of London formed a gild of S. George and founded a chantry in the chapel dedicated to that saint in the cathedral. This was a chantry ' by purchase ' for the gild bought the advowson of an existing chantry, one that had been established in 1321 by Sir Nicholas Wokyngdon. On converting the foundation to their use the Armourers continued to celebrate masses for the soul of the original founder.

In more ways than one it was undesirable that the great body of priests serving the many chantries in the cathedral should dwell in lodgings here, there and everywhere in the metropolis. It is clear that bishops and chapters realized this, for in the early years of the fourteenth century, lodgings for the chantry priests of S. Paul's were built in the churchyard on a plot of land assigned for the purpose. These buildings were known as the 'Presteshouses' or S. Peter's college, and in 1391 Bishop Braybrook compelled all chantry priests who were not members of any other college of the cathedral to dwell therein. By 1430 the number in residence in Presteshouses had reached thirty-six.

There was another college, founded by Roger Holmes, Canon of S. Paul's, and known as Holmes College. It was built as a common house for the chantry priests who served the chapel of the Holy Ghost near the north door. The dean and chapter had provided the site for the building in 1386 and by his will Canon Holmes increased the number of priests to seven.

Before the end of the fourteenth century there were more than seventy perpetual chantries in Old S. Paul's as well as one hundred and eleven obits and innumerable endowments for occasional masses—figures which are significant of the increasing belief amongst all classes of London citizens in the efficacy of soul-masses.

To serve all these obits and chantries a great crowd of priests was attached to the cathedral. The office was much envied by the country clergy, so much so that in 1392 the dean and chapter decreed that no beneficed priest should serve a chantry in the cathedral save their own minor canons. Moreover, they bore a reputation that brought little credit to the church ; for, their morning masses ended, they would resort to taverns and other undesirable places in the metropolis.

Stow tells us of a London chantry priest, though not of S. Paul's, whose conduct left much to be desired :

John Atwood, draper, dwelling in the parish of S. Michael upon Cornhill directly against the church, having a proper woman to his wife, such an one as

9

seemed to be the holiest among a thousand, had also a lusty chantry priest of the said parish church, repairing to his house ; with the which priest, the said Atwood would sometimes after supper play a game at tables for a pint of ale. It chanced on a time, having haste of work, and his game proving long, he left his wife to play it out and went down to his shop ; but returning to fetch a pressing iron, he found such play to his misliking, that he forced the priest to jump out at a window over the penthouse into the street, and so to run to his lodging in the churchyard. Atwood and his wife were soon reconciled, so that he would not suffer her to be called in question; but the priest being apprehended and committed, I saw his punishment to be thus : he was on three market days conveyed through the high street and markets of the city, with a paper on his head, wherein was written his trespass . . . he lost his chantry of 20 nobles the year, and was banished the city for ever.

The last chantry founded in Old S. Paul's was that of Robert Brokett in 1532.

At the time of the Suppression Act, 1547, the annual income of all the chantries in the church amounted to £646. 6s. 0d., of which about £245 went as stipends for the priests. The number of obits had declined very greatly, for in 1541 there were only fifty-four being regularly observed.

## SALISBURY CATHEDRAL

There were nine chantry foundations in Salisbury Cathedral at the time of the Suppression. Due to the wanton destruction wrought by the notorious James Wyatt, who had a genius for ' tidying up ' our cathedral churches, only two chantry chapels are left standing at Salisbury, both in the choir. Two others which once flanked the Lady chapel on its north and south sides were swept away by Wyatt in 1789.

Between the piers of the south choir arcade, in the second bay from the east, stands the lofty and imposing Hungerford chapel. It was founded in 1429 by Walter, Lord Hungerford, who fought in the French wars. He was with Henry V at Agincourt, and in 1417 was made Admiral of the Fleet. The chapel was originally built on the north side of the nave, in the second bay from the crossing, where are the tombs of himself and his wife, Catherine Peverell. It was moved to its present position in 1778, where it was used as the family pew. The base consists of a low stone wall in the panels of which are the arms of the baron and his two wives. On the base is a massive superstructure of wrought iron which forms a grilled enclosure. The severity of the design of the ironwork is somewhat relieved by the cresting.*

*Walter, Lord Hungerford, also built a chantry chapel in the north transept of Heytesbury church, Wilts., the stone screen of which remains intact. The three sickles of the Hungerfords are carved above the entrance.

Occupying the corresponding bay on the north side of the sanctuary is the equally large chantry chapel of Bishop Edmund Audley, who in 1502 was translated from Hereford, where he had already built a chapel to the south of the Lady chapel. This at Salisbury, dating *c.* 1520, is of the stone-cage form and rises to a considerable height. It rather lacks unity in design, being divided into two dissimilar bays, each opened up with

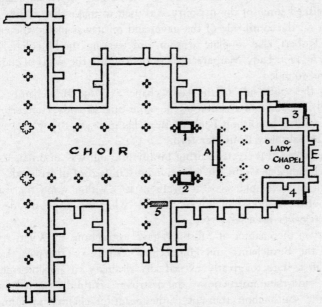

FIG. XIV SALISBURY. A. *High Altar. 1. Audley Chapel. 2. Hungerford Chapel. 3. Robert Hungerford Chapel. 4. Beauchamp Chapel. 5. Bridport Chantry Tomb.*

two stages of four-centred arches. At the angles are polygonal standards and the richly carved cornice displays the Bishop's heraldic arms and his initials (Pl. 26).

The chapel must have been one of great splendour when the niches were peopled with figures and the finely chiselled stonework was coloured. On the surface of the fan vault traces of colour still exist. Bishop Audley was buried in his chapel on his death in 1524.

Differing in character from the foregoing and of greater magnificence were the chantry chapels which, until a century and a half ago, flanked the Lady chapel at the east end of the cathedral. On the north was that founded in 1464 by Margaret, widow of Robert, Lord Hungerford, a warrior who had fought in the French campaigns under Bedford and

Talbot. At the altar masses were sung for the souls of Margaret and her husband. When the chapel was built the north wall of the Lady chapel was opened with arches, and beneath one of them was placed the tomb of Lord Robert (d. 1459) with his effigy. Large Perpendicular windows lighted the chapel. It had a lierne vault, and on the walls were paintings of the Annunciation and S. Christopher. The external stonework was enriched with the heraldic devices of the family. When the chapel was demolished some of the masonry was used to make the ' tomb,' which stands on the south side of the nave, and on it was placed the effigy of Lord Robert, clad in plate armour and wearing the SS collar. On her death in 1477 Lady Margaret was buried within the walls of the chapel she had founded.

On the south side of the Lady chapel was the Beauchamp chantry chapel, in course of erection at the same time as Lady Hungerford's. It was founded by Bishop Richard Beauchamp (1450–81) who was translated to Salisbury from Hereford.

The chapel was erected during his lifetime and was an ornate example of Perpendicular Gothic. It was covered with a roof of Irish oak, ' never known to have spiders or cobwebs in it.' Within stood the canopied tomb of the Bishop, which was ' mislaid ' when the chapel was destroyed and has never been recovered.

In 1789 the chapter of Salisbury gave instructions to Wyatt to ' take down the Beauchamp and Hungerford chapels, on the plea that they were in a state to greatly exceed any ordinary or possible means of repair,' and these instructions ' the destroyer ' faithfully carried out.

In the south choir transept is the beautiful chantry monument of Bishop Giles de Bridport (1257–62), one of the earliest of its kind and a beautiful specimen of Geometrical Gothic. The tomb stands within a gabled structure whose sides are opened with two arches supported by clustered shafts. Each arch is subdivided into two lesser arches with a quatrefoiled circle above. In the spandrels are sculptured reliefs of incidents in the Bishop's life. The whole design is that of a thirteenth-century triforium. On the tomb lies a recumbent effigy attended by censing angels at its head. To the east of the monument is a double aumbry which was used for the reservation of the Host.

## WELLS CATHEDRAL

Of the many chantries which had been founded in Wells Cathedral during a period of two and a half centuries sixteen were in being when the Suppression came. Most of them had been established by the bishops and ecclesiastics of the diocese. Amongst the earliest were those of Bishop

Robert Burnell (1275–92) and Bishop Walter Haselshaw (1302–8). To-wards the close of the fourteenth century, when the number of chantry priests attached to the cathedral had reached fourteen, Bishop Ralph Erghum (1388–1400) established a college at Wells.

Of the chapels there are two survivals, both of the stone-cage form. Situated on the north side of the nave in the second bay from the east is the chapel erected about 1420 by Bishop Nicholas Bubwith (1407–24). He founded an almshouse near S. Cuthbert's Church, Wells, built a chapel in Bath Abbey and bequeathed a sum of money for the erection of the north-west tower of the cathedral. His chantry at Wells was endowed with the manor of Bicknoller, and by his will he directed that three priests should celebrate a daily mass in his chapel in the nave (Pl. 23).

The Bubwith chapel is six-sided on plan, the angles of the screen-walls being chamfered to meet the piers more ' easily.' Unlike most chapels of this kind, it has an entrance from the nave and the aisle. Within are the remains of a reredos, the niches of which have been hacked away (Pl. 24). There is no vault, but a stone tester covers the eastern part of the chapel. At the west the shafts of the nave pier inside the chapel have been cut away and the arms of the See and those of the Bishop occur on the corbel.

More than half a century later is the Sugar chantry chapel on the opposite side of the nave in the second bay from the crossing. It was built for the chantry founded by the Treasurer of Wells Cathedral, Dr. Hugh Sugar, and dates about 1485–90. Similar in form to the Bubwith chapel, though more ornate, it is six-sided on plan and rises to the height of the pier capitals. The lower part consists of rectilinear panelling, with Per-pendicular windows above, crowned by a bold frieze. The frieze is charged with demi-angels whose wings are beautifully carved and who bear shields of the founder's arms, his initials, the arms of the See, the emblems of the Passion and a rebus, three sugar loaves beneath a doctor's cap. Much sculptured ornament is lavished on the stonework of the in-terior ; at the east end are five niches with tabernacled canopies and the stone tester above the altar is vaulted with fan tracery in which occur the arms and initials of Dr. Sugar. Like the Bubwith chapel it has a door on both sides (Pl. 18).

Until a century ago there remained intact on the south side of the choir the chantry chapel of Bishop Thomas Beckington (1443–65). Surely the enthusiasts of the Gothic revival might have raised a voice to save it when the choir of Wells was ' restored ' in 1850. ' It is at Wells,' wrote Sir Nicholas Harris in his *Life of Beckington*, 1828, ' that the lover of the arts and the admirer of the zeal and disinterestedness of the prelates of the

Middle Ages will be most impressed with respect for Bishop Beckington.' But this ' respect' failed to save the Bishop's chapel from ruthless dismemberment. Beckington was at one time tutor to Henry VI and later became his private secretary. In 1443 he was made Keeper of the Privy Seal, an office he resigned when he became Bishop of Bath and Wells. His munificence and the energy he displayed in building projects at Wells have left more than a memory, for he was responsible for the gatehouses in the close, the west walk of the cloisters, the houses of the vicars-choral and the famous Chain Gate. Beckington's chapel stood beneath an arch on the south side of the choir and was enclosed with an iron grate. Above the altar, which was backed with a reredos of much beauty, was an elaborate tester of stone with a fan vault and pendants. The cornice is enriched with vine ornament and two of the carved cusps represent angels holding shields (Pl. 27).

The chapel was completed before the Bishop's death and was consecrated by Beckington himself in 1452, on which occasion he recited a mass for his soul and for the souls of his family and all the faithful departed in the presence of a great gathering. When the choir of Wells Cathedral was undergoing restoration in 1850 the chapel was taken down and the reredos and altar were installed in the chapel of S. Calixtus in the south transept, and part of the iron grate was re-used as a parclose screen there. Fortunately the Bishop's tomb was spared to mark the site of his chapel in the choir. It is made of alabaster and has two effigies ; on the slab a figure of the bishop in pontificalibus, and within the arcade beneath, a cadaver or emaciated figure, not uncommon in tombs of ecclesiastics.*

## YORK CATHEDRAL

York Cathedral, the metropolitan church of the northern province, is almost devoid of chantry chapels, though the number of chantry foundations there is known to have been considerable. In the returns of Edward VI's reign thirty-six are recorded, but the names of the founders are not given ; the altars alone are named at which the masses were celebrated.

Probably the earliest chantry in York Cathedral was one founded by Archbishop Walter de Gray (1216–55). Gray was a capable administrator for, on his translation to York from the See of Worcester, he found the province ' a barren wilderness ' and after forty years he left it ' a fruitful

*Beckington's chapel is now restored more or less to its original condition. The stone tester covers the altar, and the iron grille, 7 ft. in height, completely encloses the chapel.

garden.' He it was who undertook the rebuilding of the south transept of the cathedral, a glorious piece of Early English Gothic, and he lived to witness its completion in 1241. On 22 March of that year he founded a chantry, dedicated to S. Michael and All Angels in a chapel on the east side of the new transept. It was endowed with the church of Millom and was served by two priests and a clerk, who sang a mass there every day for the souls of the Archbishop's predecessors and the canons of York. In front of the altar in the chapel stands his tomb, constructed of Purbeck marble and Early English in style. In general form it resembles a shrine of the period. The lower part consists of open arcades of trefoiled arches on either side with slender shafts and stiff-leaf capitals. The canopy is much like the feretrum of a shrine and has crocketed gables above the arcading. The effigy of the Archbishop beneath the canopy is in episcopal vestments ; his right hand is raised in the act of blessing and in his other hand is a crozier thrust into the mouth of a dragon at his feet. On either side of the Archbishop's head is a censing angel.

Projecting from the south side of the choir and ranging with the fifth and sixth bays from the east is the chantry chapel of Archbishop William la Zouche (1342–52). He had been Dean of York, and when Edward III embarked on his French expeditions Zouche was made Warden of the North and triumphed over the Scots at Neville's Cross in 1346. In 1350 he founded a perpetual chantry of two priests in the cathedral at the cost of 300 marks, a huge sum, part of which was spent on the erection of his chapel to the south of the choir. The Archbishop died before its completion and was buried in the nave. The reconstruction of the choir of York in the fifteenth century necessitated the rebuilding of the Zouche chapel.

More famous in the Middle Ages was the Scrope chapel at the extreme east of the north choir aisle. After the execution of Archbishop Richard Scrope (1398–1405) for the part he had taken in the northern rising against Henry IV,* his body was buried beneath the pavement of the north aisle near the altar of S. Stephen. His grave attracted pilgrims, and miracles were said to be wrought there. In time Scrope came to be regarded as a martyr and a saint. A shrine was erected on the site and he was popularly spoken of as Saint Richard Scrope. The aisle where he was buried was later known as ' the Scrope chapel,' and at the altar of S. Stephen the Lords Scrope of Masham founded a chantry for the souls of the family, in particular for the Archbishop. Shrine and altar have gone and all that is left is a plain stone slab beneath the eastern arch on the north side of the choir.

* He was beheaded in a field near Bishopsthorpe, June 8, 1405 for high treason, the first instance of a prelate put to death by any form of law, in the country.

## S. DAVID'S CATHEDRAL

The chantry chapels in the remote and secluded cathedral of S. David's, Pembroke, are unique both in position and character.

Of all the bishops who have held the See, none has left his mark so surely on the fabric of the cathedral as has Bishop Henry de Gower, (1328–47). Amongst his several undertakings there the elaborate rood screen at the east end of the nave is remarkable in more ways than one. The design of the screen front is unsymmetrical ; against the wall which forms the northern half, with its small arcade of three shallow arches, was set up an altar dedicated to the Holy Cross, whereas the southern compartment was occupied mainly by the chantry chapel of Bishop Gower.

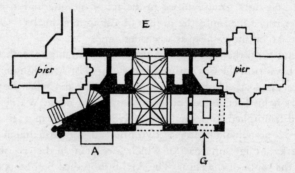

FIG. XV S. DAVID'S CATHEDRAL. A. *Altar of Holy Cross. G. Gower's Chapel and Tomb.*

The Gower chapel is opened up on its western and southern sides by a wide cinquefoiled arch with rich cuspings and within stands the tomb of the Bishop. The effigy of Gower lies on the tomb, clad in canonicals and wearing the mitre. He holds a staff in his left hand and the other hand, now broken off, was raised in the act of blessing. At his feet is a lion and on the southern face of the tomb are eight figures of the Apostles in relief. The bronze grille which once enclosed the tomb was removed during the Civil War.

Gower's screen is remarkable for its skeleton vault, similar to one in the small sacristy built by Abbot Knowle at Bristol. The Bishop and the Abbot were close friends and as the Bristol masonry bears the same banker marks as does the screen at S. David's, it seems certain that the same masons worked at both places.

Beyond the presbytery is the late Perpendicular chapel of Bishop Edward Vaughan (1509–22).

Its unusual site is accounted for by the abnormal arrangement of the retrochoir. The aisles and the Lady chapel here had been planned and were begun shortly before the earthquake of 1248, but were never completed. About the end of the century, however, the erection of the Lady chapel, some distance east of the presbytery, was resumed. Bishop Gower furthered the work by carrying the aisles of the choir farther east and they were then connected by a cross-aisle running north-south, which also served as a vestibule to the Lady chapel. The enclosed area between the presbytery and the vestibule thus formed a small court open to the sky, ' *Vilissimus et sordidissimus locus in tota ecclesia*,' the most vile and sordid place in the whole church, a description which leads us to suppose it was

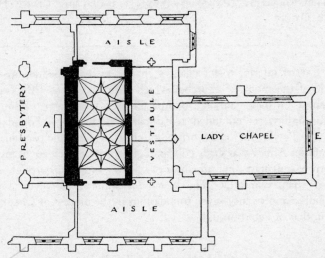

FIG. XVI THE VAUGHAN CHAPEL AT S. DAVID'S

used as a yard for rubbish. It remained so until the early years of the sixteenth century, when it was appropriated by Bishop Vaughan, who converted it into a chapel dedicated to the Holy Trinity and intended for the Bishop's chantry. The Vaughan chapel is a forgotten work of Perpendicular Gothic, and its construction was no mean undertaking.

The three lower lancet lights in the east wall of the presbytery were blocked up and to light the choir a large Perpendicular window, now destroyed, was inserted higher up, above the roof of Vaughan's chapel. A wide arch was cut in the north and south walls dividing the chapel from the aisles and a stone screen of rectilinear panelling inserted in each opening. Against the western wall of the cross-aisle was placed the altar of the Holy Trinity ; and to light the chapel from the east a three-light window was inserted in the wall on both sides of the altar. The chief feature of interest is the fan vault of two bays, a simpler version of the vault in the retrochoir at Peterborough Cathedral. The tomb of Bishop Vaughan (d. 1522) stands in front of the altar and once bore a brass. On the north side of the chapel is the tomb of Sir John Wogan, Chief Justiciary of Ireland in Edward I's reign. It was brought from a chapel which formerly occupied part of the north aisle of the choir.

**(9)** Chantry chapels in the monastic churches : Bristol, Westminster, S. Albans, Tynemouth, Gloucester, Tewkesbury, Boxgrove, Bath, Christ Church (Hants), Hexham, Oxford.

IN NO RESPECT inferior to the chantry chapels in the cathedrals are those in some of the monastic churches which escaped Henry VIII's orgy of destruction. Of these churches, Bristol, Chester, Gloucester, Oxford and Peterborough were refounded as cathedrals of the New Foundation ; others, *e.g.* Tewkesbury and Christ Church, Hants, became parochial and Westminster Abbey was made collegiate. Destitute as they are of mediaeval chapels and altars, the cathedrals of Chester and Peterborough afford little of chantry interest. The *Valor Ecclesiasticus*, however, records one hundred and twenty-seven foundations in the diocese of Chester and thirty in that of Peterborough.

## BRISTOL CATHEDRAL

Prior to the Suppression of the monasteries, Bristol Cathedral was the church of an abbey served by Augustinian canons. For four centuries it had enjoyed the generous patronage of the Berkeleys, Lords of Berkeley Castle. A worthy monument of this association is the chantry chapel on the south side of the choir of the cathedral.

The Berkeley chapel was founded in 1348 by Thomas, Lord Berkeley, the third of that name, for ' a perpetual chantry for his soul and the soul of Margaret, his wife.' It is a rectangular building of two bays which projects southwards from the choir.

The chapel was dedicated to the Virgin Mary and had two altars raised on steps and separated by a stone screen. Both have now been restored, two piscinas remain and there are aumbries in the south wall. The chapel presents us with a good example of Decorated Gothic ; the ribbed vault with its carved bosses, the foliage capitals and the ball-flower and rose ornament are typical of the period. In the western wall is a door which opens on to a stairway that formerly led to the sacristan's chamber above. The latter was destroyed when the roof of the chapel was lowered. In the wall dividing the chapel from the aisle of the choir is a wide arch beneath which is the tomb of Thomas, Lord Berkeley (d. 1321) and his wife, Lady Joan. Lord Thomas was ' much skilled at running at the ring and his elder years were exercised at jousts and tournaments.' On the front of the tomb are five shields of arms, above which is a frieze of horseshoe ornament. The arms of the Berkeleys are also sculptured on

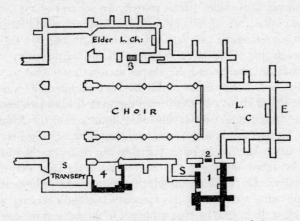

FIG. XVII BRISTOL CATHEDRAL. 1. *Berkeley Chapel.*
2. *Berkeley Tomb.* 3. *Tomb of Maurice.* 4. *Newton Chapel.*
S. *Sacristy.*

the soffit of the arch. The chapel is entered from a narrow vestibule at the west which was originally the monastic sacristy.

Lady Margaret, for whom the chantry was founded, was not laid to rest in the chapel but on the other side of the choir. In the eastern arch between the Elder Lady chapel and the north choir aisle stands an altar tomb bearing the inscriptions :

' This tomb was erected to the memory of Maurice, Lord Berkeley, 9th Baron of Berkeley Castle, who died the 8th day of June, 1368.'

' Also of the Lady Margaret, his mother, daughter of Roger Mortimer, Earl of March, and wife of Thomas, Lord Berkeley. She died the 5th of May, 1337.'

The only other chantry chapel in Bristol Cathedral is the Newton chapel, a square structure built to the east of the south transept. It dates 1332–50 and contains tombs of the Newton family of Barrs Court, Kingswood. Architecturally it is of the Transitional phase, Decorated to

Perpendicular, though alterations were made when the transept was re-built towards the end of the fifteenth century. Against the eastern wall of the chapel is a chantry tomb of grey marble with a flat canopy, dating from the early sixteenth century, and at the foot of the tomb is space for the priest. An inscription states that the tomb is that of Sir Richard Newton (d. 1448), but more probably is it a memorial to his grandson (d. 1500).*

More than a century after Thomas, Lord Berkeley, had founded his chantry at Bristol, James, 11th Earl (d. 1463), erected the handsome chantry chapel in Berkeley parish church. An account of the latter may not be out of place here. A small but admirable specimen of Perpendicular Gothic, it is rectangular on plan and stands in the angle of the chancel and the south aisle of the nave. The east wall of the aisle shuts it off completely from the church and the chapel narrows somewhat to the east, for its south wall is not parallel to the chancel wall. Internally it is divided by a stone screen about one-third from the west. It has a rich lierne vault which has carved bosses displaying the Annunciation, the Assumption, the Holy Trinity, Christ in Majesty, emblems of the Evangelists and the Berkeley arms. There is an outer portal to the chapel in the south wall. Beneath an arched opening in the chancel wall is the large Perpendicular tomb of James, the 11th Earl, on which recline effigies of himself and his second son who was slain in the French wars whilst serving with the redoubtable Talbot, Earl of Shrewsbury. On the sides of the tomb are a number of quatrefoils each containing a heraldic shield. The four-centred arch above is surmounted by a row of empty niches. The only entrance to the Berkeley chapel from the church is a small doorway in the chancel wall to the west of the tomb.

## WESTMINSTER ABBEY

The great abbey church at Westminster was not rich in chantry chapels, but of those that remain, two are of outstanding importance, *viz.* the chapels of Henry V and Henry VII.

In the Middle Ages the abbey church was much more than the chapel of a Benedictine monastery. It was a royal foundation, a coronation church, and the shrine of S. Edward the Confessor behind the High Altar was a central object of pilgrimage. Moreover S. Edward's chapel was intended for a Royal mausoleum when Henry III embarked on the recon-

---

*In the north transept of Yatton church, Somerset, is an alabaster monument of Sir Richard and his wife and in the same church is the chantry chapel of Sir John Newton, their son, and his wife, Isabel of Cheddar. Their tomb, dating *c.* 1487, is against the north wall.

struction of the choir and transepts in 1245. In accordance with the King's wishes his tomb was placed in the Saint's chapel, to the north of the shrine. Throughout the course of the fourteenth century the bays of the apse encircling the Saint's chapel were filled one by one with the tombs of the Plantagenets. To the east of Henry III's tomb was erected that of Eleanor of Castile, and the bay to the west was taken by her husband,

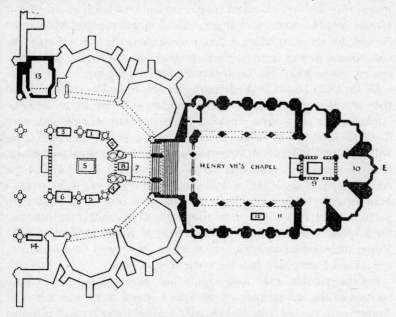

FIG. XVIII PLAN OF WESTMINSTER ABBEY. S. *Shrine. Royal Tombs: 1. Henry III. 2. Queen Eleanor. 3. Edward I. 4. Queen Philippa. 5. Edward III. 6. Richard II. 7. Henry V's Chapel. 8. Tomb of Henry V. 9. Grille enclosing tomb of Henry VII and Elizabeth of York. 10. Proposed Chapel of Henry VI. 11. Lady Margaret Chapel. 12. Tomb of Lady Margaret. 13. Islip Chapel. 14. Chapel of S. Benedict.*

Edward I (d. 1307). The encirclement was continued on the south side, the bays there being occupied by the tombs of Philippa of Hainault (d. 1369), Edward III (d. 1377), and of Richard II (d. 1399), and Anne of Bohemia. The ring of monuments was complete.

It is a matter of surprise that Richard II, to whom the abbey and convent were most dear, did not found a chantry chapel within its walls. Many were the gifts he made to obtain the prayers of the convent. A contemporary recorded that Richard gave ' to the church of West-monastery unto the value of 500 marks by year to pray for him ' and in

1391 he granted the appropriation of Aldenham church to the monks as an endowment for soul-masses for himself and his queen at the altar of S. John Baptist. Shortly before his deposition in 1399 Richard ' for his healthful estate while he lives and for the health of his soul after his death, and for the health of the soul of Anne his consort, late queen of England, [gave] to God and the church of S. Peter, Westminster, all lands, tenements, rents and services called Hoddeford and Cowhous, in the ville of Hendon and Hamstede, with appurtenances, in the county of Middlesex.' An obit for the unfortunate Richard was kept in the abbey church, the endowment issuing from property in Berkshire, Wiltshire, Middlesex and elsewhere which had been alienated for the purpose.

Of the kings buried at Westminster, the first to build a chantry chapel there was Henry V (d. 1422). Deeply attached as he was to the abbey he ' ordained the place of his sepulchre where he is now buried, and every day three masses to be sungen in a fair chapel over his sepulchre.' In his will the King left directions as to its form. It was to be a raised relic-chapel with two stairways. The altar was to be dedicated in honour of the Annunciation of the Virgin and All Saints, and eight wax lights were to burn about his tomb during High Mass and vespers every day. Masses to the number of 20,000 were to be said for the King's soul at the altar, and for a whole year thirty poor persons were to recite the Psalter of the Virgin there, concluding with the petition ' Mother of God remember thy servant Henry who puts his whole trust in thee.'

For the erection of the King's tomb and chapel drastic liberties were taken with the arrangement of the Saint's chapel at the east end. The Trinity altar and the relic-lockers were removed and a raised platform of Purbeck marble was built, projecting into the ambulatory. On the tomb was placed an effigy of Henry V covered with silver plates, the head being of solid silver. The oak core alone remains now. Platform and tomb were begun in 1422 and completed within ten years. The chantry chapel stands in a class by itself, for it is in the form of a bridge spanning the ambulatory, the western half resting on the vault above the platform. The parapet walls of the bridge are carried by four-centred arches on each side and are faced with tiers of canopied niches containing figures. In a large central niche in the south wall is a sculptured group representing a coronation, in which two mitred figures are seen placing the crown on the sovereign's head. A similar group in the north wall depicts the act of homage at the coronation. Heraldic devices, including the chained swan and the antelope of the de Bohuns and the flaming beacon of Henry V occur in the frieze above the arches, and these are repeated in the lierne vault beneath the bridge. The western parapet-wall, also enriched with a range of niches with figures, is carried by a wide arch flanked on either side by an octagonal stair-turret, built against the eastern piers of the apse (Pl. 29).

Their construction caused some damage to the tombs of Eleanor of Castile and Queen Philippa. On the faces of the turrets are tabernacled figures, including S. John Baptist on the northern and Edward the Confessor on the southern. To protect the tomb the archway was filled in with iron gates which were made by Roger Johnston, a London smith, in 1431. Within the chapel were stored the relics which had been displaced by the royal tomb and for this purpose there are recesses in the east wall and lockers on either side of the altar. Above the altar is a tabernacled reredos which still retains five of its original figures. Amongst them are the patron saints of England and France, S. George and S. Denis, and two kings, probably S. Edmund and Edward the Confessor. On a wooden beam above the chapel are Henry V's shield, helmet and saddle, placed there after use in the funeral ceremonies. The chapel was not completed until twenty years or more after Henry's death. Professor Lethaby was of opinion that the unusual form of the chapel was ' suggested by the relic-stage and its two staircases in Ste Chapelle, Paris, which the king would have known so well ' (Pl. 30).

Splendid as was the chantry chapel of Henry V, the admired of all wandering pilgrims who wended their way to Westminster, it was to be eclipsed in size and magnificence by Henry VII's chapel, architecturally the supreme achievement of Perpendicular Gothic and described by Leland as the *Orbis Miraculum* (Pl. 31.)

Dedicated to Our Lady, Henry's chapel replaced the thirteenth-century Lady chapel which stood at the eastern extremity of the abbey church.

Originally it was the King's intention to found a memorial chapel for his saintly uncle, Henry VI, which would also serve as a mausoleum of the Tudor dynasty. ' Forasmuch as we by the grace of God propose shortly to translate unto the same, the body of our uncle of blessed memory, King Henry VI . . . and we will that our tomb be [placed] in the midst of the same chapel before the High Altar.'

It was hoped that the Pope would canonize Henry VI ; the monks of Westminster would have welcomed another shrine in the abbey church. They advanced the sum of £500 for the papal licence to translate the body of Henry VI from Windsor to Westminster, but the sum demanded by Julius II for the canonization was too great, and the body remained at Windsor and was buried in S. George's chapel. Thus it was that the new Lady chapel at Westminster became the chantry chapel of the first of the Tudors. For its endowment the king obtained the Pope's permission to dissolve a number of small religious houses and his gifts included the college of S. Martin-le-Grand and certain manors.

The great care and thoroughness with which Henry VII prepared every detail of his chantry foundation is shown in his will and numerous indentures.

The clearing of the site was begun in 1501. The old Lady chapel of 1220 as well as an ancient hostelry, the White Rose, was demolished and the foundation stone of the new building laid by Abbot Islip. ' On the 24th daie of January 1502-3 a quarter of an houre afore three of the clocke at after noon of the same daie, the first stone of our Ladie chapell within the monasterie of Westminster was laid, on behalf of the King by the hands of John Islip, abbot of the same monasterie . . . and divers others.' The building was finished by 1519.

Henry VII's chapel is a complete church in itself and consists of a wide nave with narrow aisles, and a series of five radiating chapels at the east, each fourteen feet by eleven. It is entered from the ambulatory by a wide flight of steps and a spacious vestibule, and its total length is one hundred and fifteen feet. Architecturally the building is of supreme importance for here is Perpendicular Gothic at the very zenith of its accomplishment, the walls being little more than screens of glass between stone posts. The triforium is a continuous range of niches in which were housed an assemblage of one hundred and seven figures of saints and doctors of which ninety-five remain—the finest array of late Gothic statuary in the country. But most amazing of all is the fan vault with its pendants, the *tour de force* of vault construction.

Within and without, the masonry of the chapel is bespattered with Tudor devices, in allusion to Henry's right to the English crown. There are the roses of York and Lancaster, the portcullis of the Beauforts; the root of daisies for the King's mother, Lady Margaret; the dragon of Cadwallader, the British king from whom Henry claimed descent ; the greyhound of the Neville family, ancestors of his queen, Elizabeth of York; the falcon with the fetterlock, the lions of England and the fleurs-de-lis, all of which badges occur alike on the woodwork and bronze of the royal chapel.

Centrally placed at the east end of the nave is the magnificent bronze grille or closure in which stands the tomb of Henry VII and Elizabeth of York. The closure, a Perpendicular ᶠcage, was originally enriched with thirty-two small bronze figures of saints, of which only six are left (Pl. 28).

It was designed to be ' a brassen chapel within the new chapel ' and was to contain an altar dedicated to the Holy Saviour. It had been the King's desire that the closure and tomb should be erected ' in the midst ' of his chapel, *i.e.* much farther west than its present position, which was intended for the altar of Our Lady. Moreover, Henry planned a chantry

41. THE BAYNTON CHAPEL ROOF, BROMHAM CHURCH, WILTS

40. THE SALISBURY CHAPEL VAULT, CHRIST CHURCH PRIORY, HANTS

42. CHAPEL OF MARGARET COUNTESS OF SALISBURY, CHRIST CHURCH PRIORY, HANTS

43. CHAPEL AND WATCHING LOFT, OXFORD CATHEDRAL

45. WARWICK CHAPEL, TEWKESBURY ABBEY, SHOWING THE VAULTING

44. PRIOR DRAPER'S CHAPEL, CHRIST CHURCH PRIORY, HANTS

tomb for his uncle Henry VI, a two-storied structure of stone to be installed in the central radiating chapel at the east. In the Cottonian MSS.
in the British Museum is a drawing on vellum made *c.* 1500 entitled
' The monument intended for King Henry Sixte,' and showing a tomb in
the lower stage ; but the monument is on such a scale that had it been
erected it would have projected considerably from the chapel it occupied.

The remaining chapels at the east were no doubt intended for the
chantries of other members of the Tudor dynasty, and the south aisle of
Henry VII's chapel was to be the chapel of Lady Margaret, the king's
mother. It may be that the north aisle was for his son and successor.

Henry VII did not live to see the fulfilment of his wishes, for he died
on 21 April 1509 when little more than the bare shell of his chapel was
completed. The following extract from his will, dated 31 March 1509,
in modernized spelling, gives some indication of the provisions Henry
made for the completion of this ambitious undertaking after his death :

And if our said chapel and tomb, and our and our wife's images, grate and
closure be not fully accomplished, perfectly finished according to the premises
by us in our lifetime, we then will that not only the same chapel, tomb, images,
grate and closure and every one of them . . . be done best by our executors
after the manner and sum before rehearsed ; also that the said chapel be desked
and the windows be glazed with stories, images, arms, badges and cognizances
as is by us readily devised . . . and that the walls, doors, windows, aisles and
vaults and images of the same our chapel within and without be painted, and
garnished and adorned with our arms, badges and cognizances ; and for the
more sure performance and finishing of the premises and for the more ready
payment of the money necessary in that behalf, we have delivered in ready
money the sum of £5000 to the abbot, prior and convent of our said monastery
of Westminster, as by writing indented betwixt us and them . . . dated at
Richmond, the 13th day of April, the 24th year of our reign.

However, after the death of the King, his carefully prepared plans were
in part ignored by his son, Henry VIII, for the tomb of Henry VI was
never made and the ' brassen chapel ' was put up at the east end of the
nave, with the altar of Our Lady farther west. Fortunately the making
of the tomb of Henry VII and Elizabeth of York was not abandoned. In
1512 the Florentine sculptor Pietro Torrigiano entered into a contract
with Henry VIII to make it ' well, surely, cleanly, workmanly, curiously
and substantially ' for the sum of £1,500. The work was completed in
1518. Torrigiano cast the recumbent effigies of the king and queen in
bronze, ' the greatest portrait sculptures ever wrought in England '
(Lethaby).

This tomb and the similar one of Lady Margaret in the south aisle of
the chapel furnish us with the earliest-known examples of Renaissance
craftsmanship and sculpture in the country. They are wholly classic in

10

character, with pilasters, wreaths, putti and other features quite foreign to English Gothic art. On the sides of Henry's tomb are a number of wreathed roundels with paired saints in relief.

When this work was well in hand, 1516, Torrigiano entered into another contract to make the altar of Our Lady for the sum of £1,000. This altar, with a Renaissance baldachino supported at the angles by Corinthian columns stood against the western face of the closure. Though designed by Torrigiano it was set up by Benedetto da Rovezzano in 1526. Both altar and canopy were broken up in 1644 by order of the Long Parliament, a few fragments alone surviving ; but a replica was installed in the chapel in 1935, as an offering of the Knights of the Order of the Bath to commemorate the Jubilee of King George V. The remnants of Torrigiano's altar were skilfully incorporated in the reconstruction.

Some time before his death, Henry VII also provided for obits to be kept at Christ Church, Canterbury, at S. Albans Abbey and in fourteen other monastic churches as well as at the universities of Oxford and Cambridge. At S. Albans Abbey the obit was to be observed on 11 February *during the king's lifetime*, and after his death on the anniversary of his burial.

In the south aisle of Henry VII's chapel is the Renaissance tomb of the King's mother, Margaret, Countess of Richmond, who died in 1509 in the abbot's house at Westminster. A great patroness of learning, Lady Margaret founded Christ's and S. John's colleges at Cambridge and instituted chairs in Divinity at the universities. She made many gifts to her son's chapel, the building of which she watched with a lively interest. The south side was known as ' the king's mother's chapel ' and she founded a chantry at the altar there in 1505. A weekly mass was to be sung by each of the monks in turn, the celebrant receiving 3s. for his services. For the endowment Lady Margaret gave the abbot and convent the churches of Cheshunt and Swineshead, which yielded more than £50 per annum. By her will she ordained that ' our executors do make in the chapel a convenient tomb, and one altar or two in the same chapel for two chantry masses there perpetually to be said.'

Her black marble tomb in the aisle with its exquisitely modelled effigy in bronze was the work of Torrigiano. Above the head, which was painted in natural colours, is a Gothic ' gabletz ' of bronze, fashioned by an English craftsman. At the western end of the north aisle of Henry VII's chapel is a small screened enclosure which was the sacristy for the priests serving the chantries.

On his sumptuous chapel and its furnishings Henry VII expended vast sums of money, equivalent to £250,000 to-day, and the endowment must have amounted to another £100,000.

John Islip, 1464–1532, the last of the great abbots of Westminster lived
to see the chapel completed and the tomb of Henry and his queen installed within the bronze enclosure. Such a magnificent foundation must
have made the good abbot envious ; so much so, that in 1522 he planned
a chantry chapel, known as the Jesus chapel, for himself off the north
ambulatory of the choir. To this end he appropriated and walled off the
eastern half of the chapel of S. John Evangelist at the southern end of
the north transept.

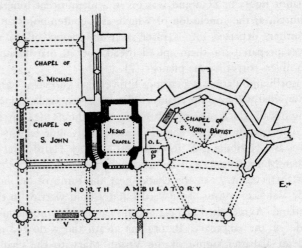

FIG. XIX  PLAN OF NORTH AMBULATORY
OF WESTMINSTER ABBEY. *Islip's or Jesus Chapel.*
*Chapel of Our Lady of the Pew. V. Tomb of Aymer De Valence.*
T. *Tomb of Sir Thomas Vaughan.*

To enclose the Jesus chapel from the ambulatory, a lofty stone screen
was erected, designed in two stories and embracing two floors within.
A Jesus altar was set up in each. The lower half of the screen consists of
mullioned windows and the doorway, and the front of the upper stage
displays a range of niches alternating with rectilinear panelling. The
abbot's name occurs in various forms on the frieze dividing the two
stages—an eye with a slip or branch of a tree, a man slipping from a tree
and 'Islip' in decorative lettering (Pl. 34).
   The central area of the lower chapel is roofed with a lierne vault, the
ribs of which form an eight-pointed star, and in the carved bosses occurs
the Islip rebus. On all sides except the west are arched recesses with
panelled barrel vaults ; in that at the east is a sculptured figure of Christ,
much mutilated. In 1938–9 the vaulting was cleaned and the ribs and

bosses recoloured. The tomb of the abbot formerly stood in the middle of the chapel but is now beneath the window, and the effigy has long since disappeared. The upper chapel, reached by a stairway at the west was intended for choristers and was no doubt used as a vestry. On its eastern wall are the remains of a painting in which can be discerned two figures of kings, one of which may be Edward the Confessor. Islip was an active builder during his rule at Westminster. He witnessed the completion of the abbey nave and he enlarged the abbot's house. He died at Neate manor house in 1532 and was given a magnificent funeral in the abbey church, at the conclusion of which, as a contemporary recorded, ' the mourners departed into a place over the chapel of the defunct, where was prepared for them spiced bread, sucket, marmylate, spiced plate and divers sorts of wine plenty ' (Pl. 32).

In the north ambulatory is a curious little chapel known as ' Our Lady of the Pew,' that was used for chantry offices.* It was made, c. 1370-5, by hollowing out the thick mass of buttressing that adjoins the Islip chapel on the east. This cavernous little chapel measures only nine feet by six and now serves as a vestibule to S. John Baptist's chapel. Hardly was it completed when Mary, Countess of Pembroke, by her will dated 1377, made a bequest for a chantry ' in the chapel near the tomb of her husband,' Aymer de Valence, cousin of Edward I and a bold warrior in the wars with Scotland. Aymer died in 1324 and his canopied tomb stands on the north side of the sanctuary. Before her death the widowed countess presented an alabaster figure of the Virgin Mary to the chapel ; the bracket on which it stood remains in situ. Until an opening was made into the chapel of S. John Baptist in 1524, the altar of Our Lady stood against the east wall. In the vault of the chapel is a carved boss of the Assumption of the Virgin and there is much colour decoration on the walls and the vault—on the latter the Virgin's symbol of the pointed stars. At the entrance are the original wooden gates with iron prickets for wax tapers.

This little chapel is often mistermed the chapel of S. Erasmus, from the alabaster niche which once held a figure of the saint and is built in the wall above. The words ' Sanctus Erasmus ' painted in Islip's time on the masonry related to the image in the niche and not to the chapel. The niche, dating c. 1485, came from a chantry chapel dedicated to S. Erasmus, which had been founded by Edward IV's queen, Elizabeth Woodville, who had twice taken sanctuary at Westminster. She repaid the hospitality of the abbots by erecting the chapel of S. Erasmus. It was built on the south side of the thirteenth-century Lady chapel and was completed by 1486.

*The derivation of ' Pew ' is uncertain, but the word may mean enclosure.

In a royal charter of 1479 the monks of Westminster were granted lands in Worcestershire as an endowment for the queen's chantry. Masses were to be sung daily in S. Erasmus chapel for the good estate of Edward IV and his queen, and on the eve of the anniversary the whole convent of Westminster were to sing Placebo and Dirige in the choir, and twenty-four candles, each 6 lb. in weight, were to burn round the hearse. On the morrow, masses were to be sung, 240 pennies to be distributed to the poor and the monks were to receive pittances.*

When Henry VII demolished the old Lady chapel the niche and its figure were set up in their present position by Abbot Islip.

In the chapel of S. John Baptist is the chantry tomb of Sir Thomas Vaughan, one-time treasurer to Edward IV and beheaded by Richard, Duke of Gloucester, in 1483. The tomb is a plain chest of Purbeck marble and on the slab is a small brass portraying the knight in armour. At the foot of the tomb, which stands in an arched recess, is space for the priest who recited the masses. Another chantry tomb in the abbey is the Chaucer monument in the south transept. When the poet died in 1400 he was buried in the chapel of S. Benedict in the south ambulatory; but in 1555 his remains were transferred to the south transept and the present tomb erected. It is of grey Purbeck marble with a canopy of four ogee arches, and there is standing room for the priest at one end. Francis Bond in his *Westminster Abbey* suggests that the tomb was brought from Blackfriars or Greyfriars when those houses were suppressed.

Obits and anniversaries were observed at Westminster for departed abbots and brethren. Flete, the monk-historian of the abbey, records an ordinance of Abbot Berkyng, 1230, that when a monk died his daily provision was to be given by the almoner for one year to a priest of good report, who in return was to offer up special prayers and recite a daily mass for the deceased. It was the custom of the abbots to make provision for their own obits and anniversaries. According to Flete, Richard Kedyngton (1308–15) over-burdened by debt, was almost the only abbot of Westminster who failed to do so. Some found means to endow a chantry. Out of the huge fortune which Cardinal Langham bequeathed to his former brethren in 1376, the sum of 1,000 marks (equal to about £27,000 to-day) was left as an endowment for a perpetual chantry to be served by four monk priests. His successor, Nicholas Litlyngton, was so

---

*In the gracious protection of S. Erasmus, Edward IV and his queen placed particular trust. Four years earlier the King made a grant to the prior and canons of S. Mary Overie, Southwark, of the church of West Tilbury, Essex, on condition that a mass of S. Erasmus was celebrated every day in the priory church, for the good estate of the King and queen and their children, for their souls after death and for the soul of the King's father, Richard, Duke of York.

loved by the monks that they granted him an anniversary *during his life-time,* and in addition they acquired lands worth £20 a year to endow a chantry in the abbey church for his parents.


# S. ALBANS CATHEDRAL

In the abbey church of S. Albans* upon which Pope Adrian IV conferred the title of premier abbey amongst English Benedictine houses, three chantry chapels have survived. Two, founded by abbots, are in the sanctuary and the other, that of Humphrey, Duke of Gloucester, flanks the Saint's chapel beyond.

Duke Humphrey, who was uncle to Henry VI, was a close friend of Abbot Wheathampstead. He was numbered amongst the 'familiares' of the house and was a frequent visitor there. The story is told by Sir Thomas More of his detection of an impostor who claimed to have been born blind and to have received his sight at the shrine of S. Alban, an incident made use of by Shakespeare in *Henry VI*, part ii. In 1441 licence was granted the Duke to make over the alien priory of Pembroke to the abbot and convent of S. Albans for the endowment of a chantry in their church. The ordinance provided for the celebration of a daily mass, for the distribution of alms and for the payment of £60 a year to the conventual kitchen. The 'good Duke Humphrey,' as he was called, was murdered in 1447 by William de la Pole, Earl of Suffolk, with the connivance of Queen Margaret and Cardinal Beaufort.

His chantry chapel stands to the immediate south of the shrine of S. Alban and was erected by Abbot Stokes, *c.* 1444. The duke was buried beneath the pavement of the Saint's chapel. It is recorded in the *Monasticon* that 'The abbot and convent . . . have payed for makynge of the tomb and place of sepulture of the said Duke within the said monasterie the summe of £433. 6s. 8d.' The chapel, an ornate example of Perpendicular Gothic is a two-storied structure. The open lower stage, which was designed to take the tomb, is spanned by three pendant arches, and in the spandrels above are shields in traceried circles. In the cornice are four shields of the Duke's arms supported by chained antelopes. Within is a fan vault with pendants (Pl. 33). The upper stage consists of a range of traceried panels with crocketed heads, alternating with niches. On the south front of the chapel the niches are filled with small figures of kings, seventeen in number ; a thirteenth-century grate of wrought iron, brought from elsewhere, shuts off the lower stage from the south aisle.

*Made a cathedral in 1877.

Long before Stow compiled his *Survey* a monument in the nave of old S. Paul's was popularly known as Duke Humphrey's tomb. At dinner-time the unfortunate folk who lacked a meal were wont to loiter in the cathedral and were said to ' dine with Duke Humphrey.' Our historian, however, identified the tomb as that of John Beauchamp, son of Guy, Earl of Warwick—' A proper chapel and a fair monument re-maineth of him ; he is by ignorant people misnamed Humphrey, Duke of Gloucester, who lieth honourably buried at S. Albans.' In confirmation

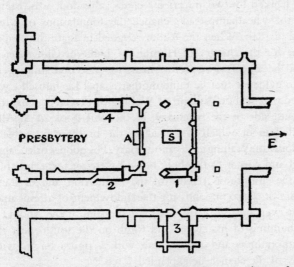

FIG. XX S. ALBANS. A. *High Altar*. S. *Shrine of S. Alban*. 1. *Humphrey Chapel*. 2. *Wallingford Chapel*. 3. *Wheathampstead Chapel (destroyed)*. 4. *Ramryge Chapel*.

of Stow's statement, the leaden coffin of the Duke was discovered in the eighteenth century in a vault beneath the pavement of the Saint's chapel.

On the south side of the sanctuary in the bay adjoining the High Altar is a low chantry chapel which until recently was attributed to Abbot John of Wheathampstead (d. 1464).

From documentary evidence, Sir Charles Peers has shown that the chapel was founded and built by Abbot William of Wallingford (1476–84) who is remembered for the stately reredos of the High Altar. The chapel is architecturally undistinguished. It is set within a wide, four-centred arch and enclosed with contemporary iron grilles. In the cornice appears a motto ' *Valles habundabunt* ' with three wheat-ears, and above is a row of quatrefoiled panels enclosing the rose-en-soleil, the arms of S. George, and a mitre with wheat-ear. The rose-en-soleil was the badge of Edward IV and it is therefore assumed that the chapel was built during his reign, between 1471 and 1483.

Abbot Wheathampstead died in 1464 and it is on record that he built a chantry chapel during his first abbacy, 1420–40, ' outside the south aisle of the presbytery in the monks' cemetery.' This chapel, long since destroyed, was erected about 1429 and was consecrated in the following year. In the wall of the south choir aisle opposite the Saint's chapel is a framed doorway flanked by two traceried recesses ; this door was originally the entrance to Wheathampstead's chapel, the foundations of which were unearthed in 1846. When the Abbot resigned in 1440, the chapel served for a time for the chantry of Humphrey, Duke of Gloucester. Wheat-hampstead became Abbot of S. Albans for a second time in 1452 but there is no evidence that he built another chapel for himself ; whereas it is recorded that Abbot William of Wallingford erected a chantry chapel on the south side of the sanctuary. In the obit book of S. Albans is a lengthy document which was read to the brethren assembled in the chapter-house on Wallingford's anniversary. His good works, 'apparent in every part and corner of this holy house,' were set forth, mention being made of the sumptuous reredos of the High Altar and of the Abbot's expenditure of £100 on lands for the endowment of a Jesus mass every Friday for ever and of a daily mass for the soul of the Abbot. Further, ' for the building of his chapel and tomb on the south, near the High Altar, with railings and marble slab with a figure on it, with other ornaments of the chapel, he expended £100.'*

From such evidence the chapel must be ascribed to Abbot Wallingford, who died in 1484. Unfortunately no tomb remains to confirm this ; instead, there is a brass which formerly marked the grave of Abbot Thomas de la Mare (d. 1396) in front of the High Altar. The entrance to the chapel is at the south-west.

On the north side of the sanctuary, facing the Wallingford chapel, is the chantry chapel of Abbot Thomas Ramryge (1492–1521) of whose career our knowledge is scanty. It is built of clunch and is amongst the finest in the country. It is a two-storied structure of the stone-cage type and completely fills the bay in which it is built, rising almost the full height of the choir arch (Pl. 35).

The lower stage is enclosed by screens composed of three-light windows above a panelled base, and the cornice is enriched with various sculptured ornaments, including the Abbot's rebus—a ram wearing a collar on which appear the letters RYGE—the arms of Henry VIII and of the cells of S. Albans, viz., Binham, Tynemouth, Wymondham, etc. The upper

* V. C. H. Herts.

story is fronted with open rectilinear panels alternating with canopied niches and resembles that of Duke Humphrey's chapel. The door of the chapel is on the south side at the western end, and in the spandrels of the arch are sculptured representations of the scourging and the martyrdom of S. Alban. Within the lower stage is a delightful fan vault and a stone slab is preserved bearing a figure of the abbot and a Latin inscription on the verge. There is much carved detail in the stonework, including the emblems of the Passion, and foliage and flowers.

Amongst other chantries in the abbey church was one that owed its foundation to the first battle of S. Albans, fought in May 1455. Three years afterwards Henry VI made an attempt, which at first promised success, to patch up a peace between the two factions. As an earnest of their desire to promote a reconciliation the Duke of York and the Earls of Salisbury and Warwick undertook to found a chantry in the abbey for the repose of the souls of the Lancastrians who had fallen in the battle. The endowment of £45 a year for this chantry, equal to £1,500 to-day, was a very welcome addition to the monastic income. Many of the slain had been buried in the abbey ; the remains of Somerset, Clifford and Northumberland were laid in the Lady chapel of S. Albans at the request of the Duke of York.


## TYNEMOUTH

Amongst the many daughter houses of S. Albans was Tynemouth Priory, Northumberland. Though the church is in a state of ruin, there remains intact the chantry chapel founded by one of the Percys, which stands in a unique position for it is built to the east of the choir, on the site normally occupied by the Lady chapel. The Percy chapel was built about 1450 probably by Henry Percy, second Earl of Northumberland, son of the famous Hotspur. The founder was slain at the first battle of S. Albans in 1455. His chapel is a low building, the roof barely rising above the sills of the presbytery windows. It is rectangular on plan, about eighteen feet in length and is entered from the priory church by a door in the centre of the eastern wall. Above the door within is a seated figure of S. Oswin, whose shrine stood in the choir, and kneeling before the saint is a figure of Henry Percy.

The most arresting feature of the Percy chapel is the intricate lierne vault, enriched with fifteen large bosses at the intersection of the main ribs 'and eighteen smaller bosses. The subjects carved on the bosses are in the main figures of the apostles and saints, their emblems and the arms of the Percys ; one of the bosses represents Christ in Majesty.

## GLOUCESTER CATHEDRAL

At Gloucester Cathedral, which before the Suppression was the church of the Benedictine Abbey of S. Peter, the chantry chapels are eclipsed in historic and architectural interest by the magnificent monument of Edward II on the north side of the sanctuary.

In the adjoining bay to the west is the chapel of Abbot William Parker who ruled the convent from 1515 until the Dissolution. It is a stone-cage structure with ranges of Perpendicular windows above a panelled base, and at each angle is a large canopied niche. The masonry bears carvings of vine leaves and grapes and within the chapel is the tomb of the Abbot on which reclines a mutilated effigy. In the panels on the sides of the tomb are the emblems of the Passion and heraldic shields of the founder, and in the pavement of the chapel are some encaustic tiles bearing the arms of the abbey and of its last ruler. Though Abbot Parker built the tomb in his chapel he was buried elsewhere.

In the first bay of the south nave arcade from the east stands the chantry chapel built by Abbot Thomas Seabroke (1450–57). It is enclosed with Perpendicular screens and retains its reredos of five canopied niches, now untenanted. Above is a frieze of lions and roses. Within an arched recess is the tomb of the Abbot on which rests an alabaster effigy in abbatial robes and wearing a mitre ; at his head are two mutilated figures of angels and there is a lion at his feet.

Between the two southern piers of the central tower is a chapel with timber screens dating c. 1514. This is said to have been the chantry chapel of Abbot John Browne (1510–14) and was dedicated to S. John Baptist. The panelling inside is covered with alternating monograms, S and B surmounted with crowns.

## TEWKESBURY ABBEY

In few churches in the land will be found so magnificent a series of monuments as that clustered about the sanctuary of Tewkesbury Abbey, Gloucestershire, which was a house of Benedictine monks. Amongst them are three chantry chapels of the stone-cage form, all of which are within a few feet of the High Altar.

On the north side of the sanctuary, in the second bay from the west, is the chapel of Robert Fitzhamon, who was a kinsman of William Rufus and Lord of Gloucester, Bristol, Tewkesbury and Cardiff. He was the founder of the present abbey, for by his munificence the monks were enabled to rebuild their church early in the twelfth century. On his death in 1107 Fitzhamon was buried in the chapter-house ; in 1241 his remains were translated to the choir and about 1395 a chantry chapel was built for his soul-masses by Abbot Parker. The enclosing walls of the chapel are stone screens, each consisting of two large rectilinear windows above a panelled base and crowned with oak-leaf cresting. The entrance is by a small door at the south-west and within is a lovely little fan vault. In the middle stands the tomb of Fitzhamon. In every way the chapel is a delightful specimen of Perpendicular Gothic (Pl. 37).

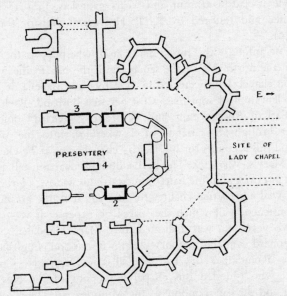

FIG. XXI TEWKESBURY ABBEY. A. *High Altar.*
*1. Fitzhamon Chapel. 2. Trinity Chapel. 3. Warwick Chapel.*
*4. Grave of Isabella de Despenser.*

On the south side of the sanctuary, opposite the Fitzhamon chapel is the Trinity chapel, built between 1390 and 1400 by Elizabeth, widow of Edward, Lord Despenser (d. 1375), for the chantry of her husband. Lord Edward fought with the Black Prince at Poitiers and is described by Froissart as 'the most honourable, gallant and valiant knight in all England, much beloved of ladies, for the most noble said that no feast was perfect if Sir Despenser was not present.' The chapel was dedicated to S. Mary and the Trinity and in its architectural character resembles the Fitzhamon chapel. Above a base faced with a series of niches are two Perpendicular windows each of five lights, and there is a cornice with cresting above. The chapel is roofed with a fan vault. By reason of its slender mullions and lighter tracery, it is of greater elegance and delicacy than the Fitzhamon chapel, though it was probably the work of the same masons. Both chapels were originally gilded and coloured and traces of mural paintings remain. In the Trinity chapel, the Coronation of the Virgin and symbols of the Holy Trinity have been identified. A unique feature of this chapel is the canopied niche which rises from the middle of the roof, and which contains a life-like figure in stone of Lord Edward, facing the High Altar and kneeling, his hands together in prayer. He is clad in armour and wears gauntlets. In 1938 the figure was cleaned and restored by R. P. Howgrave-Graham (Frontispiece and Pl. 36).

Foremost amongst the monuments at Tewkesbury is the Warwick chapel on the north side of the sanctuary in the bay to the west of the Fitzhamon chapel. It was erected in 1422 by Lady Isabella de Despenser for the celebration of soul-masses for her first husband, Richard Beauchamp, Earl of Abergavenny and Worcester. Richard's union with a Despenser brought the manor of Tewkesbury into the Beauchamp family, and this accounts for his chantry chapel being at Tewkesbury and not at S. Mary's, Warwick. The Earl, a doughty warrior, fell at the siege of Meaux in 1421 and immediately afterwards his widow, a girl of twenty-one, endowed a perpetual chantry for him and built the graceful chapel, on the construction of which she spared no expense. It was completed within two years and was dedicated to S. Mary Magdalen, S. Barbara and S. Leonard ; on the masonry a Latin inscription, Englished, ran as follows : 'Remember the Lady Isabella de Despenser, Countess of Warwick, who founded this chapel in honour of the blessed Mary Magdalen and died in London in the Minories, A.D. 1439, on S. John Evangelist's day and was buried in the choir on the right hand of her father, on whose soul God have pity. Amen ' (P. 38, 45).

The design of the Warwick chapel is not unlike that of the Wykeham chapel at Winchester, though it is less lofty and is divided into two stories, both roofed with fan vaults. The lower stage, the chapel proper, is enclosed with stone screens of rectilinear windows above a panelled base. In the panels are figures of angels holding heraldic shields. At the west end are doors leading from the sanctuary and the ambulatory. The vault of the lower stage only covers the western half and is supported by two slender shafts. The upper story is quite open, save for a range of tabernacled canopies and the ' buttress mullions ' carried up from the screens below. The vault is of a most intricate design, with delicate tracery covering its surface in web-like fashion and with pendants. The purpose of the upper floor remains a matter of conjecture for there is no stairway leading to it and it is floored only in the west, above the vault of the chapel. The Lady Isabella was not to remain a widow for long. By papal dispensation she married her husband's cousin, another Richard Beauchamp, and on his death at Rouen in 1439 she had his remains brought to this country. He was buried in the Beauchamp chapel at S. Mary's, Warwick. The countess died the same year and by her will ordained that she should be buried in Tewkesbury Abbey and a marble tomb should be erected there. All traces of the tomb have disappeared but the site of her grave, in front of the High Altar and close by the Warwick chapel, was identified seventy years ago.

## BOXGROVE PRIORY

At Boxgrove Priory, Sussex, formerly a Benedictine house dependent on Lessay Abbey, Normandy, is a chantry chapel that exhibits a curious mingling of Gothic form and Renaissance detail in the characteristic fashion of the sixteenth century. The chapel, an ' open ' version of the stone-cage type, stands on the south side of the choir and was founded by Thomas West, 9th Lord de la Warr of Halnaker (Pl. 39).

For centuries the owners of Halnaker had been patrons and bene-factors of Boxgrove Priory, and Lord de la Warr inherited the property through his wife, Elizabeth, the last of the Bonville family of Halnaker. For a few years masses for the souls of De la Warr and his lady were sung in the chapel and a vault beneath was to be their burial place. To provide room for the chapel an ' intermediate ' column in the choir arcade and the two arches springing therefrom were taken down and a four-centred arch spanning the whole bay was built. The chapel, which projects into the choir, is Gothic in its general form but the ornament and decorative detail show how surely the Renaissance was gaining the upper hand. There is a low enclosing wall, adorned with diamond-shaped panels, from which pillars rise at the angles and intermediately. Small four-centred arches spring from the pillars and above is a top-heavy canopy divided into square panels by canopied niches. The surfaces of the six supporting pillars are enriched with arabesques and in the panels of the canopy are angels and putti bearing heraldic shields of the successive owners of Halnaker. The grotesque character of the Renaissance orna-ment leaves no doubt that the carving was not executed by Italian crafts-men, but probably by Flemings or perhaps Englishmen trying their hand at the new-fashioned ornament. Within the chapel is a fan vault and at the east end above the site of the altar is the unfinished reredos, on which appears the inscription, ' Of your charity, pray ye for the soule of Thomas la Warr and Elizabeth his wife.'

In 1535, when the suppression of the priory was at hand, de la Warr wrote to Thomas Cromwell begging that it should be spared.

And so it is, that I have a poor house [priory] called Boxgrove very near to my poor house called Halnaker, whereof I am founder, and there lieth many of my ancestors and also my wife's mother ; and for cause it is of my foundation and that my parish church is under the roof of the said monastery, and have made a poor chapel to be buried in ; wherefore it might stand with the King's grace's pleasure for the poor service that I have done his Highness, to forbear the suppression of the same or else to translate it into a college of such number as the lands will bear.

The efforts of the ' poor ' petitioner proved of no avail for within a few days the priory was dissolved : De la Warr purchased the land and goods and the church was made parochial. When he died in 1554 he was buried in Broadwater church where his tomb is still to be seen.

## BATH ABBEY

In the church of Bath Abbey, a Benedictine establishment which was closely associated throughout the Middle Ages with the See of Wells, is the chantry chapel of Prior William Bird (d. 1515). During his priorate he had witnessed the reconstruction of the abbey church, a project begun by Dr. Oliver King, Bishop of Bath and Wells. So anxious was Bird to further the scheme that he devoted all his wealth to it and is said to have died in abject poverty.

The Prior's chapel is of the stone-cage type and stands in the south arcade of the abbey choir. The enclosing screens on either side are treated as two large Perpendicular windows above a range of quatrefoiled panels. Surmounting the whole are a carved cornice and cresting, and the chapel is roofed with a fan vault. The tracery and details in general lack the elegance and delicacy which characterize some of the smaller chapels of the period.

## CHRIST CHURCH PRIORY, HANTS

From the middle of the twelfth century until the Dissolution the Priory of Christ Church, Hants, was a house of Augustinian canons. The church is one of the most complete of that Order in this country, and the eastern arm, planned on cathedral lines, afforded ample space for chantry chapels, of which five remain. There are stone-cage chapels in the sanctuary, parclose chapels at the extremities of the choir aisles and chantry tombs in the Lady chapel.

One of the most splendid of its kind is the Salisbury chapel, situated on the north side of the choir adjoining the High Altar. It was founded *c*. 1520 by the ill-fated Margaret, Countess of Salisbury, grand-daughter of Warwick the king-maker, and was to be the burial place of herself and her son, Cardinal Reginald Pole. On account of the Cardinal's denunciation of Henry VIII, in 1539 the king attainted all the members of the Pole family then in England, and the venerable Margaret, then over seventy years of age, was imprisoned in the Tower of London. Two years later she was barbarously executed, and permission to convey her remains to Christ Church being refused, she was buried in S. Peter's-ad-Vincula at the Tower. The Cardinal remained in Italy until the accession of Mary Tudor and succeeded Cranmer as Archbishop of Canterbury. On his death in 1558 he was buried in the cathedral.

The Salisbury chapel is a lofty structure built of Caen stone and projects considerably on each side. As the aisle pavement is at a lower level than the choir, the north face is loftier than the south, and it is more ornate. Above a panelled base are two four-light windows on either side and at the angles are octagonal piers or standards, an intermediate one dividing the structure into two bays. On the masonry flanking each window are three canopies, one above another, but no figures have survived. Above the windows are two blind stages, the lower of wide panels and the upper surmounted by a carved cornice. On the sanctuary side two curious tabernacles rise above the cornice. The advent of the new Renaissance art is manifest in the antique ornament in low relief, unobtrusively carved in the narrow panels of the angle-piers. Within the chapel are three tabernacled niches which backed the altar, and there is a rich fan vault, in the centre of which is a carving depicting the Coronation of the Virgin together with Plantagenet devices. The commissioners appointed by Thomas Cromwell to visit the priory wrote : ' In thys church we found a chaple and a monument pr'pared by the late mother of Raynolde Pole for herr buriall, which we have causyd to be defayced and all the armes and badgis clerely to be delete ' (Pl. 40, 42).

A little later than the Salisbury chapel and quite different in character is the chantry chapel of John Draper, the last of the priors of Christ Church. It was founded in 1529, only ten years before the house was surrendered. Draper made a chapel at no great cost, for he merely screened off the east end of the south aisle of the choir, but no remodelling was carried out as for the West chapel at Ely. The screen, an elegant one of Caen stone, bears the date of its erection in Latin. Centrally placed is the doorway, with canopied niches above, and on either side is a large Perpendicular window with transoms. On the outer sides of the windows are more canopied niches. Above the four-centred arch of the doorway is a sculptured relief of a church. The base of the screen consists of recti-linear panelling and the whole is surmounted with a carved cornice. On the stonework appear the Prior's initials, J. D., and within, a canopied niche remains in the south wall (Pl. 44).

When the priory was suppressed Draper was granted a pension of 200 marks. He died twelve years later and was buried in the nave of Christ Church, but a century ago his body was transferred to a grave in the choir aisle near his chapel.

The corresponding bay in the north aisle was also utilized as a chantry chapel, of which little is known. Adjoining the Salisbury chapel on the west is the so-called Berkeley chapel, the origin of which is wrapped in obscurity. It is a stone-cage structure of late Gothic with rectilinear windows above a panelled base. On the flat timber ceiling are painted a red and a white rose. On the opposite side of the choir is a similar chantry chapel, founded c. 1520 by Robert Harys, Rector of Shrowston (d. 1525), whose rebus, a hare with the letter R, occurs in the panels.

In the Lady chapel at the east end of the priory church are two chantry tombs of Purbeck marble. In the south wall is the tomb of Lady Alice West (d. 1395), and on the north is that of Thomas, Lord West, her son (d. 1406).

Mother and son made many gifts of money to further the building of the Lady chapel and founded perpetual chantries in the church. By his will Thomas ordained that he should be buried ' in the new chapel of Our Lady in the mynster of Christ Church ' and he and Lady West each made a bequest of £18 for the recitation of 4,500 soul-masses within six months of their decease. Their tombs stand flush with the walls and must have been inserted after the Lady chapel was complete, for the arcading and panelling were cut away to admit them. Neither is of particular beauty but Lord Thomas's tomb is remarkable for the grid-like range of closely set mullions which support the canopy.

## HEXHAM PRIORY, NORTHUMBERLAND

In the choir of Hexham Priory, Northumberland, which was a house of Augustinian canons, are the remains of two chantry chapels of interest by reason of their timber screens.

In the north arcade is the chapel of Prior Rowland Leschman, which was built c. 1490. The lower part of the enclosing screen is of stone and is faced with a series of curious ogee-arched recesses above which is a three-lobed ornament quite un-English in character. The superstructure is of timber divided by muntins into a number of lights with flamboyant tracery of great delicacy in their heads. Above is a carved cornice. Only

46. DR. KING'S CHAPEL, S. GEORGE'S, WINDSOR

47. THE BAYNTON CHAPEL, BROMHAM CHURCH, WILTS

48. CHANTRY CHAPEL AT S. MARY'S, WARWICK

49

49. SOUTH FRONT, KING'S COLLEGE CHAPEL, CAMBRIDGE

51. ABBOT LICHFIELD'S CHAPEL, ALL SAINTS CHURCH, EVESHAM

50. THE GREENAWAY CHAPEL, TIVERTON CHURCH, DEVON

part of the tester which covered the enclosure now remains. At the east end of the chapel is a stone altar-slab bearing five consecration crosses. Towards the west is the recumbent effigy of Prior Leschman, wearing the habit of the canons, with the cowl drawn over his face and his hands together in prayer. On the south side of the choir is the reconstructed chantry chapel of Robert Ogle (d. 1410). It consisted wholly of timber screens and was swept away about a century ago. A few years since, however, portions were recovered and pieced together, and with the addition of some new timber a restoration was effected.

## OXFORD CATHEDRAL

At the ' cathedral Church of Christ,' Oxford, which prior to Cardinal Wolsey's suppression in 1524, was the conventual church of an Augustinian priory, is a chantry chapel of unusual form. It is built in two stories, the lower being of stone and the upper a timber gallery. It is often described as a watching chamber, for the gallery commanded a view of the shrine of S. Frideswide, a few feet distant. For whom this uncommon monument was erected is unknown. It stands at the eastern end of the arcade dividing the Latin and Lady chapels and is a lofty structure, rigidly Perpendicular in design, dating from the end of the fifteenth century. The sides of the lower stage are divided into recesses by panelled piers with crocketed heads, and carried right across the heads of the recesses is a range of small and closely set arches. Above is a cornice carved with a running vine ornament and Tudor cresting. In the north front wide and narrow bays alternate, the former having pedestal seats in their recesses. The lower parts of the narrow bays are faced with quatrefoil panels containing blank shields. At the west is a doorway leading to the upper floor. The south front is divided into nine equal bays, similar to those on the north but without seats and doorway. The interior of the lower story has a flat fan vault with foliage bosses. The timber fronts of the loft-chapel consist of a series of panels divided by buttresses with a range of open lights above, each with a depressed arch and a spired canopy. The roof is an imitation ribbed vault (Pl. 43).

It would seem that the lower story, in which is a large altar tomb, was intended to be the tomb-chamber, and the upper was the chapel proper for the celebration of the soul-masses.

# 10) Chantry chapels in collegiate churches : S. George's, Windsor ; S. Mary's, Warwick ; Manchester ; Ottery S. Mary ; Ripon ; Southwell ; Eton ; Cambridge.

CLOSELY RELATED TO the religious houses in the Middle Ages were the collegiate establishments, communities of secular canons, vicars-choral and prebendaries who banded themselves together for purposes of teaching and study. They lived a semi-monastic life, though not bound by any rule. The personnel invariably included a number of chantry priests ; at Beverley Minster there were fifteen in 1547. Of such size and importance were the collegiate churches of Manchester, Southwell and Ripon that they became cathedrals when new dioceses were formed in the last century.

## S. GEORGE'S CHAPEL, WINDSOR

Rivalling Winchester Cathedral in the number of chantry chapels is the Royal Chapel of S. George within Windsor Castle. The present church was begun c. 1480 though not completed until 1537.

Here was a glorious setting for chantry foundations. No less than eight chapels remain, all of which are legal to this day, for the royal chapel was excluded from the provisions of the Suppression Act. Edward IV (d. 1483), the first monarch to be buried at Windsor, intended that a chantry chapel should be built for himself in the new S. George's. By his will, dated 1475, he desired to be buried in the chapel 'low in the ground, and upon the same, a stone to be laid and wrought with the figure of Death.' The will made provision for a chantry, to be served by two priests and a body of thirteen bedesmen, who were to dwell within the castle. He left directions for the making of a vault for his remains, over which a chapel was to be reared. In the chapel was to be an altar for the soul-masses and a tomb bearing the King's image of silver-gilt. He had intended that there should be two chapels, one above the other. The lower one was to occupy two bays in the north aisle of the choir and was to be enclosed with an iron grille.

Sandford, writing in 1677, says that Edward IV ' lies in the new chapel whose foundation himself had laid, under a monument of steel polished and gilt representing a pair of gates between two towers all of curious transparent workmanship, in the north arch near to the High Altar.' This grille, the most splendid piece of Gothic ironwork in England was

the work of John Tresilian, a Cornish smith. Edward was buried in the
eastern bay of the aisle, his grave being marked by a black marble slab
which formed part of his unfinished tomb. The tomb had been made
abroad and was imported the year before the King's death. So weighty
a mass was it that the crane that was being used to land it broke in the
operation. In the wall of the aisle is a vice which gives access to the upper
chapel. The latter, some forty feet in length, extends over the three
eastern bays of the aisle. The vaulting beneath it, adorned with badges of
Edward IV, was kept low in order to give greater height to the interior,
and on this account the two arches adjoining the High Altar are lower

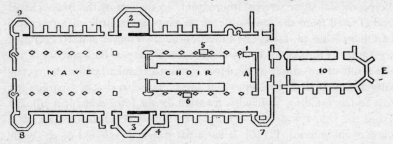

FIG. XXII  PLAN OF S. GEORGE'S CHAPEL, WINDSOR.
*A. High Altar. 1. Tomb of Edward IV. 2. Rutland Chapel. 3. Braye Chapel.*
*4. King Chapel. 5. Hastings Chapel. 6. Oxenbridge Chapel. 7. Lincoln Chapel.*
*8. Beaufort Chapel. 9. Urswick Chapel. 10. Tomb House.*

than the rest. In the western wall of the upper chapel is a small oriel or
bay window overlooking the aisle and formerly there were two similar
windows on the sanctuary side. One of these was destroyed when the
timber oriel was inserted by Henry VIII. In 1492 Edward's queen, Elizabeth Woodville, was buried by the side of her husband, by the order of
Henry VII.

Of outstanding beauty with their large Perpendicular windows are the
five-sided transepts of S. George's, both forming spacious chapels.

The north transept or Rutland chapel was founded in 1481 by Sir
Thomas St. Leger, the husband of Anne, Duchess of Exeter, sister of
Edward IV. Sir Thomas was beheaded in 1483 by Richard III and his
remains were laid beside his wife's, who had died eight years before. Their
daughter, Anne, married Sir George Manners (d. 1513), ancestor of the
Rutland family, whose alabaster tomb with effigies of husband and wife
stands in the centre of the chapel.

The south transept, similar in every respect to the Rutland chapel was
the chantry chapel of Sir Reginald Braye. None was more deserving of
remembrance at S. George's than Sir Reginald. From 1481 until his

death in 1503 he was the Surveyor of the royal chapel and was most active in promoting the building operations ; hence the frequent occurrence of his arms and badge on the stonework of the nave and transepts. He lived to see S. George's almost completed and made bequests of land and money to that end. As he was a firm supporter of the Tudors—he had placed the crown on Henry VII's head at Bosworth Field in 1485—his executors had no difficulty in obtaining the King's permission to appropriate the south transept for his chantry, though they failed to erect the tomb for which Braye had made provision.

Both transept chapels are shut off from the body of the church by large Perpendicular stone screens. Immediately to the east of the Braye chapel and entered from the south aisle of the choir is the little chantry chapel of Oliver King (d. 1503) one-time Canon of Windsor and Registrar of the Order of the Garter. In 1495 he became Bishop of Bath and Wells. As the result of his vision of the Holy Trinity he embarked on the reconstruction of Bath Abbey church in 1500.* His chapel at S. George's is a low square building, somewhat dwarfed by the lofty transept it adjoins. From the aisle a wide four-centred arch with a panelled soffit affords a view of the interior (Pl. 46). It has a flat panelled roof and on the walls are devices and inscriptions which are said to allude to the bishop's vision. After his death his body was brought to Windsor and laid in the chapel he erected. Bishop King, together with the Dean of S. George's and the Mayor of Windsor, under licence of Henry VII founded the Gild of the Holy Trinity in the parish church of Windsor. The objects of the fraternity were to support a chantry for the souls of the townspeople and to distribute alms to the poor. The members also undertook to keep certain bridges in the locality in good repair. Gifts bestowed by the townsfolk added to the revenues of the gild, which, at the Suppression, amounted to £19. 4s. 4d., out of which the priest received a stipend of £7. 6s. 8d.

In the choir of S. George's, are two chapels of the stone-cage type, though they are hidden from the choir by the lofty stalls. The earlier of the two is the Hastings chapel, founded and built by the widow and the son of William, Lord Hastings, chamberlain to Edward IV. He came to an untimely end for he was barbarously executed by the order of Richard III in 1483. His remains were brought to S. George's and buried near the tomb of Edward IV. The chantry chapel, dedicated to S. Stephen, is situated in the fourth bay from the High Altar on the north side of the choir and projects into the aisle. It is a noble specimen of Perpendicular Gothic ; its traceried windows with ogee heads are divided by slender

---

*On the west front of Bath Abbey is a representation of the angels of his vision ascending and descending ladders on either side of the great window.

buttresses and at the angles are clusters of buttresses. A rich cresting crowns the screen walls. On the walls within are contemporary paintings depicting incidents in the life of S. Stephen. The colours were restored by Professor Tristram in 1932.

Opposite the Hastings chapel, on the south side of the choir but one bay farther west, is the chantry chapel of Canon John Oxenbridge (1509–22). Dedicated to S. John Baptist, it was obviously modelled on the Hastings chapel, and though some twenty-five years later was probably the work of the same masons. Here are similar buttresses dividing the windows ; the same traceried forms and brattished transoms, the same clusters of buttresses at the angles, and cresting above. The entrance is in the same position, at the west, in both chapels. Above the door of the Oxenbridge chapel occurs the rebus, an ox, the letter N and a bridge.

The earliest chantry chapel here is the Lincoln chapel, a polygonal structure at the south-east angle of the choir. In 1481 it was made a shrine chapel by Edward IV to house the tomb of a famous thirteenth-century healer, John Shorne (d. 1290), Rector of North Marston, whose reputation attracted pilgrims in great numbers to his tomb. In 1478 licence was granted by Pope Sixtus IV for the translation of the healer's remains to a shrine in S. George's, and the chapel was then built to receive them. Miracles were reported of Shorne during his lifetime and were afterwards associated with the shrine, which Edward IV intended as a counter-attraction to the tomb of Henry VI, a Lancastrian, at Chertsey. Edward, a Yorkist, would grant no sepulchre for Henry at Windsor, nor was a chantry for the guileless monarch at all desirable. Henry's ' College of Our Lady of Eton beside Windsor,' founded in 1440, loomed large and itself constituted a chantry ' to pray for the king's health during life and when he left the light of earth, for his soul, and the soul of the illustrious prince Henry, his father, etc.' The popularity of Shorne the healer was short-lived, for in 1484 Richard III translated the body of Henry VI to S. George's and buried it on the south side of the High Altar. Later, Shorne's shrine chapel became the mortuary chapel of Edward Clinton, first Earl of Lincoln (1512–85), and his family.

The polygonal chapel at the southern end of the west front of S. George's is known as the Beaufort chapel. In it was founded the chantry of Charles, Earl of Worcester, a near relative of Henry VII, and within is the tomb of the Earl and his lady, Elizabeth, with their effigies on the slab. The chapel derives its name from the Duke of Beaufort, a descendant of Earl Charles, who in 1689 restored the bronze grille which encloses the tomb.

At the northern end of the west front is a similar chapel, which served for the chantry of Dean Christopher Urswick (d. 1521). Urswick was chaplain to Lady Margaret, Countess of Richmond, by whom he was employed in negotiating the marriage between her son, Henry VII, and Elizabeth of York. He became Dean of Windsor in 1495 and was associated with Sir Reginald Braye in the task of completing the royal chapel. In 1502 he was made Rector of Hackney, north London, and, resigning his other preferments, he retired to his house there, where he died in 1521. He was buried in Hackney parish church. His chapel at Windsor is enclosed with a screen which he put up in his lifetime, and his arms appear in the vaulting. On the wall above the chapel is inscribed a prayer, part of which reads : ' Deliver we beseech thee the souls of Henry VII and of Christopher and all whom Christopher has offended during life, from eternal death.'

Occupying the site of the old chapel of S. Edward, at the east end of S. George's chapel is an annexe or tomb-house which is now known as the Albert Memorial chapel. It is a long unaisled building with a three-sided apse at the east end and is walled off from S. George's at the west. Its erection was undertaken by Henry VII c. 1501, his intention being that it should serve as a chantry chapel and tomb-house for himself. But the walls were hardly completed when the king embarked on a more ambitious project, namely the building of the chapel at Westminster.

The abandoned chapel at Windsor was later granted by Henry VIII to Cardinal Wolsey, who proposed making it a tomb-house for himself. In 1524 he commissioned the Florentine sculptor, Benedetto, to prepare a sumptuous tomb of black marble adorned with bronze figures, for his remains. But after Wolsey's fall in 1529 the chapel reverted to the Crown and Henry VIII then paid large sums of money to the Florentine to convert Wolsey's tomb into an even more magnificent monument for himself. It was to be surmounted with an equestrian figure ' lively, in armour like a king, after the antique manner.' The monument was incomplete at Henry's death and was subsequently dismantled. The bronzes disappeared and all that remains is the black marble coffer which now forms part of Lord Nelson's tomb in the crypt of S. Paul's Cathedral.

Henry doubtless meant to use Wolsey's tomb-house as a chantry chapel for himself. He left elaborate directions in his will, together with sums of money to the Dean and Chapter of S. George's, to provide for the recitation of frequent masses for the good of his soul. After an appeal to the Virgin Mary and all the company of Heaven to intercede on his behalf, the king directed that ' Our body be buried and interred in the quire of our College of Windsor mid-way between the stalls and the High Altar, with the body of my true and loving Queen Jane [Seymour]' and that an honourable tomb with a fair grate about it should be erected.

Prior to the fall of Wolsey, Henry VIII 'contemplated burial in his father's chapel at Westminster. A bull of Clement VI dated 10 October 1525 granted an indulgence to the faithful who should make their devotions in the chapel which Henry VIII was about to found and endow and wherein he intended to be buried.' This may have referred to Henry VII's chapel, which his son would have re-endowed ; or to the revestry, now the chapel of S. Faith, in the south transept at Westminster, which Dart speaks of as ' the chapel of Henry VIII.' However, Wolsey's connections with Windsor at an end, his royal master finally decided upon S. George's chapel as his place of sepulture and he and Queen Jane were accordingly laid in the vault beneath the choir.

In the reports drawn up by the Chantry Commissioners in Henry VIII's reign, the eight chantry priests attached to the royal chapel were in receipt of £78. 6s. 8d. as stipends. The chantries enumerated were as follows ; Edward IV's, served by two priests ; the Duchess of Exeter's, Edward IV's sister, also by two priests ; and those of Lord Hastings, John Oxenbridge, Thomas Passche and John Plumer, verger. The two last mentioned were a combined chantry founded in 1493 at the altar in the chapel of the Salutation.

## S. MARY'S, WARWICK

In size second only to Henry VII's chapel at Westminster is the magnificent Beauchamp chapel at S. Mary's, Warwick. It stands to the east of the south transept of S. Mary's and like the chapel at Westminster was built as a separate structure, not forming an integral part of the church to which it was attached. That it was intended to be a chapel apart is evident from the fact that its north wall stands free of the choir wall, the narrow intervening space being utilized as lobbies or chapels. But the chapel has no entrance from the outside.

The church of S. Mary, Warwick, was made collegiate in the reign of Henry I, when it was united with the collegiate church of All Saints within the castle. Thenceforward, the reconstructions of S. Mary's through the centuries were undertakings of the Warwick family.

The Beauchamp chapel, which was dedicated to Our Lady, was built in accordance with the will of Richard Beauchamp, Earl of Warwick, who died in the castle of Rouen in 1439 in his fifty-eighth year. His will, dated 1435, gives the following directions :

I will that when it liketh to God, that my soul depart out of this world, my body be interred within the church collegiate of Our Lady in Warwick, where I will that in such place as I have desired, which is known well, there be made a chapel of Our Lady, well, fair and goodly built ; within the middle of which

chapel I will that my tomb be made. And in the meantime, my body to be laid
in a clean chest afore the altar that is on the right hand of my Lord, my father's
tomb, till the time that the said chapel and tomb for me be made, and then my
body to be taken up and laid therein. Also I will that there be said every day,
during the world, in the aforesaid chapel that, with the grace of God, shall be
thus new made, three masses.

Then follow the directions for the masses and the payment of £40 per
annum as stipends to the priests. 'Also I will that in the name of Heryott
to Our Lady, there be given to the church of S. Mary, mine image of

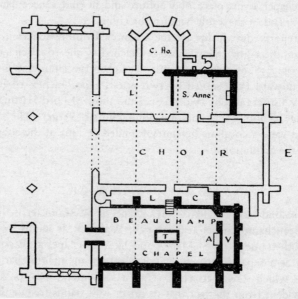

FIG. XXIII PLAN OF S. MARY'S, WARWICK. A. *Altar.*
T. *Beauchamp Tomb.* V. *Vestry.* C. *Chantry Chapel.* L. *Lobby.*

gold and of Our Lady, there to abide for evermore.' The provisions of
the will were strictly complied with. His remains were brought 'by
water as by land,' from Rouen to Warwick, and were buried by his
father's tomb, then standing at the end of the south aisle of the nave,
where is now the entrance to the Beauchamp chapel.

The Earl's executors laid the foundation stone of the chapel in 1443
and the work of building it occupied twenty-one years. The cost
amounted to £2,481. 4s. 7½d., an expenditure equivalent to £100,000
to-day. The chapel was consecrated in 1475 by John Hales, Bishop of
Coventry and Lichfield, and the Earl's body was removed from its tem-
porary resting-place to the sumptuous tomb prepared for its reception.

The Beauchamp chapel, rectangular on plan, has a total length of about sixty feet and is entered from the south transept of S. Mary's. Behind the altar at the east end is a narrow chamber which was used as a vestry or treasury. The external walls of the chapel are overlaid with Perpendicular panelling. At the apex of the eastern gable is a canopied niche, housing a figure of the Virgin and Child. The chapel is divided into three bays with boldly projecting buttresses to support the lierne vault. The bosses are coloured and gilt, and at the ridge of the vault converging ribs form a number of panels which enclose carvings of the Virgin Mary and the founder's arms. Beneath the Perpendicular windows are two tiers of recessed panels with ogee heads.

The great east window is remarkable for the canopied niches in the major mullions, the jambs and the window arch itself. There are upwards of thirty figures in the niches, representing the Heavenly Host and including S. Michael, S. Katherine, S. Barbara and S. Margaret with their emblems. The altar and the tabernacling beneath the window are additions of the eighteenth century, the originals having been destroyed in 1642.

The stalls and panelling in the westernmost bay of the chapel were the work of Richard Bird and John Haynes, London woodworkers, who made them in 1449. On the elbow rests are carved figures of muzzled bears and of lions and griffins.

Rich as was the chapel in architectural detail and painted imagery, it would have been incomplete but for the deep-toned stained glass designed to fill its windows. In the east window were 'costly portraitures of Earl Richard with his wives and children' and figures of S. Alban, S. Thomas of Canterbury, S. John of Bridlington and S. Winifred, while in the side windows were the hierarchies of angels. By a contract dated June 1447 John Prudde of Westminster, glazier, covenanted :

to glaze all the windows in the new chapel in Warwick with glasse beyond the seas and with no glasse of England ; and that in the finest wise, with the best, cleanest and strongest glasse of beyond the sea that may be had in England and of the finest colours of blew, yellow, red, purpure, sanguine and violet and of all other colours most necessary and best to make rich and embellish matters, images and stories that shall be delivered and appointed by patterns in paper, afterwards to strongly set it in lead and souder as well as any glasse is in England. . . . the executors paying to the said glazier for every foot of glasse 2s. and for the whole, £91. 1s. 10d.

Of this glass a few fragments remain in the east window.

But the interest of the Beauchamp chapel does not rest only in its architectural character and appurtenances. Almost in the centre of the chapel stands the costly tomb of the founder, which ranks in splendour and in the quality of its craftsmanship with the greatest of the royal tombs at Westminster or with that of the Black Prince at Canterbury.

The tomb of Richard Beauchamp is built of Purbeck marble and bears the recumbent effigy of the Earl in bronze. It was made by John Bourde of Corfe Castle, marbler, who covenanted ' in and about the tomb to make fourteen principal housings [niches] and under each housing a goodly quarter for a scutcheon of copper and gilt to be set in.' The sides are divided into five compartments and each end into two, each compartment containing a large canopied niche. Between the niches are narrow recessed panels with small niches above. In each of the fourteen ' principal housings ' is the figure of a weeper, cast in latten and gilt, representing some person of rank related to the earl. Seven of the figures are males dressed in mourning attire and the females wear mitred head-dresses. Amongst them are Richard Neville, Earl of Salisbury and Cicely his wife ;  Edmund Beaufort, Duke of Somerset and Eleanor his lady ; Stafford, Duke of Buckingham, the Duchess Anne ; Talbot, Earl of Shrewsbury and Margaret his wife ;  Richard Neville, Earl of Warwick, ' the king-maker ' and Anne, Lady Warwick—a glorious company of courtly personages of the period, all of whom are to be identified by the enamelled shields beneath them. The eighteen smaller niches contain latten figures of angels with scrolls in their hands. All these lovely little bronze figures were made by William Austin, citizen and founder, of London. He received 13s. 4d. for each of the noble weepers and 5s. for each angel. The main figure on the tomb is the effigy of Richard Beauchamp, which lies on a large plate ' of the finest latten.' Over the effigy is a latten hearse, made to carry a velvet pall.

In the contracts for this monument, William Austin, the London founder and Thomas Stevyns, coppersmith, undertook ' to cast and make an image of a man armed, of fine latten, garnished with certain ornaments, viz., with sword and dagger, with a garter, with a helme and crest under his head, and at his feet a bear muzzled and a griffin, perfectly made of the finest latten according to patterns, to be laid on the tomb, at the peril of the saide Austin, for the sum of forty pounds . . . also a herse of latten over the image to bear a covering to be ordained.' The effigy wears a suit of Milanese armour which is supposed to be a reproduction of the suit worn by the Earl, ' when he held his tournament victoriously for three days against all comers, presenting each of the discomfited adversaries with new war-chargers, feasting the whole company and finally returning to Calais with great worship.' The details of the armour, the buckles, straps and fastenings are all rendered with exactitude. The earl's hands are raised in adoration and he wears a garter below the left knee. The head with close-cropped hair rests on a tilting helmet and at the feet are a muzzled bear and a griffon. Round the verge of the tomb is a lengthy inscription in English on two latten plates, the words being interspersed with Warwick badges.

The hearse, one of the few remaining examples of its kind, consists of six hoops of latten connected by five long bars, moulded at the ends and enamelled with heraldic devices. At each angle is a standard for the burning of lights about the tomb.

On the north wall of the chapel is a doorway reached by a flight of steps which opens into a passage or lobby leading to the choir of the church. To the east of the lobby is a door opening into a diminutive chantry chapel, probably used for the celebration of low mass for Richard Beauchamp or for one of his family. The little chapel has a delightful fan vault with pendants and is lighted by windows in the wall of the Beauchamp chapel and by a small two-light window at the east (Pl. 48). Beneath the east window formerly stood an altar, flanked by a canopied niche on either side, which still remain, as does also a piscina to the south. There is another small chamber to the west of the vestibule. These three compartments occupy the space between the walls of the Beauchamp chapel and the choir of S. Mary's, the buttresses of the former being utilized as dividing walls.

On the north side of the choir of S. Mary's was another chantry chapel, its altar dedicated to S. Anne. Amongst the records at Worcester is a licence granted to Robert Waldene in 1401 to found a chantry of S. Anne in the church. This chapel was in all probability the rectangular building, now used as a vestry, which flanks the choir on the north. To the west is the vestibule of the chapter-house, from which it is separated by a fifteenth-century screen. Originally the only entrance to the chapel was by a door in the north wall of the choir. The chapel and the lobby are roofed with flat tierceron vaults.

## MANCHESTER CATHEDRAL

The collegiate church of Manchester,* though not to be compared in size or architectural splendour with the monastic and secular cathedrals of the Middle Ages, is remarkable for its great width, an abnormality which resulted from the accumulation of chantry chapels about the aisles of nave and choir. The internal width of the western arm is one hundred and fourteen feet, *i.e.* nine feet greater than York, which is the widest of our mediaeval cathedrals.

In 1421 the church of Manchester, hitherto parochial, was made collegiate, royal licence being granted for that purpose to Thomas de la

*Elevated to cathedral rank in 1847.

Warre, the Rector and twelfth Lord of Manchester. The new establishment was virtually a chantry foundation, inasmuch as it was ordained that masses should be celebrated every day in the church, for the good estate of Henry V, the Bishop of Coventry and Lichfield and Thomas de la Warre, and for the souls of their progenitors and all the faithful departed.

Immediately, a reconstruction of the church was decided upon, an undertaking which occupied eighty years or more. By the end of the

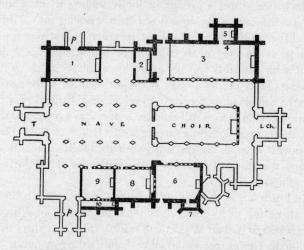

FIG. XXIV PLAN OF MANCHESTER CATHEDRAL. *1. Holy Trinity Chapel. 2. Ducie Chapel. 3. Derby Chapel. 4. Bishop Ely's Tomb. 5. Ely Chapel. 6. Jesus Chapel. 7. Hulme Chapel (destroyed). 8. Trafford Chapel. 9. Galley Chapel. 10. Brown Chapel. The screens are partly conjectural.*

fifteenth century, the choir and the nave, with single aisles north and south were nearing completion. Here was an opportunity not to be lost by the wealthy who wished to erect chantry chapels before the aisle walls enclosed the new church. The chapels then added were built external to the aisles, forming in themselves complete outer aisles and thus increasing the width of the church.

Little evidence remains of these chantry chapels for the altars have been removed and the screens which enclosed them swept away.

Probably the earliest was the chapel of the Holy Trinity, founded in 1498 by William Radcliffe of Ordsell. It occupied three or four bays at the western end of what is now the outer aisle on the north side of the nave. The easternmost bay of the same aisle was the Ducie chantry chapel, founded in 1507 and dedicated to S. James. In the pier at the south-eastern angle of the chapel is still to be seen a piscina.

Flanking the north choir aisle along its entire length is the Derby chapel dedicated to S. John Baptist. This was founded and endowed by the Stanley family, of whom two were successively wardens of the collegium. James Stanley, who held office 1481–5, was succeeded by another James 1485–9 and it was this second James, the youngest son of the first Earl of Derby, who began the erection of the Derby chapel in fulfilment of a vow made during the campaign against Scotland which ended at Flodden Field in 1513. In 1506 he became Bishop of Ely, a preferment which he may have owed to his stepmother, Margaret, Countess of Richmond. His son, Sir John Stanley, at the age of seventeen commanded his father's forces at the Battle of Flodden. When the Bishop died in 1515, the warrior John completed the building of the Derby chapel. Bishop James was buried by the north wall.

The western bay of the chapel forms a vestibule or ante-chapel and retains its oak screen. Original too is the beautiful parclose screen in the arcade dividing the chapel from the north aisle. Over the door of the Derby chapel is the shield of arms of Sir John and according to a manuscript in the library of Chetham's Hospital, there was once a brass bearing a Latin inscription, which translated, read : ' We beseech you that you aid us, James Stanley, Bishop of Ely, John Stanley, Knt., and Margaret his wife and their parents, with your prayers to the Lord Jesus Christ, who have built this chapel in His name and in honour of S. John Baptist in the year of his Incarnation 1513.' The magnificent canopied stalls on the south side of the choir were erected by the Bishop James. By his will he directed that a chantry chapel should be built over his grave, and his grandson, Sir John Stanley, accordingly put up the small Ely chapel which projects from the north side of the Derby chapel. Against the screen enclosing the chapel is the plain marble tomb of the Bishop. A brass represents him in episcopal robes, and the inscription begs ' off your charite pray for the soule of James Stanley, sometyme bushype of Ely and warden of his colledge of Manchester.'

The Bishop's son subsequently incurred the displeasure of Cardinal Wolsey and was imprisoned in the Fleet. By his will of June 1527 he made many bequests to the churches of Manchester and Cheadle and left ' penny doles to be given to poor widows, poor maidens and poor persons who would say paternoster, ave and credo for him, or pray for the souls of his father, himself and his wife and for William Handforth [his wife's father], and Ellen and Anne Stanley.' A priest was to recite a mass every day for the repose of their souls. He also obtained fraternity for himself and his family from the Abbot of Westminster, all their names being enrolled on the obit list, which was read in chapter.

He petitioned for the dissolution of his marriage in order that he and his wife might ' enter holy religion,' and in June 1528 a separation was granted at S. Paul's Cathedral and Sir John forthwith became a monk at Westminster.

The Derby and Ely chapels at Manchester remained in the possession of the Earls of Derby until the second half of the eighteenth century, when they were made over to the parishioners. On the south side of the collegiate church were five chantry chapels.

Separated from the south aisle of the choir by a fine parclose screen of the sixteenth century was the Jesus chapel, founded in 1506 by a Richard Beswicke. Though little is known of Beswicke he is described as ' an especial benefactor of the church, who built at his own charge [this] chapel and one side of the quire of the collegiate church, which cost him 300 or 400 marks or more.' He also provided the tabernacled stalls on the north side of the choir and made a gift of costly vestments.

The Jesus chapel is now used as the library and vestry. Projecting from its south-eastern angle was a small chantry chapel built by Ralph Hulme in 1507, but this has long since been destroyed.

To the west of the Jesus chapel, from which it was separated by a timber screen, was the Trafford chapel, dedicated to S. Nicholas.

The Traffords were an ancient family, who had held the manor of that name in Lancashire from the eleventh century. The chapel occupied two bays of the outer aisle to the south of the nave.

The next two bays to the west formed the chapel of S. George, which was the chantry chapel, founded in 1508 by a prosperous merchant of Manchester, W. Galley. At the Dissolution the two priests, John Barlow and Edward Smith, serving Galley's chantry were granted pensions of £6 and £4. 12s. 6d. respectively.

To the south of this chapel was a shallow projection also two bays long, known as the Brown chantry chapel.

Originally, low stone walls divided the aisle chapels from east to west and parclose screens enclosed them from the inner aisles, but none remains now, for the arcade between the inner and outer aisles was rebuilt in the nineteenth century.

All the chantry chapels, like the church of which they were a part, are late Perpendicular Gothic in character with large rectilinear windows and timber roofs. They formed a remarkable series, all being erected within a period of less than twenty years.

In Mary Tudor's reign the chantries in the church were re-established but came to an end with the death of that unhappy queen.

# OTTERY S. MARY CHURCH, DEVON

One of the most beautiful chantry chapels remaining in a collegiate church is the so-called Dorset aisle at Ottery S. Mary, Devon. The church was made collegiate by Bishop Grandisson of Exeter in 1337 and he immediately embarked on a reconstruction, making the new building a veritable cathedral in miniature, modelled on Exeter.

The only important addition to Grandisson's church was the chantry chapel built as an outer aisle on the north side of the nave. It was founded *c.* 1520-25 by Cicely, a wealthy heiress, daughter of William Lord Bonville and Marchioness of Dorset by her first husband, and was probably begun during the lifetime of her second husband, Henry Lord Stafford (d. 1523), whom she outlived by twenty years.

The Dorset chapel extends the full length of the nave from the north transept to the west front and is much wider than the aisle it adjoins. When it was built, the wall of the aisle was taken down and an arcade of five arches substituted. No doubt timber screens were installed between the piers to enclose the chapel on the south. At the same time a north porch was built, with the Stafford arms, now obliterated, above the door. The altar was placed against the west wall of the transept but disappeared when the wall was opened up. The chapel has a fan vault with pendants and the Stafford knot occurs freely in the stonework of the aisle.

# RIPON CATHEDRAL

At Ripon, which was a college of secular canons and was raised to cathedral rank in 1836, nine chantries are named in Edward VI's returns. The majority were founded by canons but it has not been possible to establish the sites of the altars at which all the masses were celebrated.

The eastern aisle of the north transept is now called the Markenfield chapel. Originally it was subdivided into two chapels by a low perpeyn wall or a screen. In one of them was founded the chantry of S. Andrew, *c.* 1240. The returns named Jeffrey Hyde and David Waller, canons, as the joint founders of S. Andrew's chantry but this may have been a later foundation at the same altar. The wall dividing the chapels was removed in the fifteenth century to make room for the tombs of the Markenfields, a family of some note in the neighbourhood. Probably they made the eastern aisle their chantry and mortuary chapel. Of the Markenfield tombs, that in the centre of the chapel is of chief interest. There is some delicate heraldic carving on the shields around the tomb, unhappily much defaced, and the effigy of Sir Thomas Markenfield, *temp.* Richard II, wears a curious collar of ' park palings ' and a badge beneath the chin with a stag couchant.

There were two chantries of the Holy Trinity at Ripon ; one described as *supra summum altare* was founded in 1342 by Sir Joseph Plompton, knt. ; and the other was spoken of as *subter altare* and was founded by John Sendall, canon, in 1461. What is meant by ' above the High Altar ' is not easy to determine. As a matter of conjecture, this altar may have stood behind the High Altar, which was situated one bay to the west of the east window ; for the sedilia then occupied the second bay from the east, being removed to their present position in the nineteenth century. The altar of the Holy Trinity ' below the [High] Altar ' presents an even greater difficulty, and may indicate a site somewhere to the west of the High Altar.

Two chantries of Our Lady occur in the records, one spoken of as ' in the Lady-loft ' and the other as ' in the church.'

One of these, termed ' the chantry of the Assumption,' was founded by William Fulfort and Robert of Kendall. The Lady-loft refers to the Lady chapel which occupied a most unusual position at Ripon, being the third floor of a building on the south side of the choir.

Some provision was made in 1515 for the founding of a chantry at Ripon by Brian Batty, but for some undiscovered reason the project was abandoned. It is worthy of mention on account of the agreement made between John, the son of Brian, and William Bronflet, a Ripon carver, for the making of ' a George upon horseback and a dragon according to the George at Kirkstall Abbey and a loft for the minster.' The carver was to make two heads and three arms for S. George, so that the spares could be used interchangeably on certain occasions. The figure would necessarily have been made of wood.

## SOUTHWELL CATHEDRAL

The collegiate church of Southwell, Notts., which became a cathedral in 1884, is shorn of all the chantry chapels it once possessed, nor can more than two or three of the altars be identified at which chantries were founded.

Built against the wall of the nave adjacent to the south-western tower was a chantry chapel dedicated to S. John Baptist. Founded in 1280 by Henry de Vavasour, one of the prebendaries, it stood on the site of the grammar school and was enlarged in the fifteenth century. Archbishop William Booth of York (1452–69) who preferred to dwell at Southwell,

52. THE KIRKHAM SCREEN, PAIGNTON CHURCH, DEVON

53. ABBOT LICHFIELD'S CHAPEL, S. LAWRENCE CHURCH, EVESHAM

54. THE MEYRING CHAPEL, NEWARK CHURCH, NOTTS

55. THE MARKHAM CHAPEL, NEWARK CHURCH, NOTTS

enlarged the Vavasour chapel and ordained that he should there be buried ;
and William's brother Lawrence, translated from Durham to York (1476–
80), added two more chantry foundations to the chapel. They were
dedicated to Our Lady and S. Cuthbert respectively. He also enlarged the
building which was thenceforth known as the Booth chapel. Archbishop
Lawrence Booth was buried by the side of his brother in the chapel,
which was used after the Suppression as a grammar school until its
demolition in 1884.

The chantry priests at Southwell formed a community that had grown
out of the vicars-choral. They received a stipend of four or five pounds a
year and in 1415 Canon Thomas Naxey gave them a house, where they
lived in common. They were required to assist the vicars-choral in the
offices in the choir. With one exception—the chantry of S. John Evangelist, which was in the gift of the vicars-choral—the presentations to
the other chantries were vested in the chapter of Southwell.

## ETON COLLEGE

The most famous of public schools bears little semblance to-day in
function or in character to ' the Kynge's college of oure Ladye of Eton
beside Wyndsore,' the charter for which was granted in October 1440.
Henry VI, then a youth of eighteen, ' to the praise, honour and glory of
the Crucified and the exaltation of the most glorious Virgin Mary, his
mother, and the establishment of the most holy church,' planned a collegiate body that was to consist of a provost, ten priests, four clerks and
six chorister boys ' to serve there daily in the celebration of divine worship,
and of twenty-five poor and indigent scholars and also of twenty-five poor
and indigent bedesmen, whose duty it shall be to pray there continually
for our health and welfare . . . and for the souls of Henry V, Queen
Catherine and all their forefathers and the faithful departed ; together also
with one master or teacher in grammar, whose duty it should be to in-
struct the said scholars in the rudiments of grammar.' The divine offices
and masses were of prime importance, the education of the twenty-five
poor scholars incidental. Henry VI's declining fortunes arrested the progress of the building operations and Edward IV, succeeding him in 1461,
might well have dissolved the Lancastrian foundation. Instead, he granted
several manors and priories to William Westbury, provost, and to the
college ' to pray for himself and Cicely, his mother, and for the soul of
Richard, Duke of York.'

On the north side of Eton College chapel is a little projecting chapel of
the kind to be seen at Lincoln Cathedral. It was built for the chantry of
Robert Lupton, a canon of S. George's, Windsor, and provost of Eton

12

from 1504 to 1535. During his long provostship Lupton was actively engaged in enlarging the college buildings. The great gatehouse known as Lupton's Tower and the contiguous ranges of the inner quadrangle are part of his work. His chapel, which was completed in 1515, is a small rectangular building, about fourteen feet by eleven and is tucked in between a deep buttress to the east and the vestry at the west. The wall beneath the window in the second bay of the college chapel is pierced with a wide four-centred arch, the lower part of which is occupied by a panelled screen of stone, thus enclosing the chantry chapel on the south. The door of the chapel is at the west end of the screen, and in the spandrels of the big arch is the founder's rebus, the letter R and LUP on a tun. The screen is surmounted with a cornice and cresting.

The tomb of the founder and the monuments of other pre-Reformation provosts stand within the chapel, but the most note-worthy feature of the interior is the lovely fan vault, from the centre of which drops a pendant bearing Lupton's arms. His obit was observed here on 27 February, his death-day. By his will, 1540, he ordained that for attendance at his obit the provost should be given 2s. 8d., the master half that sum, the usher 8d. and the scholars and choristers one penny each.

## KING'S COLLEGE, CAMBRIDGE

In February 1441, less than six months after Eton College had been founded, Henry VI signed the charter for King's College, Cambridge, known as ' Our College of S. Mary and S. Nicholas.' The Wars of the Roses interfered with the fulfilment of the king's wishes. The cloisters were never built and the chapel was not finished until Henry VIII's reign. King's College chapel was specially planned for chantries. On either side of the vast building, nestling between the huge buttresses is a range of very low chapels, each intended to house an altar for chantries and soul-masses. From the details given in Henry VI's will it is clear that this arrangement was not an afterthought : ' And between every one of the boteraces in the body of the chapel on both sides . . . a closet with an altar therein containing in length 20 feet and in breadth 10 feet vaulted under the sills of the aisle windows.' There are in all eighteen of these buttress chapels, nine on each side of the building. The three western chapels on each side are entered by small doorways in the nave wall ; in the others the buttresses dividing them are pierced, and entrance is by a doorway in the third bay of the choir from the east (Pl. 49).

All the chapels are very low structures and they are each lighted by an eight-light Perpendicular window with a four-centred head, in the outer wall. So wide are the windows that very little wall remains. The eastern-most chapels, completed *c*. 1461, are covered with delightful lierne vaults, the remainder, of a later period, having fan vaults.

In some of these chapels chantries were founded by members of the college personnel. The second from the west in the southern range was the chantry chapel of Provost Robert Hacombleyn (d. 1538), and of un-usual interest is that adjoining it to the east. This was the chapel of Robert Brassie, provost of King's from 1556 to 1558, who endowed a chantry there during the period of Mary Tudor's reunion with the Church of Rome.

As the college chapel was not completed until the reign of Henry VIII, many of the lateral chapels were probably never put to the purpose which the royal founder intended.

III Some chantry chapels in parish churches—the hospital at Ewelme—the college of Arundel.

TO PRESENT ANYTHING like an adequate survey of the chantry chapels that remain in our parish churches would require a book of much greater con-tent than this. The pages that follow supplement what has been said in the latter part of Chapter VI, Part I, and the chapels here described are in-tended to exemplify the form and character that such structures assumed in the churches of the people.

When the Chantries Act was passed in Edward VI's reign, the vast majority of chantry chapels in the parish churches of this country were either destroyed or dismantled, leaving little or no trace of their existence. The hard-headed parish folk showed little compunction in making a clean sweep of anything in their church that was no longer needed. Many a village church owes its commodious proportions to some local bene-factor or lord of the manor whose munificence made possible its recon-struction, enlargement or embellishment. As a matter of course he would found a chantry therein. Mediaeval wills furnish evidence of the abiding interest of the manorial families in their parish church. A typical instance is the Throckmorton family of Coughton, Warwickshire. The church there was built by Sir Robert, lord of the manor from 1486 to 1518, and by his will he made large bequests for its embellishment. He ordained that his body should be buried beneath a tomb ' in the midst of the church ' which he had already erected ; his executors were to glaze the chancel window with the Doom ; 20s. was to be expended on glazing the east window of the north aisle with a representation of the Seven Sacraments, and the same amount for the 'Seven Works of Mercy' in the south aisle. Images were to be set up in the church ; one of Our Lady by the altar in the south aisle, another of S. Gabriel ' at the pillar between the aisle and the chancel,' and others of S. Raphael, S. Michael and the Trinity in other parts of the church. All were to be lavishly coloured and gilded. Furthermore, he willed that certain lands should be put into the hands of feoffees to support a priest at £8 a year, who should sing perpetually for his soul and the souls of his ancestors, in the north aisle of Coughton church, thenceforward known as the Trinity chapel and enclosed with screens.

The most common form of chantry chapel in the parish church was an aisle built on one side of the chancel or nave. Normally, the nave was fully aisled before the chantry cult came into being and thus it is that many chapels are found flanking the chancel .

On the south side of the chancel of Mere church, Wilts., is the chantry chapel of Sir John Bettisthorne, which was built c. 1350 and dedicated in honour of the Annunciation. Each of the two arches dividing the chapel from the chancel is completely filled with a screen of timber resembling a huge Perpendicular window of the Severn type. In front of the altar and enclosed by an iron railing is a brass of Sir John, Lord of Chadenwycke, clad as a military figure of the period.

In the church of Chipping Sodbury, Gloucester, the chancel is flanked on the south by a spacious chapel built to serve the Gild of S. Mary. The gild was founded by Thomas Hampton and others, by licence granted by Henry VI in 1442. Its main purpose was ' to erect a chantry and provide two priests to celebrate at the altar of S. Mary, praying for the good estate of the King, and after his decease, for his soul, the founders' souls and all Christian souls.'

The chapel, erected after the middle of the fifteenth century, is unusually large for a parish church. It is two bays in length and is lighted by large Perpendicular windows in its east and south walls. A modern parclose screen of wood encloses it from the chancel. When the gild was suppressed in 1548 the endowment was valued at £18. 19s. per annum, of which £12. 4s. was paid to the chantry priests, 8s. for four obits and the remainder for the maintanence of the fabric and for the poor.

The beautiful Wilcote chapel at Northleigh, Oxon, on the north side of the chancel was made by prolonging the nave aisle to the east. It was founded some time before the middle of the fifteenth century by Lady Wilcote, the daughter of Sir John Trillowe of Chastleton, as a chantry chapel for the souls of her two husbands and her two sons. The chapel is roofed with a fan vault and beneath an ogee arch in the chancel wall is the tomb of Lady Wilcote and her first husband. The arch is enriched with crockets and finial and the stops are carved angels holding shields. On the tomb lie alabaster effigies of Sir William Wilcote and his lady, both wearing the SS collar. The knight is in armour, his hands together in prayer ; his lady wears a fur-lined coat and her head is encircled with a chaplet. On the sides of the tomb are a number of niches separated by buttresses.

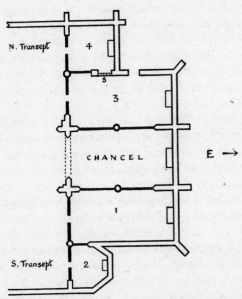

FIG. XXV PART PLAN OF ALL SAINTS, CHESTERFIELD. *1. Foljambe Chapel. 2. Colton Chapel. 3. S. Mary Magdalen Chapel. 4. Holy Cross Chapel. S. A squint. The screens are largely conjectural.*

The church of All Saints, Chesterfield, is of special chantry interest, for there were two chapels flanking the chancel on each side. The inner one on the south is the Foljambe chapel, which flanks the chancel along its entire length and contains a number of monuments of this ancient Derbyshire family. It was originally enclosed by a Perpendicular parclose screen, now relegated to the south transept. To the south of this is the Calton chantry chapel, a fourteenth-century structure which projects eastwards of the south transept. It is much smaller than the Foljambe chapel and terminates in a three-sided apse, an uncommon feature in a parish church.

The two to the north of the chancel were gild chapels. The inner one, of the same length as the chancel, was the chapel of the gild of S. Mary Magdalen and S. Michael and was enclosed by a parclose screen of wood. The outer chapel is much shorter and was built by the ' Brethren of the Gild of our Lord Jesus Christ and of the Holy Cross,' a fraternity founded by the vicar of Chesterfield and the townspeople in 1393. The altar was dedicated to the Holy Cross. In the south wall of this chapel at a distance of four or five feet above the pavement is a large squint with five openings and about five feet square, which enabled the gild brethren to view the High Altar when they assembled in their chapel.

A superb example of a Perpendicular chantry chapel is the so-called Baynton aisle in Bromham church, Wilts. It flanks the chancel on the south and was erected by William Beauchamp, Lord S. Amand, who owned the manor of Bromham in the fifteenth century. The chapel, dedicated to Our Lady, is extremely ornate in character. It is five bays long and is lighted by Perpendicular windows in the east and south walls (Pl. 47). Above the windows are carved figures of angels bearing shields and the buttresses are weighted with crocketed pinnacles. The embattled parapet is covered with small quatrefoiled panels and cresting and there are heraldic shields in the panels of the crenels. Above the eastern gable are canopied niches. The chapel has a timber roof gorgeously coloured in red, blue, and gold ; and thirty-two shields of arms are displayed in the panels (Pl. 41). Lord S. Amand was not buried in the chapel he had founded, but on the north side is the tomb of his mother, Elizabeth, with a brass beneath the canopy. In the middle of the chapel stands an altar tomb of Purbeck marble, on which lies the effigy of Sir Roger Touchet (d. 1457) who was buried beneath. Sir Roger married Richard Beauchamp's mother after the death of her first husband.

The other memorials are of the Baynton family, cousins of the S. Amand who succeeded to the Bromham property in the early sixteenth century.

The founder of the Beauchamp chapel at Bromham erected a similar chantry chapel at S. John's Church, Devizes. It stands to the south of the chancel and here again are Perpendicular windows, crocketed pinnacles surmounting the buttresses, a battlemented parapet richly sculptured and a large canopied niche crowning the eastern gable. The interior is equally ornate, the timber roof enriched with no less than 288 traceried panels.

Chantry chapels attached to chancels were not always of the aisle type. In form, position and size they differ considerably, sometimes being little more than shallow projections from the north or south wall. At Sawley church, Derbyshire, the Booth chapel of the late fifteenth century is a panelled bay projecting from the south side of the chancel and lighted by one four-light window. Within is the tomb with an alabaster effigy of John Booth (d. 1496), the treasurer of Lichfield, wearing the habit of a canon. He was a member of a local family of wealth and repute, one of whom became archbishop and two, bishops. His brother was rector of Sawley at the time of John's death.

Even smaller is the Barnard chantry chapel in Luton church, Beds., a curious little sunken recess in the south wall of the chancel. It was founded by Richard Barnard, Vicar of Luton (1477–92). The front is opened up with three pendant arches, the spandrels enriched with quaintly carved ornament, including a rebus—a chained bear and a hand holding a pot of spikenard. The structure has a lierne vault, the ribs of which spring from angel corbels. The pavement of the chapel is eighteen inches below the level of the chancel floor. There is no tomb within but a recumbent effigy in a recess beneath the west window of the south aisle of the nave is said to be that of the founder.

Of more ample proportions were the many excrescent chantry chapels, which as a rule were only built when nave and chancel were fully aisled. The Hall chapel at Grantham is a good example. When, in 1495, Thomas Hall, a wealthy merchant and alderman of the town, founded a chantry and wished to build a chapel for the masses, the great church of S. Wulfram had its full complement of aisles, so this chapel was built projecting from the Corpus Christi aisle, which flanked the chancel on the north. It is a low building, and is of greater length north to south than east to west, a peculiarity rarely met with. It is well lighted with Perpendicular windows and has a battlemented parapet. Within is a piscina on either side of the altar, and an arched tomb recess bears the founder's arms.

At Long Melford church, Suffolk, is a charming little chantry chapel erected by John Clopton of Kentwold (d. 1497), one of the many benefactors through whose efforts the church was largely reconstructed in the fifteenth century, and whose names appear in several places on the battlements. John Clopton was at one time Sheriff of Norfolk and Suffolk and a staunch supporter of the Lancastrian cause. He narrowly escaped beheading after a term of imprisonment in the Tower.

The aisle to the north of the chancel is known as the Clopton aisle—' the advanced aisle without the church on the north side ; . . . and here John Clopton worthily deserves to have his memory preserved. . . . He built the four first pillars and arches on the north side.' So wrote a seventeenth-century chronicler. His chapel is a low building, rectangular on plan, situated at the east end of the Clopton aisle and is entered from the latter through a small fan vaulted chamber which has a fireplace and may have been the chantry priest's room. The only opening into the sanctuary is the arch over the founder's tomb in the chancel wall. The tomb is supposed to have been used as the Easter sepulchre; ' the sepulchre being always placed . . . at the north end of the High Altar ; between that and Mr. Clopton's little chapel there is a vacant place of the wall, I think, upon the tomb of his ancestors.'* The Purbeck marble tomb has no effigy but its front is adorned with quatrefoil panels containing shields. Beneath the arch are slight traces of paintings which are said to have been portraits of John Clopton and his wife. At each end of the tomb are recessed seats. In the west wall of the chapel a squint affords a glimpse into the Clopton aisle. Above the sedilia and the tomb arch is a row of traceried panels with heraldic shields of the family and this is surmounted by a range of twelve canopied niches. Considerable traces of colour decoration remain, notably on the roof timbers.

The aisle to the south of the chancel was the chapel of the Jesus Gild. At the altar, which had a carved reredos depicting the Crucifixion, the gild priest recited masses and obits for deceased brethren. At the east is a small chamber which gave access to the priest's lodging, a two-storied building between the chancel and the Lady chapel. The upper floor of this house no longer exists.

In fully-aisled churches, chantry chapels were commonly built as outer aisles of the nave. Save for the screens which enclosed them, a number remain fairly intact. On the south side of Tiverton church, Devon, is the famous chapel built in 1517 by John Greenaway, a prosperous wool merchant and a considerable benefactor. He erected the south aisle and the western porch of the church and founded an almshouse in the place of his birth. The Greenaway chapel, two bays in length, stands east of the porch and rises to a greater height than the aisle it flanks. The external stonework is lavishly adorned with carvings of ships, woolpacks and horses. On the porch and the lofty parapet, which seems somewhat top-heavy, are sculptured some twenty-one scenes in the life of Our Lord, below which are galleys of various kinds and other carvings associated with the founder. Within the chapel at the east end is the tomb of John Greenaway (d. 1529), and in the wall above are brasses of himself and his wife, Joan (Pl. 50).

*Chantry tombs elsewhere were used as Easter sepulchres. At Stanwell, Middlesex, Thomas Windsor (d. 1486) by his will founded a chantry for ' an honest and well-disposed priest ' to pray for his soul, etc., and directed that his body should be buried on the north side of the choir of Stanwell church and a ' plain tomb of marble and of a competent height ' be erected ' to the intent that it may bear the Blessed Body of our Lord and the sepulture at the time of Easter to stand upon the same ' before which tapers were then to be burned.

Even more splendid is the Lane chantry chapel at Cullompton church in the same county. It was founded in 1529 by John Lane, a clothier and a person of some consequence in the trade ; an inscription which runs 'Wanpat custos Ianuarii' has been rendered 'Woolwarden of the Wapentake.' The chapel forms an outer aisle on the south side, extending the whole length of the nave. Here again is prolific ornament ; ships, merchants' symbols and grotesque beings appear on the external masonry. In niches set in the faces of the Perpendicular piers dividing the chapel from the aisle are fifty figures of saints. The most beautiful feature is the lovely fan vault, resembling that in the cloisters at Gloucester, except for the lumpy pendants. The fans spring from angel-corbels bearing implements of the wool industry. Few parish churches in the country possess so fine an example of fan vaulting as this at Cullompton.

At Porlock church, Somerset, the south aisle of the nave, separated from the body of the church by timber screens, served as the chantry chapel of the Harington family, lords of the manor in the fifteenth century.

It was founded by John, fourth Baron Harington of Aldringham, a stout warrior who fought in Henry V's campaign in France and there died in 1418.

The chantry calls for notice mainly on account of the canopied monument of the baron and his lady which stood within the chapel but was moved to its present position, beneath the eastern arch of the south nave arcade, when the chantry was suppressed. Above the altar tomb is a lofty canopy consisting of wide four-centred and cusped arches with trefoiled circles in the spandrels. Unhappily one side of the nave arch cuts through the canopy. On the tomb lie alabaster effigies in good preservation of the founder and his lady, Elizabeth Courtenay. The knight is clad in cuirass, baldric, belt and sword and his lady, at whose feet is a boar, wears a coronet of fleurs-de-lis. Both figures have their hands together in the act of prayer.

S. Mary's Church, Scarborough, has a unique series of chantry chapels, four in number, which are built side by side at right angles to the south aisle, extending from the transept to the porch. Each is roofed with a pointed barrel vault and is separately gabled. The dividing walls remain internally and there is a tomb recess and a piscina in each chapel except in the westernmost. They were built for the chantries founded by Robert Galland (d. 1380), Robert Rillington (d. 1381), Agnes Burn, c. 1390, and the bailiffs and commonalty of the town, c. 1396 ; and were dedicated to S. James, S. Stephen, S. Nicholas and Our Lady respectively.

Two beautiful little chantry chapels of the excrescent kind are to be seen in the churches of S. Lawrence and All Saints which were built within the precincts of Evesham Abbey.* Both of these chapels were founded by Abbot Lichfield (1514–39), and in each case they project from the south aisle of the nave. That in All Saints, known as the Lichfield chapel, is rectangular on plan and rises the full height of the aisle. There is no window in the eastern wall (Pl. 51). Bold buttresses support the fan vault within and the battlemented parapet is pierced with rectilinear panels. In the vault are shields of the abbey arms and the initials of the founder's name. The Abbot was buried beneath the pavement, a stone slab with a brass inset formerly marking his grave. Opening from the aisle into the chapel is a lofty four-centred arch, the soffit of which is covered with rectilinear panelling. The timber screen now enclosing the chapel is modern.

The chapel in S. Lawrence is dedicated to S. Clement, the abbot's Christian name. It is very similar to the Lichfield chapel but is square on plan. From the angles spring traceried fans and a pendant is dropped from the spandrel at the ridge. The stonework of the vault bears the common Tudor devices, the rose and the portcullis ; and the arch opening into the chapel is almost a replica of that in the Lichfield chapel (Pl. 53).

In those churches that were cruciform on plan, the transepts provided most convenient sites for chantry altars. An outstanding instance is the Kirkham chapel in Paignton church, Devon, which occupies the small south transept, in area no larger than a bay of the adjoining aisle. The main feature is the monumental stone screen which encloses it from the aisle and which incorporates two tombs of the Kirkham family (Pl. 52). This superb structure is opened up with three arches, the middle one forming the entrance to the chapel, and the lateral and wider arches supporting canopies above the tombs. On each tomb lie two effigies, probably of Robert Kirkham and his wife, and their son, and Joan his wife. The lavish detail and the figure-sculpture which adorn this monument render it one of the most ornate of the period, though it is much mutilated. The jambs of the doorway are overlaid with panelling ; intricate vaulting ribs cover the arch soffits and niched buttresses support the canopies, which are clusters of crocketed gables. On the traceried pedestals which rise above the gables are angels bearing shields. The fronts of the tombs are enriched with deep ' housings ' containing weepers telling their beads, and inter- mediately smaller niches have angels bearing the instruments of the Passion. Figures of the twelve apostles occupy the niches of the buttresses dividing the three big arches.

---

*These two churches were chapelries of the monastery, All Saints being parochial and S. Lawrence used by the pilgrims who came to pray at the tomb of Simon de Montfort in the abbey church.

The sculptured figures on the transept side of the screen are of saints and female weepers together with the four Evangelists. On the walls at the head and feet of the tombs are relief panels carved in freestone depicting the Visitation, the Coronation of the Virgin, the Mass of S. Gregory, and SS. Antony and Roch. There is much lesser detail carved in the hollows of the mouldings—subjects from the Old Testament such as the Sacrifice of Isaac, and Samson with the gates of Gaza.

Writing of the iconography of the Kirkham screen, the late Mr. G. M. Rushworth said, ' the scheme embodies the whole Christian faith as it was understood in the later Middle Ages. The angel hierarchies suggest the divine government of the universe . . . the apostles stand for the Church and its creed ; the Evangelists for its gospel, the doctors for its authorized interpreters, while the women saints represent the Church militant and triumphant.'*

At East Horndon church, Essex, are two small chantry chapels, two stories high and built of brick. They project transeptwise from the north and south walls of the unaisled nave. By whom and when they were founded is not known. The northern, which is the smaller, measures only nine feet by six feet and in the east wall a stairway leads to the upper floor. The balustraded front of the upper stories of both chapels were put up in the seventeenth century.

Very few chantry chapels of the stone-cage type remain *in situ* in our mediaeval parish churches. Two deserving of notice are to be found in the large church of Newark, Notts. In the north arcade of the choir stands the chapel founded by Thomas Meyring. By his will, dated 13 August 1500, he directed his body to be buried in the north part of the choir ' between the two pillars next the altar, where at the time of Easter it is said to be set up the sepulchre of Jesus Christ.' He bequeathed certain tenements in Newark and an acre of meadowland to ' a discreet priest to pray for my soul,' and for the building of the chapel over his grave he left to be sold ' all my clipped wool and all my floke of sheep.' He ordained that the priest should recite ' one requiem mass on the weekday for my soul . . . and on the principal feast days shall say, *if he be disposed*, mass, etc.,' and anthems, psalms, Placebo and Dirige on other days named. His chapel is open on the chancel side with one four-centred arch and is kept flush with the piers ; as a result it projects into the north aisle, where is a flight of seven steps leading up to the entrance at the west. The chapel rises to a height of eight feet in the aisle and the screen-wall there consists of two tiers of rectilinear lights above a panelled base. On the latter are heraldic shields of the Meyring family and its connections. The

*Transactions of the Exeter Diocesan Architectural and Archaeological Society*, 1927.

top is finished with a battlemented parapet. There is no tomb in the chapel and it is doubtful whether the founder was buried in Newark church. The wooden altar is modern (Pl. 54).

Immediately opposite, on the south side of the chancel, is the chapel of Robert Markham, which dates *c.* 1508. The Markham family, connected by marriage with the Meyrings, came from Cotham near Newark and were distinguished for their services to the State. Robert's father was an ardent supporter of the Yorkist cause and after the battle of Towton Field he was created a Knight of the Bath for his loyal services to Edward IV. His eldest son, the founder of the chantry here, married Elizabeth, daughter of Sir William Meyring. By his will, dated 16 June 1505, Markham ordered his body to be buried ' in the chancel of Newark church on the south side of the High Altar.' His tomb bore the legend ' *Orate pro animabus Roberti Markham armigeri et Elizabeth uxoris ejus.*' The Markham chapel is very similar to that of Meyring, projecting in the same way into the aisle with a door at the west, approached by steps. On the chancel side it is open, with one four-centred arch, and the aisle front is a stone screen of rectilinear panelling. In the panels of the base are the arms of the Markham, Meyring and Bozom families, and the long panels above are divided into two tiers by a transom. Here, as in the Meyring chapel, there is no cusping in the heads of the panels. In the lower range of openings at the east end are two painted panels depicting the Dance of Death, and there is a double squint. Common to both chapels are the angle buttresses and an intermediate one, but neither has a vault or roof (Pl. 55).

Undoubtedly built as a chantry tomb is the extraordinary monument in the Babington chapel on the north side of the chancel at Kingston-on-Soar church, Notts. It consists of an elaborately carved canopy supported by four massive columns and was obviously designed to house a tomb, probably of Sir Thomas Babington. As the monument is not earlier than *c.* 1547, the tomb which would have been used as a chantry altar, was never made. This curious if not grotesque monument now forms an archway from the Babington chapel into the chancel. It bears no inscription but is adorned with a mass of carving of great variety. There are no less than two hundred figures of babes with their bodies half hidden in casks, the rebus of the family name, ' babe-in-tun.' The panelling of the columns at the angles is likewise enriched with figures and heads, and groups of joyous babies encircle the capitals. A number of heraldic shields of the Babingtons and of families connected with them appear on this striking monument (Pl. 56).

In everything but name, the bede-house of mediaeval England was a chantry foundation. When a chapel for the bedesmen was built as part of the establishment, it needed to be of some size, and was sometimes an aisle grafted on to the parish church. No better example is extant than the chapel of S. John Baptist at Ewelme church, Oxon, founded by the ill-fated William de la Pole, Duke of Suffolk. In 1437 royal licence was granted Pole and his wife, Alice, to found a hospital at Ewelme for twelve poor men with two priests to minister to them, one to be master and the other, ' a well-disposed man apt and able to teach and inform children in the faculty of grammar ', in the free school which was to form part of the establishment. The endowment was not to exceed 200 marks a year ; the master and the ' well-disposed man ' were to receive £10 a year and each bedesman £3. os. 8d. The original buildings, which were completed by 1443, remain intact to-day. Only a few years earlier, Pole had built the nave and chancel of Ewelme church and now he added an aisle to the south of the chancel as the Hospital chapel, dedicated to S. John Baptist. It is as wide as the chancel and of the same length, and the stalls for the bedesmen are still in use. In the open roof, built of Spanish chestnut, appear a number of carved angels at the intersections of the moulded timbers. Leland, the ' king's antiquary,' *temp*. Henry VIII, recorded an inscription on the walls, ' Pray for the sowles of John, Duke of Suffolk, and Elizabeth his wife.' In the statutes of the hospital, the founder ordained that the almsmen should attend the offices in the chapel and should recite prayers at the tomb of the founder or of the duchess's parents for the souls of Henry VI, the Duke and Duchess of Suffolk, their parents and all Christian souls. As in other foundations of like character, attendance at the divine offices was to be strictly observed and late-comers were sub-jected to a fine of 1d. or 2d. out of their weekly allowance of 1s. 2d. William de la Pole, who was created Duke of Suffolk in recognition of his services to Henry VI and Queen Margaret, was the third husband of Alice Chaucer, daughter of Sir Thomas Chaucer. It was this alliance that brought the manor of Ewelme to the duke. The tomb of Sir Thomas (d. 1436) and his wife, Matilda, stands in the chapel. It is unfortunate that Pole was not buried here. After his banishment in 1450 he was captured at sea and put to death on board the vessel *Nicholas of the Tower* and his remains were conveyed to Wingfield church. Duchess Alice survived her husband for twenty-five years. Maybe for political reasons, she erected no tomb for him. Her son John, who married Elizabeth, daughter of the Duke of York, certainly intended that his mother, after her long widow-hood at Ewelme, should not be so readily forgotten. Her tomb in Ewelme church that he set up is unsurpassed in splendour and craftsmanship by any to be seen in a parish church of this country (Pl. 59).

The altar tomb of the duchess stands within a rectangular opening in the wall dividing the chapel of S. John Baptist from the chancel. The panelled jambs and lintel of the opening form a perfect frame for the monument. On the tomb lies the alabaster effigy of the lady, clad in rich robes and resplendent in colour. Her hands are together in prayer and she wears the Order of the Garter on her arm and a coronet on her head. Above her head is a traceried ' gabletz.' The tomb is designed in two stages ; the upper consisting of a range of alabaster angel weepers bearing shields and housed in niches. They are charming little figures with red wings and gilt hair, against a background of gold. The lower stage is opened up with a series of two-light traceried windows to afford a view of the emaciated figure of the duchess in a shroud—a strange conceit for the monument of a noble lady. Above the panelled opening in which the tomb stands is a deep cornice divided into three ' bays ' by octagonal standards which form pedestals for some fourteen wooden angels. Each bay has three demi-figures of the heavenly host, their hands together in prayer, and the whole is surmounted by a row of panelling and cresting.

Chantry colleges were in the main attached to parish churches, and when the Chantries Act was passed and the colleges dissolved, such churches once more became solely parochial. This was not always so desirable as it might seem. In churches like Fotheringay, where the college had built a spacious choir for its own offices, the parish folk who had hitherto worshipped in the nave now found themselves with a large church on their hands which more than sufficed for their needs. The maintenance of the fabric was no light undertaking ; so to lessen the burden the redundant choir was often taken down.

A remarkable survival of a chantry choir attached to a parochial nave —the two forming one architectural whole but internally divided by brick walling, and ecclesiastically separate to-day—is the church of S. Nicholas with the Fitzalan chapel at Arundel, Sussex.

Until the last quarter of the fourteenth century S. Nicholas was both monastic and parochial, being the church of a Benedictine priory dependent upon Seez Abbey. In 1380 the priory had declined so greatly and the buildings were so neglected that the convent was dissolved. For long there had been a chantry college attached to the chapel of S. George in Arundel Castle, and Richard, fourteenth Earl of Arundel, now obtained licence of Richard II to transfer the college to S. Nicholas' Church. The statutes drawn up in 1387 provided for a master and twelve chaplains, who were required to reside in the college buildings and never absent themselves. The masses to be sung were specified and included a number of celebrations at various altars so that the parishioners and others might hear them.

The parishioners lost nothing by the changes that were being effected, for within a few years a cruciform church with a central tower was being reared in place of the old Norman church. It was probably completed during the early part of the fifteenth century. The nave, eighty-two feet in length, with north and south aisles and the transepts were allocated to the parishioners of S. Nicholas; and eastwards was, and is, the collegiate choir, known as the Fitzalan chapel. It was about the same length as the nave and was flanked on the north by the chapel of Our Lady, with a sacristy at the east.

Filling the whole of the eastern arch of the tower is the original iron grille which effectively shut off the collegiate choir from the parish church.*

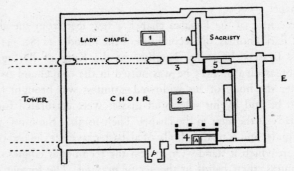

Fig. XXVI PLAN OF FITZALAN CHAPEL, ARUNDEL *originally the Choir of the College of Holy Trinity. 1. Tomb of Eleanor and John Fitzalan. 2. Tomb of Thomas Fitzalan. 3. Tomb of John Fitzalan. 4. Chantry Chapel of William Fitzalan. 5. Chantry Chapel of Thomas Fitzalan.*

For the housing of the brethren of the college, ranges of buildings were grouped round a quadrangle to the south of the Fitzalan chapel.

More pertinent to our subject are the Fitzalan chapel and the chantries and tombs therein. This was the choir reserved for the chantry priests. The daily offices and the soul-masses for the founders and their descendants were recited here for more than a century and a half. The chapel is some eighty-two feet long and is lighted by four large windows in the south wall and a wide seven-light window at the east. The Lady chapel, part of the original structure, forms an aisle on the north and is divided

*In the nineteenth century the Duke of Norfolk, claiming the Fitzalan chapel as his private property, built a wall at its western end to separate it structurally from the rest of the church, an act which was the subject of litigation between the Duke and the incumbent of S. Nicholas in 1879. The wall remains, and so it is that in the eastern half of the church the rites of the Roman Catholic Church are observed to-day and the western arm is an Anglican church.

from the choir by an arcade of three arches. At the altar here a daily mass was sung as ordained by the founder, Richard, Earl of Arundel, Surrey and Warren. He was beheaded on Tower Hill in 1397 and was buried in the church of the Austin Friars, London.

In 1455 a chantry was founded in the Lady chapel for Eleanor, Countess of Arundel, who by her will provided for a daily mass for her soul and that of her husband for a period of twenty-six years. She left a sum of 2,000 marks as an endowment. The Purbeck marble tomb of Eleanor and of her husband, Earl John (d. 1421), stands in front of the altar of the Lady chapel.

In the centre of the Fitzalan chapel, a few feet from the altar, is the tomb of Earl Thomas, the second son of the founder (1381–1415), and of Countess Beatrix, his wife, daughter of the King of Portugal. When Earl Thomas died in 1415 he was buried in the chapel and twenty-four years later the body of his widowed countess was brought from Bordeaux to be laid by his side. Soul masses were celebrated for the Earl and his lady at the altar in the chapel. Their tomb is the most splendid of all at Arundel and is made wholly of alabaster save for the bed of Purbeck marble on which it stands. On it rest the recumbent effigies of the earl and countess, their hands in the act of praying. The former wears the SS. collar and at his feet is the Fitzalan horse ; there are dogs at the lady's feet. More remarkable perhaps than the effigies are the Gothic canopies, or ' gabletzes,' above their heads, for there is a niche in the back of each canopy, an unusual feature in tomb design. Round the sides and ends of the tomb are no less than twenty-eight weepers—clerical figures holding books in their hands—standing in shallow niches divided by buttresses. The tomb is comparable in magnificence with the Beauchamp monument in the Lady chapel at Warwick.

There are other tombs of members of the Fitzalan family for whom chantries were founded in the chapel, in particular that of Earl John (1408–35). This, which is also of alabaster, stands on the south side of the Lady chapel in the easternmost arch of the arcade dividing the chapel from the choir.

On the slab of the tomb is the effigy of the warrior earl who died at Beauvais from wounds received in the French wars. The figure is clad in plate armour of the period, the feet resting on the Fitzalan horse. Beneath the slab the tomb is opened up on all sides with Gothic arches to display an emaciated corpse.

Surpassing all the Arundel tombs in architectural splendour is the chantry chapel of William Fitzalan, eleventh earl (d. 1488), and his countess, Joan, the sister of Warwick the Kingmaker. The chapel is built against the south wall of the choir, a short distance west of the altar (Pl. 57).

56. THE BABINGTON MONUMENT, KINGSTON-ON-SOAR CHURCH, NOTTS

57. **THE** CHAPEL OF WILLIAM FITZALAN, ARUNDEL

*Sussex*

58. THE CHAPEL OF THOMAS FITZALAN, ARUNDEL

59. THE TOMB OF ALICE, DUCHESS DE LA POLE, EWELME CHURCH, OXON

In general form it resembles the De la Warr chapel at Boxgrove, and to secure greater width for the chapel much of the choir wall was cut away. It is rectangular on plan and consists of a low enclosing wall pierced with Perpendicular panels. Above is a huge canopy supported by buttressed standards at the angles and by intermediate standards which divide the front into three open bays, each having a flat cusped arch. The canopy front is enriched with a mass of trivial ornament in low relief, the chief features being the crocketed gables above the arches. The gables are carried up to an ornate frieze, from which rise the tall pinnacles of the standards. About a foot in front of each standard, and of the same height, is a twisted column crowned with a purposeless tabernacle. The whole structure is built of Petworth marble. Within, the eastern half of the Fitzalan chapel is occupied by a massive two-storied structure of Purbeck marble which served the double purpose of altar and tomb. The western part of the slab of the lower stage forms the altar, which still retains its two prickets for candles. The upper stage, on which rest the effigies of Earl William and the countess, is enriched with niches, the western face serving as the altar reredos with rectilinear panelling and a canopy above. The effigy of the countess wears a coronet and a necklace composed of roses and suns, the badges of Edward IV and the Yorkist family. At the feet of the earl is the Fitzalan horse.

The chapel is roofed with a ribbed vault with pendants and is entered at the west by a door in the wall of the choir. The decadence that is manifest in the architectural treatment of this chapel is even more apparent in the later chantry chapel adjoining the altar on the north side of the choir (Pl. 58).

It was founded by Thomas Fitzalan, the twelfth Earl of Arundel (d. 1524), and consists of a large canopy carried by four carved columns. The detail of the whole structure is a mixture of Gothic and classic motives, amongst which are several heraldic devices which are repeated on the panelled wall at the rear.

Set in the pavements of the choir and the Lady chapel are a number of brasses, some of which mark the burial places of the priests of the college.

The college of the Holy Trinity was dissolved in 1544 and ' the site, lordships, manors, lands, tenements and other hereditaments ' were purchased from the Crown by Henry, Earl of Arundel, the last of the Fitzalans. With the exception of the choir and the master's house, the collegiate buildings were destroyed, and during the Civil War the choir itself was wantonly damaged. In 1886, however, it underwent a thorough restoration by the Duke of Norfolk and is now used as the tomb-house of the Howard family.

13

# APPENDIX A

## CHANTRY CHAPEL IN A HOSPITAL

ATTACHED to the Hospital of S. Mark called Gaunt's Hospital, at Bristol* is a beautiful little chantry chapel in a state of almost perfect preservation, which was founded by Sir Robert Poyntz of Iron Acton, d. 1520. It flanks the sanctuary of S. Mark's Chapel on the south side and is a choice specimen of late Perpendicular Gothic.

The Poyntz family were connected with the Berkeleys by marriage and Sir Robert was a friend of Henry VII and Henry VIII. He took part in the reception of Katherine of Aragon, the bride-to-be of Prince Arthur, in 1501, and he attended Henry VIII at the Field of the Cloth of Gold. Shortly before his death he founded a chantry in S. Mark's Hospital, Bristol, and built the ' chapel of Jesus ' in which his soul-masses were to be sung. Apparently the chapel was not finished at his death, for in his will, dated 19th October 1520, instructions were given for its completion and furnishing, as well as for his burial and the celebration of the masses. He ordained that he should be buried

In the church of the Gaunts beside Bristol in the chapel of Jesus, which latter I have caused to be new edified and made at my cost and charges, on the south side of the chancel of the said church and the overpart thereof behind the presbytery there. . . . The said new chapel which I lately edified *is not in all things perfect and finished*, yet according to mine intent, that is to wit, the glazing of the windows thereof and making of two pews within the said chapel in the lower end of the same, mine executors shall finish and perform all the things being yet undone and shall also garnish the same chapel and certain images and the altar of the same with altar cloths, vestments, book and chalice and all other things thereunto necessary. . . . The master of the house of the Gaunts is to take issues [of certain manors named] to provide an honest and considerable priest to sing mass at the altar of the said chapel of Jesus. . . . the said priest to have for his salary £6. A solemn obit [is] to be kept for my soul in the said church of the Gaunts on the day of my departing [i.e. decease] ; in the evening placebo and dirige by note, and on the following day a mass of requiem by note. And four tapers of wax, every one of them a pound weight be brenning upon my herse about the Crucifix at all times during the said dirige and mass, and 6s. 8d. sterling to be distributed in alms to the poor. The said priest shall always be tabled and lodged within the house of the Gaunts.

His executors were to provide ' a fine small marble stone to be laid over the middle of the vault ' which Sir Robert had already prepared for his burial, ' with a scripture making mention of all the bodies that lie buried in the same vault and of the days and years of their decease.' (*Transactions Brist. and Glouc. Archl. Soc.,* IV.)

Instead of placing a stone over the vault as directed, his executors built an altar tomb, the weight of which caused the roof of the vault to collapse in 1730, with the result that the tomb was broken up and destroyed.

The Poyntz chapel, which was restored in 1830, is rectangular on plan and measures 18 feet by 12. It is entered from the west by a portal with panelled

*The Hospital was founded in 1220 as an almonry to feed 100 poor persons, but it was in effect a chantry establishment for the souls of Maurice and Henry de Gaunt. In this respect it is comparable with S. Katherine's Hospital by the Tower (p. 33).

jambs and is lighted by Perpendicular windows of three lights. The doorway and windows have four-centred arches. In the thickness of the north wall are two lofty recesses some five feet wide and four feet deep, also with four-centred arches. Their purpose cannot be determined with certainty but as there is room enough in each for a priest to stand, they may have been intended for the celebration of low masses, though no traces of altars remain. Their walls were formerly enriched with rectilinear panelling, now hacked away. In the arch spandrels of the recesses and of the western portal is carved the founder's rebus, a clenched fist (poing). Large tabernacled niches, eight in number, to house the ' certain images ' are ranged round the walls of the chapel. The floor is paved almost entirely with enamelled tiles of the sixteenth century from Spain, said to have been brought here by Bristol merchants, and interspersed with them are a few English encaustic tiles bearing heraldic devices. The most beautiful feature of the chapel, however, is the fan vault, in the spandrels of which appear carvings displaying the arms of Henry VIII and Katherine of Aragon and of Sir Robert Poyntz and his lady, Margaret Woodville.

# APPENDIX B

## Chantries in S. Stephen's, Westminster

What S. George's Chapel was to Windsor, the royal collegiate chapel of S. Stephen was to the Palace of Westminster.

Of S. Stephen's Chapel nothing remains, for it was destroyed in the disastrous fire of October 1834, which reduced the Palace to a ruin. The present chapel was originally the undercroft or lower chapel, known as S. Mary-in-the-Vaults.

There are records of many chantries that were founded and obits kept in the royal chapel, a number of which were for the canons serving the college. The endowments, rarely on the small side, amounted to a considerable sum. Thus, in 1399 £50 was bequeathed for the perpetual obit of Dean Sleford, and a like amount in 1425 for the obits of Canon Orgrave; in 1471 an endowment of £100 was made to ensure a daily mass and the obits of Canon Crecy and Thomas, Lord Stanley.

Of particular interest is the chantry founded in 1455 for the soul of William Lyndwood, Bishop of S. David's and Keeper of the Privy Seal. In that year licence was granted by Henry VI to Robert Pyke, clerk, and Adrian Grenebough, the Bishop's executors, to establish a perpetual chantry for the healthful estate of the King and his consort, Margaret of Anjou, and for their souls after death, as well as for the soul of the departed Bishop. It was served by two priests, one to sing the masses in the chapel of S. Mary-in-the-Vaults and the other in the chapel of S. Mary of the Pewe. By his will Bishop Lyndwood bequeathed 600 marks to the college, that being part of a sum due to him from the Crown for the completion of the cloisters and other buildings of S. Stephen's. On his death in 1446 the Bishop was buried in S. Mary-in-the-Vaults. During the restoration of the chapel in 1854, the coffinless body of an ecclesiastic with a crozier was discovered embedded in the masonry of the north wall, and the remains were believed to be those of Bishop Lyndwood.

The chapel of S. Mary of the Pewe, mentioned above, is not to be confused with the cavernous little chapel of the same name in Westminster Abbey (*q.v.*). It stood to the south of S. Stephen's on the site of what was known later as Cotton's Garden. The original chapel was destroyed by fire in 1452 and was rebuilt by Antony Woodville, Earl Rivers and brother of Lady Grey who became the wife of Edward IV. By his will the Earl made an endowment for a priest to sing masses for his soul in the chapel which he had reconstructed.

# APPENDIX C

## CHANTRIES IN THE GUILDHALL CHAPEL, LONDON

IN the now forgotten Chapel of the Guildhall, London, a collegiate church founded in 1299 and dedicated to Our Lady, S. Mary Magdalen and All Saints, were a number of chantries for London citizens. In 1354 Adam Franceys, mercer and twice mayor, Peter Fanelore and Henry Frowyk clubbed together to found a chantry college of five priests who were to sing a mass daily at the altar of Our Lady in the Guildhall chapel; but not until 1368, after Fanelore's death, was their intention fulfilled. The endowment of this joint chantry issued from rents of two tenements in the parish of S. Vedast and one in S. Giles, Cripplegate. The custos (trustee) was a William Brampton, and of the five priests serving the chantry college, one was the warden, receiving a stipend of 13 marks a year and the others 10 marks each.

In Riley's *Memorials*, under the date 1379, is given the presentation of a priest to the chantry of Roger Frowyk—doubtless a kinsman of the above Henry—in the Guildhall Chapel.

To the memorable Father in Christ our Lord, the Lord William [Courtney] by the grace of God, Bishop of London, his humble and devout servants John Hadlee, mayor of the City of London and John Ussher, chamberlain of the Guildhall of the same city, the honour and reverence due unto a Father so great. We have presented unto your fatherly goodness, our dearly beloved in Christ, Sir William Whittyn as being a fit chaplain to fill one of the five chantries in the chapel of the Most Blessed Virgin Mary in the Guildhall aforesaid, within your diocese, which was founded for the souls of Roger Frowyk, and Mary his wife and all the faithful deceased; the same being now vacant and unto our presentation by virtue of our offices at this time belonging; humbly and devoutly entreating that you will deign to admit the same William to the said chantry, and him canonically to institute in the same; and graciously to do other such things as upon your pastoral office are incumbent in this behalf. In witness whereof to the above we have set the testimony of the seals of our office. Given at London, 17th day of the month of November 1379, etc. (*Letter Book H.*)

A similar presentation, dated 28 March 1411, addressed to Bishop Clifford of London entreats 'your fatherly reverence that you will graciously deign to admit William Test to the chantry aforesaid' and ends 'may the Most Highest preserve your fatherly reverence for the healthful rule and protection of His Holy Church for length of time happily to survive. In witness whereof, etc.'

Another chantry in the Guildhall chapel was founded by Thomas Knebworth, fishmonger and mayor. In 1515, two years before his death he arranged with the Wardens of the Fishmongers' Company that they should find thirteen poor and honest bedesmen to pray for his soul in the chapel, for which office they were to receive 8d. each. Knebworth was buried on the north side of the choir where his tomb was erected. It was mutilated at the Suppression, but ' within these forty-four years,' says Stow, ' was again renewed by the Fishmongers.'

The Guildhall chapel which was rebuilt in 1430 was demolished in 1822.

# GLOSSARY

**Ambulatory.** *A procession path or aisle round a choir.*

**apse.** *A semicircular or polygonal eastern end of a choir or a chapel.*

**aumbry.** *A small wall recess used as a cupboard.*

**Barrel vault.** *A stone vault in the form of a tunnel.*

**bay.** *One compartment or unit of design in a nave, a choir or a transept*

**boss.** *A carved keystone at the junction of two or more ribs in a vault.*

**Clerestory.** *The nave-wall above the roof of an aisle of a church.*

**corbel.** *A projecting stone bonded into a wall to carry a weight.*

**crocket.** *A clump of carved leafage applied to the slope of a gable or an arch.*

**crossing.** *The central area of a cruciform church, where nave, choir and transepts meet.*

**cusp.** *A projection formed by the adjacent foils of an arch.*

**Decorated gothic.** *A name given to English architecture of the fourteenth century.*

**Fan vault.** *A vault built up of inverted trumpet-shaped cones, the surfaces of which are enriched with tracery.*

**finial.** *A carved bunch of foliage at the top of a pinnacle, gable or arch.*

**four-centred arch.** *An arch of depressed form struck from four centres.*

**Latten or laton.** *An alloy similar to bronze.*

**lierne vault.** *One in which ribs cross from boss to boss producing star-like designs.*

**Mullion.** *A vertical stone bar dividing window-lights.*

**Ogee arch.** *One that takes the shape of a reversed curve, the lower part-convex and the upper concave.*

**Parclose.** *A side screen, usually of timber, enclosing a chapel or a chancel.*

**pendant.** *An elongated boss or voussoir which appears to hang from a fan vault.*

**perpendicular gothic.** *The final phase of English mediaeval architecture, characterized by an emphasis of the vertical line.*

**pier.** *A mass of masonry or a clustered column built up in courses and supporting an arch.*

PISCINA. *A water-drain in a wall near an altar.*

PRESBYTERY. *The eastern part of the choir of a large church.*

QUATREFOIL. *A design composed of four lobes or foils.*

RECTILINEAR. *A name given to windows and panels of the Perpendicular period.*

REREDOS. *A screen which backs an altar.*

RETROCHOIR. *The part of a church which lies east of the choir.*

SANCTUARY. *That part of a presbytery in which the altar stands.*

SEDILIA. *Wall seats on the south side of the sanctuary for the celebrant and assisting priests.*

SOFFIT. *The underside of an arch.*

SPANDREL. *The triangular area of walling above the side of an arch.*

STOP. *A carved stone terminating the dripstone of an arch.*

TABERNACLING. *Elaborate canopy-work, polygonal in form, over a tomb or a stall.*

TESTER. *A flat canopy suspended above an altar or a tomb.*

TIERCERON VAULT. *One in which a number of extra ribs spring from the same point as the transverse and diagonal ribs.*

TRACERY. *The curved stone forms in the head of a window.*

TRANSOM. *A horizontal stone bar across a window.*

TRIFORIUM. *An intermediate stage between the arches of a nave or choir and the clerestory.*

VICE. *A narrow spiral staircase.*

WEEPER. *A small figure of stone or bronze which occupies a niche in the side of a tomb.*

# INDEX

*The numerals in heavy type refer to the figure numbers of plates*